The Book of Letters
American Correspondence

D H Fortin & Rev. Les Seto

Photo of Les Seto by Bernadette Seto

By D H Fortin & Rev. Les Seto

WestBow Press books may be ordered through booksellers or by contacting:

WestBow Press
A Division of Thomas Nelson & Zondervan
1663 Liberty Drive
Bloomington, IN 47403
www.westbowpress.com
1 (866) 928-1240

ISBN: 978-1-9736-5476-6 (sc)
ISBN: 978-1-9736-5478-0 (hc)
ISBN: 978-1-9736-5477-3 (e)

Library of Congress Control Number: 2019902158

Print information available on the last page.

WestBow Press rev. date: 03/14/2019

Don would like to thank his mother, Reverend Vina Bonnie Fortin-Laform, his wife Elizabeth Mitchell, and his four children, Rachael Fortin-Melton, Christopher Fortin, Alison Fortin, and William Fortin.
Les would like to thank his mother Carolyn Seto, his wife Bernadette Seto, his son Kili Seto, and his daughter Mewlan Seto.

Both authors would like to thank their editor, Rhonda Aronis.

Preface

The following chapters are a reflective work about the times and events that occurred in the lives of two men who grew up in different parts of the United States in the same years. Les Seto, an ordained Missouri Synod Lutheran minister and I, Don Fortin, a career correctional prison worker developed a lasting friendship in 1997 while attending Bethany Lutheran Church in California.

Our combined interest in longhand letter writing was apparent. After sixteen years of church leadership at Bethany, Les continued on to his home state of Hawaii as a minister at Waikoloa Lutheran Church in Hawaii, where he retired after eleven years of service. In all, Les served forty years in preaching the Gospel.

I fulfilled decades developing myself as a correctional officer, sergeant, lieutenant and counselor at California state prisons including San Quentin.

The common bond of being a letter writer compelled Les and I to correspond with the news of little Vacaville (pop 96,000) and about an even smaller village of Waikoloa for many years when we became separated by the Pacific Ocean.

Reading The Book of Letters, the reader recalls seminal events that occurred in recent years. America is changing at a rapid pace with events like hurricanes, mass shootings, fires in California that are familiar. The manner in which it is recalled makes for a place marker in Americans' modern struggle to adapt to Life by overcoming fear from an uncertainty of the unknown. Les teaches the reader how to do this, both in Bible scripture and in prayer.

In alternating chapters, I describe how letter writing personally affected me and the many inmates I encountered and encouraged throughout my time as a senior counselor. Les gives a personal account rarely revealed by a minister. He struggled to elevate his career reaching out to children and adults through his masterful understanding of God's Word as well as his years managing charitable foundations.

It is evident that writing is a most honorable method of sharing. It is applied in these chapters to show how you can be a blessing to a friend by thoughtful writing of times in your life where answered prayer enabled you to overcome defeat, loneliness and sadness. It certainly applies to inmates seeking change in their lives.

Examples of both obscure and of famous writers who communicating through poetry, songs, letters and books are included to show how Don and Les developed the desire of letter writing. You'll meet Thomas Jefferson, Fanny J. Crosby, Amy Carmichael, Reverend Billy Graham, an unnamed poet, and lots more. You'll see through their eyes, the healing by reaching out to others with ideas, kindness and sharing by writing. It may be one of 'the thousand points of light.' Enjoy!

Don Fortin

Contents

Chapter One

CAUSE AND EFFECT ORIGINS OF MY WRITING

I wonder when rain and wind will subside. Dawn's sky is grayish dark, and a lonely whistling wind is so close, that I shudder. The peace of other days is lost in the deep thoughts that lie within me. What a time this is.

I am standing on a slight elevation surrounded by my family and I feel I am in a wilderness in my thoughts. Solemnly, I think, Will peace return to me?

To dwell in a self-made cave of doubt, shivering from memories, is not good for my soul. So, I must find strength in what my mother taught her children. I sense this in my destitute reverie about my mother. I am fifty-two, a husband, and a father of four children. In this moment, I am barely an adolescent thirteen-year- old. I never anticipated this kind of reaction. In my world of Peter Pan, no one ever grows old, much less dies.

It's not easy to lose a friend, but when it is a loved one, we know that it hurts. When a man loses his mother, it is dreadful. Even now, describing this is not for the faint-hearted.

So, I focus on the silence and memories come to remind me. When I listen to the nearby birds that God created, they bring a song, like a letter that I particularly loved from my boyhood. These words come softly, reminding me of truth.

God's songbirds seem to bring these beautiful words to me. My keen sadness drifts away, replaced by soothing calm. I find this strangely wonderful.

I know my mother is in heaven. In spite of this faith, often there is a need for cheerful companions, something most people desire. I read the letters a pastor and friend, Les Seto, wrote to me in the early stages of our endeavor at writing both Sister Vina's Boy, my memoir, and his soon-to-be published book, Gentleness in the Old Testament (final title to be determined). I saw a pattern of gentle humility in the writer. Having known him for eighteen years, I could see in his writing, frank, hopeful encouragement, and above all, a sense of who God is. That comes through in Les's letters as you, dear reader will soon discover. Pastor Les ministers in the Hawaiian Islands and I live in Vacaville, California.

Les and I have been corresponding with letters since 2006. Some of the excerpts of these letters are found in this book and date to close to a year before we agreed to try our hands at becoming authors. Les, of course, has written weekly sermons, usually given in thirty-minute messages to his congregation. Les has done this every Sunday for more than twenty-five years. Tenderness in the writings that I have come to enjoy in my dear colleague may be from an unseen fountain of courage developed from situations that tested Les's "intestinal fortitude," as actor John Wayne famously termed it. It is Les's peace of mind and kind heart that only God gives to those who've come to know Him personally through the work of God's Son, Jesus Christ.

The Origins of My Writings

Every story must start somewhere. As an Old Dominion kid, my story picks up in the poor America that some have thumbed their noses at. Fortunately, I was oblivious to that disdain from an early age. My dad was a career sailor and my mother was a homemaker, a business worker, and a reader and singer of God's Word. I was a short and skinny boy, from what I suspect was malnutrition, and I had dirty-blond hair. Even as a child, my soul ached for fellowship. I have four siblings, and at one point, we were living slightly above poverty.

As poor folks will say, poverty seems evil when it is upon the sufferer. "Brother, Can You Spare a Dime?", a Depression-era tune, for me, was on equal status with "Jesus Loves Me." As with many in the south, life slowly passed day by day until I was a teenager. This placidness I fondly remember in my youth. There were some family times that were from meal to meal as Mother struggled on a navy allotment check to meet our needs. I seemed to have been unduly lonely, with just a few friends. Still, life continued peacefully, and I led a carefree, pleasant and often adventurous existence. I did not always live in the southland.

My kin in the 1950'-s were from the Napa wine country. Our family moved to San Diego and briefly live in Sacramento, as we followed dad's navy career, marginally becoming migrants. Mother always said, "God is with us" because she had an all-abiding faith. Mama was strong, and her hands steadily directed her four children, as she ushered us into the house of God.

Come what may, Mother let her Bible fall open to a single verse when she was confronting any obstacle; it could be spiritual, financial, or an illness affecting our physical health. From Bible verses, she would receive a blessing knowing with certainty what her focus should be. She prayed and meditated, and quickly found comforting melody in her life.

Mother Teaches

Being a youngster, I was always studying whatever went on around me. My sisters and my brother were close to me, like little chicks in our nest with Mother as the mother bird. We worshipped the Lord from Mother's teaching and gladly rejoiced in the Spirit of God. We children weekly stepped into the hour of prayer with its reverent solitude. This was a liberating enjoyment during gospel reading. The high-ceiling, white clapboard church with its corner doors open to all, remains on Mount Vernon and Detroit Streets, in Port Norfolk, the quiet, austere section of Portsmouth, Virginia. It remains as I remembered it from fifty-five years ago.

The church sits, as do the homes in the southland, nestled beneath magnolia and old oak trees. A memory of a blue, cloudless sky on an Easter morning comes quickly back, with joyful southern voices singing Hallelujah in harmony with God's angels. I felt peace. This amazing peace soaks through my bones and fills my heart until I feel almost as light as a feather. It is perfection amid all the other feelings I might have on a slow Sunday.

During that summer, was a tent revival meeting and more carefree joy came in those evenings as the Fortin kids sat in folding wooden chairs, our shoes scuffling in the sawdust chips beneath our feet. Hands clapped in unison to songs. Godly men on the revival stage were dressed in beautiful matching suits, and sang gospel hymns with their bass, soprano and tenor voices harmonizing and pouring out into the hundreds of worshippers. Their voices went up, out of the tent flaps, and soared into the wide-open Virginia night sky.

We were indeed blessed, the anointed children of our mother, Sister Vina Fortin, to be God's children. My, my, you should have heard the gospel music and God's own word delivered by the evangelist who boldly, earnestly pleaded with the people.

"Jesus teaches, "Come to me all you who are weary and burdened and I will give you rest" (Matt. 11:28, New International Version). What rest? The rest of Christ's peace in your lives and the assurance of eternal life'."

And come, they did, men and women down the aisles to the rough wooden altar to kneel and surrender their hearts to the glorious, precious peace of Jesus Christ. I too, was in that throng.

Dad missed some of this, because he was far away onboard the navy ship. He sorely needed the Christian fellowship, and we missed him. We kids were loved and comforted by Mother's gladness those nights. Mother reminded us that God would provide our every need if we followed her lead and trusted in Almighty God. Later in our home, we were refreshed from the church meeting beneath the tent.

We learned to be conscientious and to show good manners, being thankful for everything given to us. Before bedtime, Mother would say, "'Write to Dad, Donnie; remember to say how happy his last letter made you feel.'" She would provide pen, paper, and a stamped envelope. She would address the envelope to his ship, the USS Newport News CA-148, Naval District. Somewhere, far on the other side of the world, Dad would receive that connecting touch from the America he was serving, a letter from back home.

Around 1962, as a preteen, I began learning to play guitar as I sang, equally gospel and Beatles songs. I rode my bike up Lee Avenue between the Atlantic Ocean at one end, and down through Black Town, where our street intersected with Detroit Avenue. It was glorious riding past fields, railroad tracks, and blackberry bramble bushes in those sunny days before the coming of the rainstorms of our lives.

Family Letters Connect

In the Portsmouth schools, we Fortin kids learned the aspects of writing and were made to practice our penmanship. Mother took pride in her own beautiful lettering style, writing innumerable letters. She told us stories of her namesake, Aunt Vina who lived in New York. Auntie spent her entire working life as an editor for National Geographic magazine. Mama showed us Auntie's beautiful letter with its perfect lines that looked as if it were from Abraham Lincoln's era. Mama knew your best calling card in future employment was your penmanship. Mother taught evening courses at Portsmouth Business College to women who desired to be secretaries or court stenographers. Mother's trait of writing extended to her Bible, in which she notated and underlined many pages, leaving a lasting testament to her prayer requests that numbered in the hundreds.

By the light of a table lamp, we four children sat in our cozy kitchen and carefully wrote letters to Dad, telling him about our progress in the elementary school on Elm Avenue (and later at Hunt Junior High School and Woodrow Wilson High School). I wrote about our family pet, Buttons, a German Shepherd. I wrote about summer camp and how I busied myself selling Grit newspapers or delivering neighbors their copy of the Portsmouth morning newspaper. My sisters wrote of their own fun adventures and how they missed Dad. James sat quietly from his baby chair, watching his siblings as Mother directed our activities.

It was easy to paint a word picture for navy seaman Norman A. Fortin. His return letters announced a boy's duty to his mother during my father's absence. Reading his descriptive words, I would wonder what the ocean looked like at dusk as his mammoth ship got underway out of a harbor headed home across the Pacific and the Atlantic, all the way to Norfolk. I imagined Dad and his buddies lined up against the ship rail after their duty shift ended or down below deck on the heavy cruiser playing a game of Acey-Ducey, while Sinatra's crooning amplified over the ship's public address system.

I knew even then the value of letters, and how we could keep up relationships over the miles when separation leaves you with questions. I never felt abandoned, but frequently wondered about other boys with their dads who returned home from work at suppertime.

Once in junior high, we had a parent day when the students brought their dad or mom to talk about their career. I longed for Norman Fortin to share with my classmates about his naval duties, but I settled by bringing our 8mm Kodak motion projector and showing a reel of Dad aboard the USS Chilton APA-38 and his sailor buddies listening to the ship's band, and then swimming in the blue Adriatic Sea, marksmen with their rifles at the ready should an interested shark wander too close to the swimmers. Dad grinned back at me and waved at the camera—but it was a silent ten-minute film and then the spinning end of the tape flapped noisily as the reel ended. My teacher said, "You must be very proud of your dad, Donnie." I was very proud of him and I pulled out Dad's latest letter to show my classmates. Time has generously preserved that sweet memory. Time indeed moved on.

The years passed and I grew up and had four children of my own. I began working in my chosen occupation as a corrections counselor. I had the privilege of providing new arrival inmate orientation sessions with fellow counselors and select Life prisoner facilitators in the chapel.

Often when I addressed the men, I spoke of separation from family. I mentioned the 2 a.m. hour of desolation that inmates endure when the noisy prison has finally settled down, and grown men find themselves awake on their bunk, alone in their thoughts, reading the rare letter from home from their sweetheart or their son or daughter. I would speak to these men of my joy of receiving a ship's envelope addressed to me that was a personal connection from thousands of miles away from my dad. I'd tell the inmates how much I cherished the letters from my dad and how he instructed me to be the 'man of the house' while he was away. I told these inmates they were someone's father or son and that they were gentlemen, (men full of gentleness), when they wrote to encourage their children. As my mother had done with me, I asked the inmates to write about their recent return to school, and how it was good to learn and receive an education while in prison and how they didn't waste their life 'doing time,' but through education, 'let time serve them.'

My clerk, a friendly approachable man named George, moved about the chapel room distributing envelopes, paper and pencils to the men, and he let them know he too was writing to his daughter back home. On George's face there was always a look of sincerity. I could detect bittersweet recognition from the normally calloused convicts, that they may never have enjoyed a moment as a boy when the carrier delivered mail to their house. Many of the men didn't even know their dad.

At times George assisted a man writing to his kids, even loaning him a stamp until the new inmate's funds arrived. It was in these moments, sequestered in the prison chapel, that I came to understand a powerful option that men can change and persevere in their relationships with their children. This was what mother knew many years earlier.

After training, I would occasionally find an inmate at my office door wishing to speak to me. More than once, the inmate at my door would say:

"Mister Fortin, I leave tomorrow to parole back into society. My kids are picking me up and taking me home. I just did not want to leave without saying thank you, Mister Fortin".

With a guarded choking back of a tear, he would bid me farewell. Would the man return as a parole violator? The state provides assistance to inmates, $200 gate money and a thirty-day re-entry program prior to the inmate's exit. That is not a lot of meaningful rehabilitation for these men. In my opinion, more should be done to combat recidivism. Powerful family contact through letters helps.

Fortunately, some men do not return to prison (about thirty percent). Several of these reformed men left phone messages for me that they had successfully completed their parole. One of these parolees, a very gentle African American, came to my church with his family to proudly introduce his two grown sons to 'Mr. Fortin'. He had driven fifty miles from Sacramento after his own church service, to Bethany Lutheran church, a few miles from his former prison home. While I had been out of town that Sunday, he promised another Sunday school teacher that he would return the following week. He kept his promise.

What a pleasure to have this ex-life prisoner and his sons meet my daughter and son in my classroom at Bethany. Persistent kindness has its reward. I can truly tell you that letters serve to be a wonderful tool inside and outside of prison, to encourage the change in behavior so needed in those men's lives.

Chapter Two

THE MAN FROM HAWAII 1965-1968

"And the Word was made flesh, and dwelt among us, (and we beheld his glory, the glory as of the only begotten of the Father,) full of grace and truth" (John 1:14, King James Version).

There is astonishing power, such as salvation and eternal life, in the Word made flesh, Jesus Christ. How perfect is this description of Jesus? Just as words contain might and strength, so does the ultimate Word, Jesus Christ. On a much lesser but nevertheless significant magnitude, there is power in everyday words that are spoken or written. "Heaviness in the heart of man maketh it stoop: but a good word maketh it glad" (Prov. 12:25, King James Version). When used aptly, common words have the God given power to make hearts glad. How mighty then are carefully spoken words?

King Solomon inspired by the Holy Spirit goes on to say, "Pleasant words are as an honeycomb, sweet to the soul, and health to the bones" (Prov. 16:24, King James Version).

Cheerful words by the Lord's working can even bring health to our bones. Incredible, isn't it?

The book of Proverbs continues this theme of the energy found in words: "A word fitly spoken is like apples of gold in pictures of silver" (Prov. 25:11, King James Version). Words have the creative force from God to beautify any dismal and dark condition we may be experiencing. As golden apples in a painting framed with silver will brighten a room, so will just one appropriately chosen word do the same for our souls.

Words can be shared in many formats including books, essays, poetry, speeches, commentaries, and songs. One format that many have used throughout the millennia is simple letters. Many of the books in the Bible contain letters such as Daniel, Ezra, and Nehemiah. Many books are letters of themselves such as the Epistles of Paul, Peter, and John, including Revelation. If letters have aptly chosen words from Scripture or words that reflect Scripture, those words will bring encouragement, comfort, peace, and many of the fruits of the Holy Spirit. As Don Fortin did in Chapter One of this book, I shall attempt in Chapter Two to convey that letters have the potential to transform lives by the power which God gives to well selected words.

Unexpected. Unsure. Unworthy. Unqualified. Those were my reactions when I opened Don Fortin's letter in November 2015. Sitting at my compact walnut desk on a breezy, 82° F. afternoon in the desert region on the Big Island of Hawaii, I read Don's invitation to collaborate with him on a Book of Letters. I hesitated for a number of weeks to reply because I was aware that I only have a fraction of the intensity, zeal, and devotion that Don has toward the craft of writing.

Over the past decades, I am estimating that Don has hand written over 4,000 pages of daily journals, letters, essays, books, church newsletter articles, and poetry which he has neatly collated in dozens of thick, three-hole ring binders. These writings do not include the tens of thousands of official pages that he has written for the State of California, as part of his duties as a correctional counselor. As to the non-work related 4,000 pages of writing that Don has compiled in binders, I am confident that some of his thoughtful descendants in the centuries to come will be curators of these jewels of memories, observations, and commentary. Maybe people a thousand years from now will read what it was like to live in the United States, on both coasts, the east and west, in Old Dominion and California, during historic, turbulent times when cultural, political, and spiritual, norms from the most ancient of times were overhauled in five decades. Don fastidiously wrote his hand-written chronicles, correspondence and literature during his sparse, spare hours in between working full time (and overtime) for the state of California, carrying out of his duties as a devoted husband and father of four children, and actively serving in his church.

Don has certainly "paid his dues" as musicians and artists say about those who have done the gritty, grimy, humbling, labor of crafting their skills. Don courageously read his poetry to audiences at a county fair and shared his writings with erudite relatives and friends, opening himself up to possibly brutal, candid criticism, or worse, indifference. Don evinced Ben Franklin-like initiative and energy in self-publishing at least four books. He has enthusiastically sold his books person to person.

Along with putting forth tremendous persistence and dedication into his writing, Don has also been an exemplary student of the art of writing. He has taken creative writing courses in college. He has read a myriad of books on improving one's skills in writing. He has learned from and immersed himself in the masterpieces of literature, such as the works of John Bunyan, Ernest Hemingway, John Steinbeck, Harper Lee, and T.S. Eliot. Don has earned the privilege of being called a bona fide writer. It is then with much esteem and respect for Don's accomplishments, that I embark with him upon this joyful collaboration.

As Don recounted in the previous chapter, he began his writing endeavors as a child by corresponding with his father Norman Fortin who served in the U.S. Navy and was often on a ship thousands of miles from Don and his family. Don's mother Vina encouraged Don and his siblings to write often to their dad, and in doing so, Don gained a deep appreciation for and a rich satisfaction in the art of writing. Don then related how as a correctional counselor, he incorporated letter writing as a means for inmates to improve their lives by learning skills in communication, strengthening ties with family members, boosting their morale, and building self-confidence. Letter writing became a tool for the inmates with whom Don worked, to rise above obstacles they were facing.

In contrast to Don who began writing letters in elementary school, I did not begin consistently writing letters until I was a sophomore in high school. The first letters I wrote were not even in English. My second-year French class teacher Mrs. Constance Wence, adorned with beautiful silver hair and a summer day cheerful smile, encouraged all her students to sign up for a pen pal in France. She had obtained a list of high school students in France who were interested in corresponding with teenagers in the U.S. The students in America would write letters in French to their pen pals in France, and the French students would in turn reply with letters in English.

Mrs. Wence's offer sounded exciting, and so I signed up to become a pen pal. My pen pal was a boy in a rural section of central France. Unlike Don, who would have kept these precious letters, I did not safeguard the letters between my French friend and me, and so I do not have them for which to refer. I recall that the French student's first name was Jacques, and that he had a keen interest in the United States, and in the Pacific Ocean islands.

Because France had a close connection with Tahiti, Jacques was fascinated in knowing how it was to grow up on an island in the middle of a vast ocean. Jacques expressed in his letters how serious he was about doing well in school, how he aspired to one day go to a liberal arts university, how he helped his family with chores around the house, and how he would like to visit the United States. I shared with Jacques about the classes I had in high school, how I thought that the French language had many more subtle nuances than English, and how I admired the French people's appreciation for art, architecture, literature and scholarship. Jacques and I corresponded for about a year and a half, and I learned how letters are a powerful tool in fostering good will and understanding among people from different countries.

During the summer of 1965, I, a crew cut, awkward teen, transitioned from my sophomore to junior year at Hilo High School. In that season, I learned how letters fill a compelling need to share excitement, joy, sadness, and concerns with persons not present when eyebrow-raising events take place. In July 1965, I traveled outside of the Hawaiian Islands for the first time in my life. Six other high school students and I formed a youth delegation from Lutheran Church Missouri Synod congregations in the state of Hawaii. We attended a youth gathering in Squaw Valley, California, near Lake Tahoe, along with 3,000 youth from Missouri Synod churches in the United States. The 1960 Winter Olympics had taken place there five years prior, and so many of the facilities at Lake Tahoe still had an international look and feel to them. At the convention, we listened to guest speakers including columnist Ann Landers and folk singer Pete Seeger. What Landers said and what Seeger sang was troubling to my soul. They both spoke grim words about changing times, not all positive.

Living on an island 2,300 miles from the next closest state in America and being only fifteen years old, how naïve I was to the tremors taking place in Vietnam, the Middle East, university campuses, impoverished urban neighborhoods as in Watts and Detroit, race relations, free speech, women's rights, and drugs. The unrest taking place in these sectors would shake our nation to her very core. As Pete Seeger sang his song, "Turn, Turn, Turn" from Ecclesiastes 3, he was transmitting to us in the audience the message that tumultuous changes were soon going to jolt us all. As King Solomon prophesied, the world and the U.S. were turning, turning, turning.

How shaken was I to realize that we were all living at a pivotal time in world history? I had an urgent need to share with my family and friends the experiences that took place and the messages I had received at Squaw Valley. Letters were my outlet to release the dizziness and buzzing inside me. The world as we knew it was about to be transformed in ways never imagined, for better and for worse. Writing letters to my parents and friends helped me to have a better understanding to the bright and the dark movements gaining momentum across this land "from California to the New York highland" as Seeger sang.

During the gathering of youth at Squaw Valley, I also met and became close with a group of youth from Minnesota. Probably due to the dissimilarity that the Minnesotans were from the frigid north, and I was from the balmy tropics, we were fascinated with each other's homeland. Following the conference, four of the Minnesota youth corresponded with me off and on throughout our high school years. We exchanged letters about two to three times a year. In Hawaii where I lived, the sun rose at around 6 a.m. and set at about 6 p.m. the whole year round. But through letters from my friends in Minnesota, I could visualize 9 p.m. sunsets in the summer and 5 p.m. darkness in the winters. I shuddered as I read about the thousands of mosquitoes ascending as the Minnesota sunlight waned on a July evening. I marveled at the description of two feet of snow cushioning the farmland. Such was the miracle of words in letters from friends five time zones apart.

After the Squaw Valley gathering, the seven of us in the youth group from Hawaii rode in a VW bus driven by our chaperone, a pastor of the Lutheran Church Missouri Synod near Pearl Harbor, Reverend Louis Marting. With what seemed to be a perpetual smile on his face, Pastor Marting drove us from Squaw Valley to Los Angeles with overnight stops in Carson City, Sacramento, San Francisco, Monterey (John Steinbeck territory, an author I admired even in middle and high school), Carmel, San Louis Obispo, Yosemite, and Terra Bella along the way. I wrote letters to my parents and friends during the trip, and after I returned, they kindly commented how much they felt the enchantment I was sensing as I wrote about activities on the VW bus trip such as playing softball at a church picnic in Sacramento, riding a cable car in the city by the bay, eating freshly caught abalone at a restaurant on Cannery Row, seeing a 3,000 foot "waterfall" of orange glowing embers descending down Glacier Point in the evening, seeing miles and miles of citrus trees with ripe fruit in Terra Bella, visiting the gigantic campus of UCLA with a Lutheran chaplain giving us a tour, and riding in a tea cup at Disneyland.

My letters, however, were not always uplifting and inspiring. My immaturity as a fifteen-year old revealed itself in some of my sarcastic comments written in my letters to my friends. Without praying and asking God to edit any untrue statements in my letters, I remarked how snobbish and conceited two youth were in our VW bus travel group. These two youth attended an elite, private high school, which just about every high school student in the state who did not attend that school hated. The school was Punahou High School, the ivy league high school, in Honolulu. That would be the school which former U.S. President Barack Obama would attend about ten years after the Squaw Valley youth summit and the VW tour of California. I wrote with extreme prejudice and resentment that the two youth looked down upon the other five of us, lowly public-school students. Years later I realized how sinful I was in making those false accusations. I knew that my friends who received my letters would laugh at my snarky remarks of the private school youth. However, I had no evidence to prove that the two students from Punahou High School were arrogant and cliquish. Years later I repented to God of my baseless and unfounded criticism that I shamefully wrote in some of my letters in the summer of 1965.

The letters and excitement of the mesmerizing summer of 1965 in California did not end when the 10-day VW tour was completed. The road trip through California wound down and in spite of the transgressions I committed in my letters on the trip, the Lord graciously granted me the undeserved privilege of spending two more weeks in California. My Uncle Harold and Aunt Miyo Ueki invited and took me in to spend time with them in their home in Redwood City, located south of San Francisco. While there, my uncle took me on two fishing outings. The first was to Half Moon Bay where we caught about a half a dozen foot long, silver and dark green mackerel off the pier. When we brought them home, my Uncle Harold cleaned them, and my Aunt Miyo fried them for dinner.

My uncle, aunt, their three daughters and I enjoyed the delectable mackerel from the frigid waters of the Pacific Ocean. The second fishing trip that my uncle planned was to breathtaking Morro Bay where our group of youth from Hawaii had just visited in the VW bus. In the blue-black, dark, chilly hour before sunrise with majestic Morro Rock towering over us, my uncle and I casted our fishing lines from a white sand beach into the breaking surf. We placed our rod and reels into metal stakes and sat on aluminum pole, plastic mesh beach chairs. Shortly after daybreak, my Uncle Harold's pole suddenly bent sharply downward, and he rushed to pick up his rod. He started reeling in the monofilament line but stopped reeling when whatever was on the line made a surging run out toward the sea. When the ocean creature tired, my uncle then reeled in more line. This sequence of reeling in line followed by the fish pulling out line went on for about a half hour. After a valiant fight on the part of the fish, my uncle, somewhat exhausted and breathing hard, pulled the fish into shallow water inside where the waves were breaking. My uncle and I recognized that my uncle had hooked a four-foot halibut. It's pure white under belly flashed in intervals as it splashed on the surface of the water. Finally, Uncle Harold pulled the fish up on the sand. It was an impressive halibut, about forty-five pounds. With much delight, Uncle Harold cleaned the fish at an area with a water spigot. He then placed the filets into a cooler, and we drove homeward to Redwood City with gratitude for the fine catch at Morro Bay. I had friends in Hilo who were avid fishers and so with elation, I wrote to them about the two fishing outings I had taken and how well my uncle did. My friends shared that they were very interested in learning how people in states other than Hawaii fished and that they read with interest what I had recounted. Again, it was through letters that emotions and information were transferred from one person to another.

After living eighteen years in the same three bedrooms, white, with brown trim, pine and redwood single wall constructed home, I left Hilo to attend college in Portland, Oregon. The transition was stark for a small-town boy. Hilo at that time had a population of 25,000. Metropolitan Portland was about twenty times bigger with a population of about 500,000. The food was very different. In our family of Japanese descent, we ate rice 365 days a year. At the college dorm where I lived, rice was served 20 times during the whole school year. Most people in Portland spoke with almost perfect grammar and with a smooth accent. I spoke with a dialect consisting of English, Hawaiian, Japanese, Chinese, Portuguese, and Filipino words, with choppy, abrupt utterances. During my years in Oregon, as beautiful as that state was, I would long to be back in the islands where the environment, food, and language were familiar to me.

In 1967, like most college students from low to middle income families in Hawaii and probably in most parts of the U.S., I did not telephone my parents long distance and neither did they call me. I was only allowed to call home if I had a serious injury requiring hospitalization. Communication was to be done through letters. My mother and father faithfully wrote monthly letters to me with my mother writing three fourths of the letters. I was inconsistent in many areas of my life, but I did reply to each of my parents within two weeks. The priority of writing to and receiving letters from my parents transcended my lack of discipline.

Many times, my parents brought relief for my homesickness through their wonderful letters. They wrote about how Hilo High School was doing in basketball, a topic that greatly interested me. They passed along greetings from my friends whom they met at the grocery store or the service station. They wrote about a huge tuna, which my dad had caught on his sampan. They reported on who was elected as the mayor of the county. They gave a health report on my fraternal grandfather and maternal grandmother. They described how an earthquake jolted them but did not cause damage. They related how excited everyone was with the lava eruption. My parents updated me on my younger brother's activities, which included surfing, playing drums in a school rock music band, and hunting wild pigs and pheasants.

In turn, I wrote to my parents about the tough subjects I was taking including Greek, German, Economics, Geology, Public Speaking, and English Composition. I lamented how much I missed them and home. I related innocuous events such as how surprised I was on the day after Thanksgiving when I bit into a turkey sandwich, which my classmate's mother had made at their home. The sandwich had cranberry sauce in it, a condiment that I had never had in a sandwich. At first, I was taken aback by it, but I let my parents know that afterward, I really liked it. In my letters to my parents, I often shared plans for upcoming activities such as riding with a classmate who drove his family camping trailer all the way from Portland to San Diego for spring break in 1968, the same week that Martin Luther King was assassinated in Tennessee and rioting and fires erupted in major cities.

In my college years away from home, I probably wrote seven letters a month to family and friends, and I received about the same number of letters back. All total, over the four years in college, I wrote about three hundred letters and received as many as I sent out. None of those six hundred letters were so poignant as the four letters I received from my cousin Terrance Ogata, a Specialist 4 in the U.S. Army, while he was in Vietnam during 1970 to 1971. In his first three letters, he described riding in helicopters with his protector, his rifle, always clutched close to his side. He expressed disdain toward college protestors back in the states who had no idea of what soldiers like him were going through. He told me how he yearned for the day when he would complete his tour and see his beloved girlfriend once again.

Each of his four letters were written on wrinkled, thin paper and sealed in crinkled envelopes probably due to being carried in his tightly organized back pack as he wrote a page or two whenever he had a break. In his fourth letter written in January 1971, he wrote with heightened emotions about how dangerous his circumstances were and how at any second, he might need to pick up his rifle and fire, and how he yearned to see his girlfriend again. As I had done after receiving each of his three previous letters, I wrote a letter back to him, encouraging him and letting him know that I was praying for him and thanking him for his service to our country. Three weeks later my parents called me on the phone, the only time in my four years of college that they phoned me. In a tender, composed voice, my mom said, "Lester, I have some sad news to tell you. Terrance died in a helicopter crash on February 23, 1971."

I was stunned as I heard my mother's somber words. Terrance died in a helicopter crash while on a mission over Laos. The tumultuous forces about which Pete Seeger had sung to the 3,000 Lutheran Missouri Synod youth at Squaw Valley five years prior in 1965 had struck a staggering blow to my family. The massive global, social, cultural and political upheavals of the 1960's and early 1970's had become all too personal. These pandemic movements all played a role in the loss of a Special 4 U.S. Army soldier who simply wanted to go home, marry his hometown sweetheart and raise a family.

If making a long-distance phone call required a catastrophic event so was flying home from the continental U.S. to Hawaii during the school year. Many college students were in a similar situation as I. When we left home for college in September, we did not return home for Thanksgiving, Christmas, New Year's, or any holiday. We flew back to Hawaii the next May or June when the school year ended. Only the devastating loss of an immediate family member warranted flying home for a funeral. The death of a cousin, uncle, aunt, grandparent, or friend did not qualify as a reason to fly home. And so, I was extremely thankful for letters from my parents and my aunt who described the honorable, military funeral that took place at Terrance's Methodist Church in Hilo of which he was a member. Since I could not be there for Terrance's funeral, letters from my parents and my aunt were the only means that I would know what took place in the weeks and months after Terrance's passing.

In the decades after I returned home from college, my letter writing became subdued. I got married and along with my wife Bernadette raised two children while holding down a job and volunteering a lot of time at our Missouri Synod Lutheran Church. I feel badly that one of my college friends Bud Grossmann, who lived in California and then on the island of Oahu in Hawaii, faithfully wrote me letters at least once every two months. I, however, was negligent in not replying to many of his carefully thought out letters. I later felt very badly about not reciprocating his generosity, and so I am now hand writing letters to Bud as he did to me for about three decades. I hope to recompense him for all the priceless hand-written letters that he mailed to me back in the 1970's through the 1990's.

Another devoted letter writer for whom I am thankful to the Lord is the person with whom I am currently collaborating, Don Fortin. In 2006, I moved to Hawaii from Vacaville, California where my family and I lived for sixteen years and where I met and became close friends with Don, his wife Liz and their children Alison and William. Since 2006, for the past ten years, Don has written me at least 120 handwritten letters, with precise, unmarked three-quarter inch side margins and half-inch top and bottom margins. In legible ball point stroked script, he has sent me at least a thousand pages of letters with topics ranging from the pleasant valleys surrounding Vacaville, the sparkling wisdom of students at Bethany Lutheran, Vacaville Christian, and Buckingham Schools; restful vacations on the shore of Lake Tahoe, walking his and Liz's adorable dogs Jake and Coco, home improvement projects on Ruby Drive, energized crowds at San Francisco Giants ball games, caring for family, commentary on current events, teaching Sunday school at Bethany Lutheran Church, attending worship services at Faith Community Church, exceptionally helpful tips on improving one's writing skills, and recommendations on great books to read. I have saved all one thousand pages of Don's letters in three ring binders, five of them total. I gain much encouragement and opportunities for reflection as I read them. Each letter includes many uplifting messages from the Bible.

Don's letters especially helped me through 2016, when my 91-year old mother Carolyn Seto was under hospice care at my home and was becoming frailer with each passing day resulting in the Lord taking her home to heaven on October 10, 2016. While caring for my mother and while volunteering as a pastor of a church, the Lord worked through Don in encouraging me to keep writing the draft of a book on Gentleness in the Old Testament. The manuscript began with the theme of gentleness in a harsh world, but as I got deeper into writing the manuscript, I began to focus attention upon the outpouring of gentleness found in the section of the Bible that many consider to be cruel and legalistic, the Old Testament.

It was through Don's many letters that year that I was able to carry on with my manuscript despite most of my waking hours being needed to care for my mother and the church that I serve. All praises are given to the Lord of power and mercy whose kindness and support are often conveyed through letters. By the grace of God, letters from compassionate Christians like Don, my parents when they were living, Bud, and other friends and family have gotten me through challenging times. Hopefully this book will give you encouragement to write letters to lift the hearts of friends and family in your lives, which would welcome a message of joy, peace and love centered in Jesus, who is God's living letter of love and life to all creation. As we consider the value of letter writing, may we remember that we are all "letters" of Christ to a world that desperately needs cheerful words.

"You yourselves are our letter, written on our hearts, known and read by everyone. You show that you are a letter from Christ, the result of our ministry, written not with ink but with the Spirit of the living God, not on tablets of stone but on tablets of human hearts" (2 Cor. 3:2-3, New International Version).

Chapter Three

HOW WE STARTED OUR WRITING

Many American writers have achieved success in their creative endeavors; but even the best, in my humble opinion, had critical internal conflict. One such writer went on to publish a truly great American novel, calling out the instant crisis of Americans who became homeless gypsies migrating across vast country in search of work, food, and shelter. The book is "The Grapes of Wrath" (October 1938). The author was John Steinbeck, Nobel Prize winner for "Wrath".

What were Steinbeck's internal conflicts? Why did the ideas seem like "random target practice shot gun patterns" and how did it add to, or detract from the author's work? I'll share a few paragraphs from "Working Days-The Journals of The Grapes of Wrath" by Steinbeck. You'll see how events and outside interruptions (external and internal) acted to create a pulse or trigger in the work of this exceptionally unyielding writer. The temptation was to digress, divert his attention, or even ban the writer's progress completely—and this is how it impacted Steinbeck.

"Entry #52, August 16, 1938—10:45, Tuesday: Demoralization complete and seemingly unbeatable. So many things happening that I can't not be interested...I almost feel that it would be a good thing to go up there to write [The Biddle Ranch] but I won't, I guess. All this is more excitement than our whole lives put together. All crowded into a month...Too much, too much. I should not try to write books in the summer. It is just too much. Too much. I feel like letting everything go. But I won't. I'll go, and I'll finish this book. I have to...I simply must get this thing out of my system. I'm not a writer. I've been fooling myself and other people...I'll try to go on with work now. Just a stint every day does it. I keep forgetting..." (Steinbeck pp. 56).

What Steinbeck's finely tuned mind was trying to do was to reassert the need to place a firewall between the crashing intrusive thoughts about his real-world problems and compartmentalize his rational story-telling thoughts. He became so overwhelmed that particular day, and on many other days, that he wrote to express an idea that he was really not at all a true writer.

Yet in the subsequent entries, Steinbeck 'willed' himself to go at a savage rate of writing 2,000 words daily to complete the book that would be his masterpiece. The firestorm of threats, both the legal sort, and even his personal safety weighed heavy on Steinbeck, and these things would have caused lesser writers to fold up their tent and drift off into the night sans a book. Whatever the challenges were, against all odds, Steinbeck continued, and in November, his book was done.

In January 2016, when Les and I began our discussion of co-authoring this book, there were the usual hints of excitement ("Ah, were going to publish!). There was also the extraordinary pressure on each of us, much like the Oroville, California dam that began to crumble from the monsoon of rain; and these things augured a severe threat to our writing.

These pressures were Les's mother's advanced, end-stage Alzheimer's disease and the attendant 24/7 care that fell to him, his brother and his wife, Bernadette Seto. Several of our letter exchanges revealed the narrow band of early am or very late pm hour that Les had available to write. His mother's need for constant close supervision was almost deadly to all Les's other pastoral and family duties.

He never expressed to me, any malice; nor did he evidence the harboring of any ill will towards life for the uncomfortable situation he found himself in. Rather, he continuously gave God the glory for the tiny pieces of free non-church related writing time allotted to him. I was energized by Les's thankful and humble attitude of giving care to his mother. His comments to me exuded gratefulness of being able to write at all.

I've known Les for sixteen years in his capacity of being my pastor of our place of worship "Bethany" in Vacaville. I had served on church committees, so I knew that time and motion studies revealed that during a long stretch of years, Les had put in over 270 hours of work each month. This was in comparison with a normal 40-hour week /160-hour month!

Even then, Les wrote out his sermons of the 45-minute variety during the week to be delivered twice at Sunday services. Many hours were given in preparation of those deliveries. If a survey of pastors of differing faiths or denominations were done, perhaps we would not find this polling much different from church to church. Amazingly, pastors will confide that the research and writing of sermons provides an escape or catharsis release from the pressure of long days of home visits, counseling, meetings, planning, organizing, directing, budgeting, and supervising the church staff and allocation of offering funds. The letters or sermons must have an altruistic value because Jesus said it is better to give than receive.

Most of America's gifted servants of God are equipped to run large corporate entities, yet the call of discipleship outweighs other vocational pursuits.

I offer as evidence these precious comments contained in Les's letter dated Thursday, June 23, 2016 at 5:58 am. Les wrote: "I am praising the Lord for another hour of non-church related writing where I can either respond with precious friends like you or work on my gentleness manuscript. After this hour, I will devote the next sixteen hours in caring for my mom, [Carolyn Seto], spending time fulfilling my pastoral duties for Waikoloa Lutheran Church and doing my domestic housekeeping chores. Then at 11 pm tonight I shall enjoy my daily second hour of exceptional joy as I resume writing related prose. Finally, at midnight I shall indulge myself with six hours of blissful rest. How remarkably blessed I am to have such a marvelous daily schedule."

Now lest anyone think Pastor Seto was being coy, consider his next paragraph in that letter that defined his balancing of his situation to other islanders he knows.

"I think about some of the hotel employees with whom I worked part time from March 2013 to September 2014. They worked two full time jobs with no days off to support their families. They had almost zero time off for fulfilling activities…I am not entitled in any way to complain."

There is a scripture that states, "As iron sharpens iron, so one person sharpens another" (Prov. 27:17, New International Version). I believe this is the bond of men and women when they lift one another up in supportive words and actions. As I read Les's letter that day, I began to assess my own situation of which I was just then going through day by day, little by little. In May of 2016 one of my dearest friends who happened to be my father-in-law passed away at age 94. My painful grief I was able to redirect in letters to Les. He consoled me, all the while giving me the perfect words to encourage me to continue in the completion of my book, "Sister Vina's Boy." I was in the revision stage of the book at that time before I could draft a cover letter to have a publisher consider accepting the book for publication.

All this while, Les was making tremendous strides writing the saga of his own book on gentleness in the Holy Bible's Old Testament. Many things confronting me seemed as overwhelming as ever could be imagined. Family care issues and acute illness as well as the death of Dad seemed to strangle my peace right out of me. Les and I exchanged chapters of our two separate books via postal services and I could see how his work in each chapter reflected his own personal constitution—he was amplifying his belief in the power of inner strength, derived from God to help balance the daily on-going real-life drama. So, I could see the curative power of Les's writing, both to be an encourager to me in my endeavor, and to acquaint me with how biblical figures or characters of old were able to persevere in their own struggles. I seem to have a new prospective and understanding of the commonly used expression "of biblical proportion", when someone talks about huge events occurring in their life.

Les and I are 6,000 miles apart and are still able to bear one another's burden as we poured out our souls in letters. We do not unload trivial or awkward burdens on one another and then seal the envelope and dismiss our private angst. Rather, we try to postulate how we can rise above the trending problem, by writing out our situation, relating it on a scale of high and low comparing against what biblical characters, or our own current mutual neighbors at Bethany endure.

By carefully describing the events of a particular day or night, my letters made Les feel that he was there accompanying me through all the normal daily activities, as well as traumatizing events. Busy and enjoyable events were included for balance. In this way, I often was able to clean out the funky debris in the deep furnaces of my logic and memory and refuel allowing my subconscious memory to reengage and shift into high gear, in all aspects of my life. My writing improved because of this investment. Treatment for this and other ills is explained in clear and situational ways in the wonderful book "The Art of Slow Writing" by Louise DeSalvo. Ms. DeSalvo writes in a concise, well-rounded "how to" manner for fledgling would be writers. Many of the examples of well-known authors and their harrowing struggles to complete their masterpiece novels are well documented in her book. I found beautiful remedies to writer's block, and how to remove other nagging impediments to writing within the pages of "The Art of Slow Writing."

I am amazed, in my other vocation of being a teacher to children from 6th grade to high school seniors, at their lack of penmanship skill. Many of the students confide in me that they do not know how to read or write in script. But many of these same students are willing to be taught. I suspect that texting on smartphones is the culprit in this case. Letter writing in the old reliable style of plain unlined paper with ink pens, and the beautiful script of bygone days, to me, is the ultimate form of communication. If done right, it just cannot be beat.

Being that I am engaged in teaching, I must winnow out of my thoughts, the ideas that seem to percolate in random unordered manner. I try to use sequential thinking; but this is not always possible; and you cannot always offer an environment for children or young adult students to thrive in intellectually and nurture their self-esteem, in order to match their physiological needs— thus says Mazlo's Hierarchy of Needs. At times, a substitute teacher, as I find myself these days to be, cannot rely solely on the teaching plans for the day. No, subtle encouragement comes by means of story-telling, prompting (by exercises of breathing), and the art of engaging awkward and resistant students to participate in group learning activity. There are other oddities in current teaching.

Housekeeping sanitation in the classrooms where I work is a direct responsibility of each teacher, since none is available through official janitorial services. Students who have been given detention, may be asked to vacuum carpets, wash white boards or sanitize desk tops. Rarely if ever is heavy cleaning accomplished easily. Then comes the knack of teaching the students whatever the formal lesson plan has been set up by the assigned teacher for the day. Many times, the material is vaguely familiar, and the students themselves are asked to become mini-tutors for others. I refer to these helper-students as 'junior professors' as our Principal likes to suggest. This then becomes an elevated risk, low yield to allow power and prestige to be given to marginally and socially adaptable kids. Sometimes it works and occasionally it backfires as I discovered one rainy, closeted day when kids wanted freedom to roam outdoors and weather did not permit this; instead they sat sullenly in hardback student chairs.

I have shared in my book "Sister Vina's Boy" of one rainy February afternoon when a classroom of sophomores decided to play a prank on me. It seemed they reverted to three-year-old's and doing all the no-nos. I merely gave up the ghost and sat staring at the class from the teacher's desk. What they did not see was that I was silently praying to Father God that my thoughts, words, and deeds would accept His guidance to my actions.

After twenty minutes of unruly acting out behavior, there came a peace—first, upon me—then upon the students and I did not lose control. Only my self-pride was assaulted that day. Still love conquers all.

I returned after several days of absence and picked up right where I'd left off. A version of "The Ransom of Red Chief" by O

Henry, became the latest Chapter 17 entitled "Teaching Kids" in my book. Every experience, bad and good, is worthwhile to promulgate your training to permit a teacher to grow and expand in their chosen avocation. As an educator, I believe it is vital to convey "I won't waste your time if you don't waste my time." Each class hour is designed to cover X amount of material to provide stepping-stones and building blocks to that subject course. Any deviation results in blank spots in the child's knowledge base. Ergo, the lack of training students of cursive handwriting is a failure of their skill development.

By writing about these class pranks, and by sharing both my poor sense of self-worth as a teacher that day, and humbling episodes of difficult teaching moments—I overcame the scary, diminishing strength-zapping anguish that all true teachers encounter.

I have profound respect for teachers. Sometimes it seems that some parents send their sugar-fueled hellion forth at dawn of day, depositing the half awake, then suddenly, feverous kid; the child becomes a whirling dervish spinning top into the unsuspecting first period teacher's classroom. This child can easily be multiplied to twenty-plus students in the poor teacher's room. And parents wonder why Junior can't write, read, or multiply!

Hopefully, the teacher begins the hour with bowed head, and reverent silent prayer. The adventure then begins. No teacher I've met ever feels bored, but many teachers are quite worn out by the turn of the school calendar to June.

I am fond of talking with and writing about the teachers I have met, or better said, the actors on today's world's stage. You must be a quintessential actor to get all the information out to the students in a calm and undistracted manner. Here's what Ezra Pound, author of "The Cantos" had to say about this matter.

ABC of Teaching

"The teacher or lecturer is a danger. He very seldom recognized his nature or his position. The lecturer is a man who must talk for an hour. France may possibly have acquired the intellectual leadership of Europe when their academic period was cut down to 40 minutes.

I also have lectured. The lecturer's first problem is to have enough words to fill 40 or 60 minutes. The professor is paid for his time and his results are almost impossible to estimate...no teacher has ever failed from ignorance. That is empiric professional knowledge. Teachers fail because they cannot "handle the class." Real education must ultimately be limited to men who INSIST on knowing, the rest is mere sheep herding."

Chapter Four

HARNESS THAT INTERNAL CONFLICT

Memorial Day, May 29, 2017

"I do not understand what I do. For what I want to do, I do not do, but what I hate I do" (Rom. 7:15, New International Version).

Internal Conflict

"When Johnny comes marching home again, Hurrah. Hurrah.." (Civil War Song by Patrick Gilmore, Public Domain)

Writing at my desk in my wife's and my two-bedroom cottage, two hundred miles southeast of Pearl Harbor, on an overcast, sultry Memorial Day 2017, my thoughts focus upon the men and women of the U.S. military, particularly the heroic, unselfish Johnny's and Jennie's in our nation's history, who did not "come marching home again" to the "Hurrah, Hurrah", the cheers of their family, friends and hometown residents. They did not come marching home again to jovial, celebrating crowds because they had given their lives in the line of duty as infantry soldiers, sailors, aviators, medics, chaplains, and other support staff.

In the previous chapter, Don began by calling our attention to the internal conflict that all people experience, including those striving to become writers. Today I struggle with an inner conflict related to how self-absorbed I was as a young adult when I hid behind, first, my college student draft deferment, and then, secondly, my high draft lottery number 273, and did not volunteer to serve my country. I was not a physical draft dodger, but in my soul, I was one. I chose not to serve our country while millions of Americans in my demographics did, of which more than fifty-eight thousand died, including my cousin Terrence Ogata and five of my high school classmates. On this day of remembrance, I struggle with the inner conflict of my guilt, shame, and remorse. I also somberly thank God for the sacrifice Jesus made in dying for the forgiveness of my sins, and for the sacrifice that legions of Americans in the history of our nation made in dying for the liberty of their fellow citizens, including an unworthy one such as I.

Inner conflicts such those churning inside me today can have a wholesome outcome. The painful tension of contrition for one's trespasses humbles us and drives us to rely upon Jesus for full pardon. That is a beneficial result. However, inner conflicts, as Don aptly pointed out can also block us from completing worthwhile endeavors such as inner conflicts at times halted John Steinbeck's progress to complete his masterpieces.

Internal Conflict in Beginning Writers

In December 2015, Don mailed me a gift, a classic book on creative writing. The name of the book is Becoming a Writer by Dorothea Brande. In this very helpful manual, Brande recognized how debilitating inner conflicts can be to beginning writers. She wrote,

Every writer goes through this period of despair. Without doubt many promising writers ... turn back at this point . . . [They conclude often wrongly that] they "cannot write dialogue," or "are no good at plots," or "make all the characters too stiff." When they have worked as intensively as possible to overcome the weakness, only to find that their difficulties continue, there comes another unofficial weeding-out." (Brande pp. 43)

Brande, however, does not leave her writer apprentices mired in their despondency. Instead she reassures her novices, "No ordeal by discouragement which editors, teachers or older writers can devise is going to kill off the survivor [the writer who refuses to give up]" (Brande pp. 44).

During the months of October through December 2015, I was feeling the despair and discouragement, which Dorothea Brande described in her book. At the beginning of October 2015, I had started writing a manuscript on gentle people in the Bible. But after almost a month and a half, I only had mustered 1,424 words on paper, the equivalent of about six, double-spaced, typed pages. Many seasoned writers can type that many pages in a day. For me, it had taken six weeks. At that rate, it would take an eternity to complete a manuscript for a book.

I fell back into a debilitating pattern of mine, which was to blame failures or lagging progress upon factors such as a lack of time or too many required responsibilities. I attributed the painfully slow advancement of writing a manuscript upon the sixteen hours a day which I devoted to the care of my 90-year-old mother with Alzheimer's and the responsibilities of being a pastor of a small church. I also fought with the voice inside of me that said, "Your writing is so ordinary, uncreative and unimaginative. Who will ever want to read it, let alone publish it?" I used these internal struggles as reasons for not progressing as I thought I should have after a month and a half.

Internal Conflict: Never an Excuse

It was during my dark cold days of the soul that Don both admonished and encouraged me to keep writing no matter how down I was feeling. In a letter penned to me a week before Thanksgiving, Don pleaded with me to not procrastinate in writing my manuscript. He implored of me,

As you and I have quoted Mr. [Benjamin] Franklin, it bears repeating, "Never put off until tomorrow what you can do today." These hints are geared to me foremost; although . . . you may find it as a stimulus to galvanize our writing into a dedicated, disciplined pursuit.

In another section of that letter, Don inspired me by sharing how the Lord had given him the strength to write daily in his journals despite many adversities. He was alluding that there are no excuses for a person seeking to become a writer to not scrawl even a few modest words every day. Don disclosed,

The journals I addressed each daily entry was to "My Heavenly Father," and I can say that after two million words, my penmanship greatly improved. Whether the content became fresh and vibrant, only the reader can truly say. I wrote some of those journal entries under somewhat high emotional distress, sitting adjacent to my son, Christopher during 18 months of his tri-weekly, two-hour dialysis, usually amidst nurses, doctors, and the steady hum of the loud popping and whirling motors of the blood cleansing in those machines.

Some days I was like Walter Mitty, lost in the oddly distracting vortex of some familiar writing of childhood, church meetings or the day's events. I often wrote in my car glancing up to watch my daughter, Alison or my son, Will, competing in soccer practice or out in the front of Ali's clarinet teacher's house on Buck Avenue. Sometimes I had the exquisite leisure time to sit out in our patio amidst the roses and write on our glass top table. All the while our faithful Jake, the family dog, was at my feet. I wrote in the public library while awaiting my children as they received math master tutoring and once, I wrote while awaiting court room jury selection and another time while sitting in the sound studio as Will blasted his trumpet at practices with teacher, Mrs. Charlene Mays or U.S. Air Force Sergeant M. Jaime Lantz. Wow, I wrote many a six or seven-page recitation in Vacaville Music Store with guitar strumming, horn tooting, etc.; all the while engaged in my inner stories, as you know.

From what Don, the writer of two million journal entry words, chronicled, I came to realize that there were always minutes in the day or night that I too, could work on my manuscript. A son's dialysis treatments, soccer practices, math tutoring sessions, a daughter's clarinet lessons, a son's trumpet lessons, jury duty, the stress of working in a penitentiary, teaching Sunday school, and volunteering in other church activities did not deter Don from writing daily. There was no way that I could claim to not have enough time to write even a few words daily for my manuscript.

Mentoring by example. That was what Don was doing. He was saying that he found time to write even though his day was filled with sixteen hours of spousal, parental, career, and volunteer commitments. Despite these obligations, he managed to eventually write two million words of journal entries. I could not use my sixteen-hour days of caring for my mom and tending to my duties as a pastor as obstacles preventing me from writing a manuscript on gentleness. Don was saying to me that if he could carve out time to write every day by the providence of God, so could I. No excuses, no sympathy, period.

Harnessing Internal Conflict: A Strict Schedule

Two weeks after sharing with me how he managed to write daily in his journal, even during demanding commitments, Don wrote in a December 1, 2015 letter to me,

You must write nightly or daily . . . Start early in the morning. End before you tire. I recall Hemingway saying that he threw out many of the early pages in each book after he labored over it for days. The idea was to begin with spontaneity.

Concerned about my internal conflict which was holding me back in my writing, Don then further advised me in a December 9, 2015 letter: "Dedicate yourself to a specific hour or two each day. Spend other parts of your traveling day in observing others."

It was then that I made the commitment (as Don noted in Chapter Three) to write for one hour in the early morning (6 a.m. to 7 a.m.) and one hour in the night (11 p.m. to 12 a.m.) Knowing, however, that I would continue to have mornings or nights where I would be struggling to formulate sentences, Don later exclaimed in his December 1, 2015 letter to me, "Les, the main problem is to write and get as much verbiage on paper as quickly as possible. I believe this creates those juices and allows free flowing ideas."

Don was saying to me that no matter how inept I felt in not having anything profound to communicate, by the power from the Holy Spirit, I just needed to keep writing and not lose momentum. Even if the sentences I scribbled seemed ashen and dry, Don instructed me to write them anyway. He said that I could later go back to refresh and reword them. The key was to keep inching forward. To remain immobile meant falling miles behind with each passing day.

His words were echoing what Don's literary role model, Dorothea Brande, had also pleaded in Becoming a Writer,

Now; strike out at once. . . If a good first sentence does not come, leave a space for it and write it in later. Write as rapidly as possible, with as little attention to your own processes as you can give. Try to work lightly and quickly, beginning and ending each sentence with a good, clear stroke. Reread very little – only a sentence or two now and then to be sure you are on the true course (Brande pp.142).

By the grace of God, the exhorting of Don and Brande's book Becoming a Writer shook me out of my doldrums. The Lord granted words, which became sentences, and sentences, which grouped into paragraphs, and paragraphs, which stretched into pages. Only by the kindness of Christ, the verbal flywheel inside me started spinning, and the manuscript started advancing. From Thanksgiving to Christmas 2015, the manuscript moved from 1,424 to 3,493 words. Because of the Holy Spirit at work, more than twice the number of words were added to the manuscript in four weeks, than in the previous eight weeks.

The sheer or mere number of words in a document, of course are meaningless and worthless unless there is intense prayer, humility, thought, care, discernment, imagination, and brutal pruning associated with them. The advice which Don and the book he sent, Becoming a Writer, helped me to understand the importance of another kind of internal conflict, the interaction between a writer's spontaneity and discipline.

Mandatory Internal Conflict: The Unconscious Versus the Conscious

While Don admonished me for allowing myself to be immobilized in writing due to excuses and frustrations and although he commanded me to basically write, even if the words seemed gibberish, he also wrote many pages on how to go back later and revise, rework, reposition sentences that I had jotted. When I read Dorothea Brande's Becoming A Writer, I realized that Don was prescribing a principle, which Brande formulated. This insight was that excellent writing is almost always the result of our unconscious spirit having the freedom to run wild in the field and our conscious mind then reigning in the unconscious into the training enclosure for productive purposes.

In a letter written on September 29, 2015, Don pleaded to me by quoting Hemingway who once chided F. Scott Fitzgerald with the command, "Write, man, write." Don was goading me to let my unconscious spirit sprint out of the corral, and gallop on the hillsides. But then with as much forcefulness, Don instructed me to figuratively bring the horse back into the enclosure to train and discipline it. His letters tutored me on how to move, eliminate and add words to sentences that I had written in a surge of energy and verve. He persuaded me that revision was needed to improve the power and quality of a manuscript. Exceptional writing is the product of the ongoing internal conflict between the unconscious and the conscious.

In a November 27, 2015 letter, Don wrote about the need for the conscious to keep the unconscious from going in all directions and directing its unbridled energy into a focused goal. He quoted from other books, which he recommended to me and which I read and found to be very helpful just as Becoming a Writer was.

I am far from mastering any rules of grace, which Don shared, but I am striving to at least come close. While Brande is the specialist of the unconscious, you must be the expert of the conscious. Understand the necessity of both faculties and understand that these two forces will often conflict with each other, but when both forces are respected and followed, the result will be outstanding prose or poetry. May I as an apprentice working to become a writer always remember this principle. Don will help me, I'm sure.

The Internal Conflict of Passion and Humility

In mid-December 2015, I sent to Don the first draft of the introduction to my manuscript on gentleness in the Bible. Don read it, and on the day before Christmas Eve 2015, he wrote a letter, which brought to my attention an offensive odor which pervaded the introduction, and which could permeate the whole manuscript. Here is what he stated:

I was drawn to . . . a particular quote of yours, ". . . Many (or some) weeks I, as a pastor and a non-profit organization administrator spent fifty percent of my time basically bringing self-centered egos together to work on projects." Because of your use of two locales: church work and non-profit work . . . you, the author could be misconstrued in the intended reader's mind (Editor or Publisher) that you were defining such people in a slightly judgmental way. Perhaps you could put in a second caveat, . . . to the one you already have that "some of the nicest people work in churches and non-profit organizations." You could say something like Paul did in the Bible and acknowledge being a sinner too. Something that would make you the equal. Because, to my way of thinking, people in church and or non-profit organizations tend to be volunteer oriented and work many extra hours, giving their best.

Perhaps, too, you could add a dose of Ben Franklin or Abe Lincoln by saying, "God must have loved the common face for He made so many of them (us)!" You see how Lincoln took a well-known fact of life and in his words, made himself a little more of the average man which takes the sting out of your "truth statement" . . . just as Saint Paul revealed in his own temperament.

Don was right. His candid remarks were justified. His point was that I definitely had a passion to encourage everyone to be gentler as Jesus was, but I in my zeal, as the carrier of this message, was getting in the way. I did not realize that I was coming across as a Pharisee or a self-righteous "better than thou" person. It was as if I were saying, "You, hypocrites, who attend church; you say you love

Jesus, yet you spend fifty per cent of your time arguing with each other. You vipers who volunteer at non-profit organizations. You say you have compassion for people, and yet you spend half of your time grumbling about how the non-profit organization is being run." I was also conveying, "Look at me, all of you complainers. I serve in this church or in that non-profit organization for pure, altruistic reasons. I am not like you, the reader. My intentions are sincere. Yours are not."

Believe it or not, it was not my conscious intent to convey that haughty message. But maybe the self-centered unconscious in me was trying to convey that odious and blasphemous message of superiority without my conscious catching and censuring it. Don helped my conscious side see the arrogance I was portraying. As Dorothea Brande and Don understood, the spontaneous and unfiltered spirit of the conscious doesn't realize how others will receive a message, and so it is up to the conscious voice to rebuke the unconscious when statements go against what Jesus teaches.

My conscious mechanism failed to detect my sinful ego, and Don alerted me so that I could make necessary corrections. I revised the introduction to my manuscript and struck out any words or statements that could be construed as condescending. I also added the Apostle Paul's words which Don cited, "This is a faithful saying, and worthy of all acceptation, that Christ Jesus came into the world to save sinners; of whom I am chief" (1 Tim. 1:15, King James Version).

In the revision, I made sure to let the readers know that I often fail to be gentle, fair and kind to persons. At times I am impatient, short tempered, and dismissive in my interaction with family, friends, co-workers and co-volunteers. In my revision to the manuscript introduction, I emphasized that I needed the gentleness of Christ more than anyone.

Often, I have a passion to correct wrongs in such sacred settings as churches and non-profit organizations. My passion to make things right, however, conflicts with the reality that I am no better than those whom I am trying to correct. I stand a convicted sinner in need of God's grace in Jesus Christ. Thanks be to Christ who forgives and transforms through the Holy Spirit all who repent and place their lives into His hands.

As God so ordained it, Don reminded me that I need the Holy Spirit to temper my passion so that I do not fall into the fatal trap of thinking that I am better than anyone else including the readers to whom I am writing. All glory be the Lord for working through Don to make me aware of my arrogance. How wonderful it is that God designed a conscious component in all of us to inwardly conflict with our unconscious when our unconscious gets out of hand. How blessed it is for friends such as Don who will stir up this healthful inner conflict within us. The result will be more humble and gentle servants of Jesus.

"What a wretched man I am! Who will rescue me from this body that is subject of death? Thanks be to God who delivers me through Jesus Christ our Lord!" (Rom. 7:24-25, New International Version).

Chapter Five

WAITS FOR NO MAN

The truth is, we all have desires. With those desires, we also have borders and constraints that seem to keep us from reaching fulfillment of our goals toward happiness. If wanted, we can detour around the borders that limit us. If that sounds confusing to you, bear with me. You'll see that we can cherish and make it work for us as writers. On the surface that sentence seems like a conflicting statement. We do well to realize our most valued treasure is time. You have heard that time waits for no one.

I enjoy Poets & Writers Magazine, and in Volume 45, Issue 3, dated May/June 2017, an article mentioned the National Endowment for the Arts (NEA). Each of that article's authors wrote about the obstacles they encountered and overcame in the pursuit of writing prose and poetry. One said: "I knew that I would write no matter what, and I wrote my way through jobs, classes, and child bearing." (Larimer). She went on to say this regarding a NEA grant she received, "I used the money for rent, utilities, supplies, and child care." The fellowship bought me Time."

In the same article, page 60-61, Benjamin Percy wrote: "If I could have any super power, it would be to stop or stretch time." There is never enough of it. Here is the math of 2011: Two young kids, one still in diapers; two teaching gigs at a traditional and a low

MFA program which translates to maybe a thousand manuscript pages in need of editing; one leaky roof; one totaled car; one novel under way; twelve speaking gigs; ten book reviews; six short stories; $40,000 in student loans." Does this sound familiar?

Benjamin wrote: "The NEA fellowship allowed me to slow down and carve out time, so that I could properly research and pour all my creative energy into a book that I couldn't have written in such a harried, exhausted state… …the gift of time which is in such short supply for all of us."

So, we see within the borders of our lives include decisions to write and set aside slots, or bands of time. This tells me the aspiring writer has obstacles, or distractions that violate the serenity of his agreed upon journey of becoming an author. We'll discuss how to overcome this menace to one of our soul's greatest joys.

In a letter dated Wednesday, July 29, 2015, at 4:02 p.m., Les Seto wrote to encourage me. In my earlier letter to which Les was providing his response, I had complained that no teenagers had shown up on a Sunday for a scheduled class. This was his comment (and why letters can help to mend frustrations and doubt and restore one's mind to be courageous).

He wrote: "With regard to your June 15th letter, I was greatly inspired by your calmness, maturity, faithfulness and joyful heart even though no teenagers attended your Sunday class. Many Sunday school/confirmation teachers would have been bitter, resentful and angry that they, as instructors, made the effort to prepare and be present to teach, only to have thoughtless, inconsiderate parents and teachers not bother to show up or even contact the instructors to be excused. Yet you graciously and gently with malice toward none used the valuable time for reflection, prayer, scripture reading and, as God would ordain it, a priceless dialogue with Don Henrich, a church elder."

Les filled several pages reflecting to me his spiritual, and often mentally draining challenge he had met, not just one Sunday as with me, but a near decade of shepherding his flock of Lutheran members at his tiny Waikoloa Mission in Hawaii. I have quoted before "Iron sharpens iron." Both Les and I have prayerfully compared the difficulties Christians around the world endure in the name of Christ's ministry to our own burdens. We have found it motivating, and in doing so, our spiritual eyes open once these reflections are shared. We remember God is always in control and the power of prayer changes things beginning with each one's sharing of his faith.

Saint James tells us: "Confess your faults one to another, and pray one for another, that ye may be healed. The effectual fervent prayer of a righteous man availeth much" (James 5:16, King James Version). James knew well that as the leader of the new Christian sect in Roman-occupied Jerusalem, he could not allow his faith to be bent and bowed by all the oppression he withstood. James wrote that strong verse to encourage us today.

My view of the power of prayer was born out of tumultuous times when I felt that Satan was giving me no quarter. When we fear destruction and are in a season of persecution by the enemies of Christ, we do well to remember James' strong prescription to ward off the disease of unbelief. We rejoice while we go through trials of our faith.

In his letter, Les wrote to put things in perspective for me. I knew, from other comments, Les's path was not a bed of roses. It seemed as a pastor, myriad arrows from the enemy were testing Les. He commented how he perceived trials coming at him in attacks on the church he is humbly leading.

"With the tiny church membership of our congregation in Waikoloa, I, for the past 9 years, on every Sunday morning as I drove to the golf course club house where we worship, said a prayer which goes like this, "Lord, there is a possibility that no one may show up for church this morning besides me and our keyboard accompanist. If that happens, please block my bitterness and antagonism from overcoming my heart. Grant me the serenity to accept the situation, and please build in me greater faith to trust even more in your divine providence."

Christian fellowship provides this encouragement. As newborn Christians, we thrive on and are spoon-fed the Word of God. We are children being trained up in the way we should grow. But as we mature beyond the toddler behavior, we become available to the full banquet of spiritual food God has in store for us. Trials and persecution seem to steel and strengthen us.

Saint Paul said, "When I was a child, I spake as a child, I understood as a child, I thought as a child: but when I became a man, I put away childish things" (1 Cor. 13:11, King James Version).

Likewise, a Christian's need to overcome uncertainty of the future, is to control time. Sometimes we need to write out our concerns and view them in writing revealed as what they are: obstructions and immature excuses. Once these impediments to our forward motion are dribbled out into the light of day and are freed from our mind, we see the detrimental power is minor. A once great wall becomes a mere hurdle to leap with faith.

Keeping a Positive Attitude

I once had a kindly supervisor at San Quentin prison listen to my comments in his office. Sergeant Worty let me explain my concern.

"Sergeant, I read in the Independent Journal Marin newspaper that they want to raze San Quentin to the ground and build high-rise condos on this waterfront property. Do you think that's true?"

Sergeant Worty who later retired with 55 years of correctional service, smiled at me and said:

"Hey kid, you know I worried about that rumor the first twenty-five years I worked here. But the second twenty-five years, I haven't given it much thought."

By the way, that was thirty-seven years ago and the Bastille by the Bay, also known as California State Prison San Quentin continues to serve the people of California very well. I took away from Sergeant Worty, a maxim I'd read that was attributed to Samuel Clemens aka Mark Twain. "Don't worry about the small stuff, and it's all small stuff."

That remark symbolized an unwillingness of staff to hightail it out of danger. I came to respect this trait from my years of rubbing shoulders with the badge-carrying men and women at that sometimes dangerous, daunting, workplace.

I learned at San Quentin: 'always be on your toes', 'don't take anything for granted', and 'cherish the strong bond of friendship of your co-workers'. When I was writing my memoir, Sister Vina' s Boy, I reflected on my employment as a correctional officer, sergeant, lieutenant and counselor, while working at four prisons. I remembered how certain words of wisdom came to me during unsettling times that helped me to survive and thrive. There were kernels of wisdom like 'Walk slow and drink plenty of water,' 'don't be in a rush, and stay hydrated on the Big Yard or on the tiers.' 'A man's word is his bond' (remember to always keep your word—and don't give it lightly—if you don't want to do a certain thing, say so. The other man will move on down the tier and find someone else to do his bidding).' 'Others will not always believe what you say—but they will believe what you do,' (action speaks louder than words one hundred per cent of the time). 'Never make promises you can't keep."

These diamonds have been passed down from generations of officers at San Quentin since it first opened for business in 1855.

Books of Wisdom come Disguised in Tattered Covers

Although I was only at Quentin four years, I came to realize that the penitent heart of a grizzled convict contained much sorrow from his younger wayward days. The errors and mistakes hung heavy in his thoughts. Old prisoners might share their wisdom with select officers and sergeants like I was at age 28 when I first entered the Inspecta-Scope Gate at San Quentin. Old cons watched you closely keeping the proverbial ear to the ground to determine whether you, the newest fish employee, could be counted on to enforce all the rules the inmates and staff must abide by.

Once old 'Lifer cons' could see an established maturity in a young officer, they might share some of their years of collected experience and earned knowledge. To me, it all boiled down to what I learned in my mother's Sunday school class that Mrs. Fortin called the golden rule. Although the lifer didn't name it as such, it carried the same idea: 'treat everyone the same way you want to be treated.' In prison, there are no credit cards and a man's word is truly his bond.' Once it is known your word can be trusted, nearly the whole population gets the word and will understand your motivation to be fair when dealing with the men. In repayment for this kindness, I began to say to all younger inmates in a friendly, non-confronting way: 'Don't do time; let time work for you.' As their sergeant, some paid attention to me.

I took the initiative to refer to each inmate I met, as 'Gentleman.' I found men, whether convicts in prison blue outfits or not, will usually respond well when I, the employee took care to bring the man up to my level of thinking, and not descend to his form of behavior. Some staff resisted this knowledge, never seeming to learn this pivotal point of dealing with men who are under restraint.

After years of observing incarcerated men's interaction up close, I acquired a survivalist mentality. With daily prayer for guidance a man assigned to work in the belly of the beast can walk the toughest beat in the state. For me, it was the assurance of Jesus' promise, "I will never leave you nor forsake you." What better wingman (Jesus) could you have?

In Les's letter, he happily recounted the many blessings he received. He mentions many positive things in his island community with respect to church and civic duties. I wrote back to Les on August 8, 2015, from our vacation at Chinquapin, Lake Tahoe, California. That day there were thunderheads rolling across the mile-high lake beneath a gray, black sky. Will, our son, witnessed a fishing boat capsize tethered to a buoy at the Chinquapin pier. Meanwhile, I reported that incident and Lake Berryessa fires burning uncontrolled in the Napa Mountains back home.

Les knew the areas I mentioned and how July 4th fireworks ignited hot spots in a pastureland adjacent to the state prison of Vacaville. Rejoicing that the fires were extinguished without major property loss or death was a reason to celebrate God's love for His children in Vacaville.

I took notice of Les's next letter of July 7, 2015 and I included my comments in response:

"Your letter had such an agreeable layout that I know you carefully dissected each topic and gave an astute understanding of my stories I love to express to you."

"Writers are described as lonely occupiers of this oddly urgent vocation of writing. Though I confess, I may be an exception to the rule; I seem to have friends enough, and I do not require uninterrupted quiet to write. I'm comfortable writing during brief lulls as a substitute teacher in a learning space full of students, whom I am teaching Spanish or Physics. I am rarely distracted; perhaps this is because of the concentration required of me during those many years inside the prison walls and fences." Old convicts had taught me well, it seemed.

As I did not know Les's formal writing mode or his method of composing, I asked:

"What conditions or environment are required when you compose letters, etc.? I imagine you writing out a sermon as though you might be addressing friends by name, or at other times when your sermon seeks to actively win souls to Christ. Maybe you might envision yourself as a street evangelist talking about the love of Christ to strangers. I don't know your techniques, although I'd be much appreciative to hear how you create your sermons. You haven't said it, but it is hoped that my letters to you could be read aloud to others, like Mrs. Seto's teen Bible class students, or fellow members of a church committee. While this may appear to be a selfish delusion of grandeur, it is not."

"Writers need to justify sharing their compositions to an audience, and I feel this is a good thing. God-centered themes and true accounts of miraculous workings of God's hand in our lives, bears retelling. Jesus told his remaining eleven disciples, "And he said unto them, Go ye into all the world, and preach the gospel to every creature" (Mark 16:15, King James Version). He was not speaking only to preachers, but to all who are saved from sin and are called according to His purposes."

I continued in this vein:

"I've always held high the value, as you do, of writing with good penmanship, an orderly topic with secondary emphasis on Christian application. The true, hidden pure world of Christ is what I enjoy translating into in my writing."

At this point in our 16-year friendship, I took the proverbial 'Nestea plunge' and dove right into my belief that Les should produce a book. Wow! In retrospect, I was pushy and aggressive, pursuing an idea that would, if it reached fruition require hundreds of hours and full use of Les's faculties as a thinker and interpreter of God's Word. I did not act timidly; perhaps the denouement was in the next paragraph.

"You know, Les, that twenty years of scripture-quoting sermons being written weekly for the edification of your calling has been a training ground for a novel or autobiographical letter. God has been preparing you for more—much more."

This was the baited line designed to hook Les into what might become an achievement for God.

Sermons reached a hundred or so in Les's tiny church mission at that time. A published book reaches millions of readers dependent upon the message. I strongly believe that the Word of God is sharper than a two-edged sword and is able to pierce through the darkest stubborn heart. So, I proceeded with my sales pitch to Les. In a college business class, I'd been taught the ABC's of salesmanship are: "Always Be Closing" the deal. I continued with a nugget as an appetizer for what I believed would be a feast for my friend. Knowing Les to be a great admirer of the writings of the Apostle Paul, and Paul's scribes Mark and Luke, I proceeded with this reasoning:

"Just as Saint Paul had his training in tent making and his study of the Jewish teachings in the Torah, so he was being prepared to start all those early Christian Way churches in Asia Minor. Still, what stands many hundreds of years on is Paul's wonderful letters to the churches. What proof positive to today's writers of encouraging gospel-filled letters."

"Someone, someday may happen upon our sharing of the good news and say, "I need to put this out to many because it contains something that might meet the void in the lives of the poor, hungering, masses of readers."

Then to illustrate the scarcity of good stories applied to modern day situations, I gave an illustration.

"With the exception of the TV and radio evangelists, not much is coming out of the church to cause the sinners' ears to perk. Society gets plenty of sex, violence, and ungodliness on TV, in movies, magazines, and news. But where's the truth being shared; that Jesus does heal; that He satisfies every need; that Jesus is just outside our heart's door waiting to come in when invited?"

I felt that this line of reasoning would supplement my own inner need to express that I also needed to document God's saving grace in my life, and to do it in a short volume on my mother's prayers that led me back to God. So, it was, that the letter took a turn for self-discovery and fulfillment within me to begin a book that started in January the next year and was completed in April.

At that moment, I only had a desire to write. I had not discovered Dorothea Brande's beautiful words in her 1932 book, Becoming A Writer. I knew in my heart, I had a testament, a homage to my mother that was beginning to beg its writing. Isn't that strange? I may sense the importance to do a thing, yet I redirect it to another person to start and then achieve. Sometimes a suggestion later becomes personal work for me to complete. This all came about from a conversation within my mind. It is strange how writers come upon these moments!

Never lacking in my demanding of the best from others, I proceeded in my letter adding this tickler for Les:

"God will hold us accountable for not only our sins of commission, but our waste of that precious talent He gave to His servant (that of omission). God is ever near, and He is so merciful. This is true, Amen. What we fail to hear is the still small voice within the Christian, be he scribe or layman.

Again, this theme rose within me.

Years before I had an experience involving an inmate story that happened to me. This is to illustrate that God is no respecter of persons. This story came flowing through my letter, on page 5 of 10 to Les. See how a man of faith sharpens the iron of another man's faith with his obedience to God's calling. The story is more about acting on Godly impulse; it demonstrates the authority of the power of God's Word manifested thousands of miles from a first point of contact. You will remember that I credited my mother's prayers to lead me back to Christ. An African American Godly mother had been praying nightly for the safety and salvation of her son, an inmate. This incident came now, as I recalled a blessing God had revealed to me. It was about the power of prayer in the heart of a prisoner named Cedric. I continued, writing quickly, easily:

"Once in 2002, I walked into a prison classroom. I saw a young, slender inmate, who addressed me courteously, with, "Good morning, Mister Fortin, how are you?" I noted his cheerfulness among unsmiling inmates.

"Cedric," I said, "How are you, creature?" He smiled even more, his suddenly angelic face beaming. "I know what you mean, Mr. Fortin. Jesus told you to preach the gospel to every creature." We had daily moments in passing and exchanging scripture, as my schedule of work was very busy. Cedric was a regularly featured speaker in a small, but potent inmate orientation for newly arrived inmates. I tell you, Cedric was not ashamed of Jesus and Jesus will acknowledge us, as well as prayer-warrior Cedric's mother, before Father God."

I continued in my letter to share this little event to make a point:

"You never know the audience that reads or hears your letter, testament or story…

"Several weeks passed. Cedric came before the inmate orientation group and he spoke with power of God's redeeming 'second chances.' Imagine an inmate speaking to a captured audience of detainees talking about second chances. You cannot know the power of the Holy Ghost to free a sinful man's heart to hear that message, and the room was filled with 70 men, plus the usual eight inmate speakers. Mr. Van Bemmel, a teacher was present with other counselors. But when I couldn't imagine any more of a blessing coming from thin, devout Cedric, his words truly blew me away with his story.

"Cedric said his mother had called him last evening. She'd received a phone call from Cedric and he'd mentioned that brief morning interchange between him and I—her son trying please his Lord and Savior, Jesus Christ, and I, a prison counselor. Cedric paused, his voice low and he said directly to me:

"You know, Mister Fortin, my mom stood up in her church in Clearwater, Florida last Sunday. She was telling me that she testified before 350 people over 3,000 miles from here, how God had answered her prayer and put Mister Fortin in my life to bless me and help me. This while my mother couldn't be here to strengthen and encourage me."

Then Cedric continued:

"I hope you don't mind me telling this story, but I wanted to say how great the power is of telling somebody about Jesus."

As Cedric sat down, once more I understood what Jesus meant when He told His disciples: “Cast thy bread upon the waters: for thou shalt find it after many days” (Ecclesiastes 11:1, King James Version).

Chapter Six

TIME: A LITTLE IS A LOT

"Lord," she replied, "even the dogs under the table eat the children's crumbs" (Mark 7:28, NIV).

In Chapter Five, Don correctly diagnosed that many would- be writers fall to the wayside because they are not able to hurdle the obstacle, the illusion, of "not enough time." However, Don also emphatically reassured us that we can all rise above the imaginary blockade of "not enough time" because God gives us His grace. As the Lord declared to the Apostle Paul, "My grace is sufficient for you, for my power is made perfect in weakness"(2 Cor. 12:9, New International Version).

Almost every letter that Don sent me was a testimony that God's grace miraculously changes crumbs of time into giant loaves of art. Except for letters that he wrote while summer vacationing with his family at Chinquapin Resort on the shores of Lake Tahoe, California, or while sipping iced tea on his patio on a sunny July afternoon in Vacaville, California, Don wrote his precious epistles with only crumbs of time sprinkled here and there, sprinting from one errand or assignment to the next. He penned many of his letters, short stories, poems, journals, and books by interspersing a sentence or two in between pressing chores.

In an August 8, 2015 letter, Don wrote, ". . . I do not require uninterrupted quiet to letter write. I'm just as comfortable writing during a lull as a substitute teacher in a learning space, such as at Vacaville Christian School or Bethany Lutheran School." God blessed Don with the concentration and the discipline to write in any setting. At a table in a noisy dining area at McDonald's, or under the shade of an oak tree among the silent vineyards of Suisun Valley, California, Don could "Write, man, write" by the grace with which God supplied him.

If Don were a major league baseball player, he would be one of those rare players who would be able to tune out all distractions when he was up to the plate to bat. He would not hear the rowdy boos, the trash talk, the malicious slurs, the personal insults, and the offensive language directed at him. He would just "Hit, man, hit" without needing the absolute, polite silence enforced at golf matches when players are about to tee off, or at tennis matches before a player serves. No, Don could write wherever and whenever God gave him a crumb of a minute.

The millions of quality written words that Don composed under less than ideal conditions prove that the following words of the Apostle Paul are true,

"For I have learned, in whatsoever state I am, therewith to be content. I know both how to be abased, and I know how to abound: everywhere and in all things, I am instructed both to be full and to be hungry, both to abound and to suffer need. I can do all things through Christ which strengtheneth me" (Phil. 4:11-13, King James Version).

How amazing it is that in the seventy plus letters that I have received from Don over the past ten years and have bound in five three-hole-punched binders, not once did Don write, "I apologize for the delay in writing you. I just didn't have enough time to write over the past weeks." The sentence, "I didn't have enough time to write" is not found in any of Don's writings to me. In stark contrast, my letters to Don and to others often begin with the sniveling excuse, "I apologize for not having enough time to reply to you sooner. I'm sure you can understand how hectic life can be at times." I am guessing that very few persons if any have ever heard Don express the words, "I didn't have time to write you." Don has learned the secret that crumbs from the Lord, including specks of time, are more than sufficient to eventually transform into a letter, journal entry, poem or book, or an opportunity to do something worthwhile for Christ.

If my favorite writer ever meets Don Fortin one day and learns how the Lord has blessed him with the gift to write in between life's countless necessary duties, she would be very pleased with Don. He epitomizes the kind of "crumbs are welcomed here" writer that she had in mind.

Through their actions and their words, my favorite writer and Don give much inspiration to apprentices, not yet writers, like myself. Somehow and somewhere we wishful not yet writers have gotten the false impression that the only way to write a publication is to spend eight or ten consecutive hours of writing day after day until we complete a manuscript. With such an unrealistic understanding, it is no wonder that I waited for my whole adult life, about fifty years, to begin working on a manuscript for publication.

As the Lord would have it, Don was truly instrumental in urging me to get started. The turning point was in the late summer of 2015.

Time.... Long Overdue

We've heard the adage, "The best time to plant a tree was twenty years ago. The next best time is now." The "now" for me took place during the waning days of summer in 2015.

Since Don and I began corresponding in 2006, he has often encouraged me to write and publish something that would give glory to Christ in a wider arena than the rented golf clubhouse where the tiny congregation I serve meet for Sunday Bible study and worship. Even though I have co-authored and published a Bible study book and two Portal of Prayers daily devotional booklets for Concordia Publishing House, those three publications came with very specific guidelines as to genre and design, and I had never taken on a manuscript from scratch, where all literary categories and motifs are open to me.

I had often thought about writing a novel or a devotional type book based on Biblical or other historical characters. I was like thousands of others in my generation who thought, "Maybe someday I'll write the next great American novel" or more modestly "Maybe someday I'll write a book that will actually get published." Or more realistically, "Maybe someday, I'll write a book that I will actually complete." Don Fortin was unique. He was not like me or thousands of others in my generation. Don not only thought about writing a book, but he actually wrote not one, but three books, and had the all-American gumption and initiative to self-publish them. I only "thought about writing" and I probably would never have started on such an adventure if left to myself. I would have been still "thinking about it" up to the day when the Lord would say to me, "Time's up. Please put your pen down on the blank page in front of you. You may be excused."

In an August 8, 2015 letter, Don once again challenged me as he had often in previous letters to "Write, man, write" a book. He exhorted,

"You know, Les, that 20 plus years of Scripture quoting sermons being written for the edification of your calling has been a training ground for your novel or autobiographical letter. God has been preparing you for more—much more. Just as Saint Paul had his training in tent making and the study of the Jewish teachings in the Torah, so he was being prepared to start all those early Christian Way churches in Asia Minor. Still, what stands so many hundreds of years on is his wonderful (Luke transcript) letters to the churches. What a proof positive to young writers of encouraging Gospel letters. Someone someday may happen upon our little sharing of the Good News and say, "I need to put this out to many."

Then in that same August 8, 2015 letter, he became more intentional as he wrote, "God will hold us all accountable for not only our sins, but our wasting of that precious talent He gave to his servants—us." I understood Don's message clearly. The precious talent to which Don was referring was the talent from God that he thought was in me and could be used to share the Good News of Jesus Christ in creative ways conceived by God.

Over the past decade, whenever Don would plead with me to begin writing a manuscript to be published, I used different excuses. I first used the alibi that I was working two jobs, one as a pastor and the other as an administrator for a non-profit, and I also needed to check on my mom every day at her home. Then later when my mom needed more care and moved in with my wife Bernadette and me, I quit my non-profit organization job but continued to serve as a part time pastor. And so, at that time, whenever Don would admonish me to start writing something to be published, I gave the excuse that I was too busy being a part time pastor, and a full-time caregiver for my mom.

When a person has been thriving on crumbs and yet has been thriving hears excuses such as mine, he or she has very little sympathy. Such was the case with Don. Instead of writing, "I completely understand your busy schedule. With all that is going on in your life, you would do well to hold off on starting to write a book. I won't bring up the subject of you writing a book again." No such pity did Don shower upon me. Instead in a letter dated August 20, 2015, Don sent me three crisp and charming short stories about childhood experiences in Portsmouth, Virginia and Lakeport, California. He wrote these delightful three short stories within a few days, not a few months. By his actions and his accomplishments in writing those three stories, generated by God, he was pointing out to me, without saying or writing his thoughts, that a lot can be accomplished with only a few crumbs of time.

Don then closed that August 20, 2015 letter with these persistent words:

"Have you begun any personal writing (for publishing)? I know there are several good books within you and God's Word is within you. I recently wrote to good retired Pastor Vern Oestmann encouraging him to write an autobiography which I volunteered a Biblical title called Cast a Long Shadow – he is, as you know, both a physical large man and a spiritual man of enormous size and value. . . In God We Trust . . .Don."

A person on a mission. A Christian with a vision. That was Don. Not only was he imploring me to write and publish, but he was also doing the same with other Christians, too, such as dear Pastor Vern Oestmann. Don's vision, his mission, was that many Christian pilgrims from all walks of life would be sharing the common, one message, of God's love for the whole world and how He sent His Son Jesus to save us. Don could see millions of not yet saved people reading these books and being directed to Christ for their salvation all by the work of the Holy Spirit. Don could visualize millions of already saved persons being strengthened and enriched in their faith, through the words of Scripture that would be conveyed through the Christian books being written.

Different Letters, Same Day

Not relenting at all in exhorting persons like me and Pastor Oestmann to begin writing a novel or a non-fiction book related to the Good News of Jesus, Don wrote in a September 23, 2015 letter,

"What are your insights to these thoughts? Recall I said to you once or twice (my note: Don was being playful here. He had spoken to me many times about this subject) – you must write and put down the wisdom in words that God gives you for sharing. Your letters strengthen me immeasurably. What if hundreds or thousands could hear what is in the heart of you, a friend of God? Perhaps that is why you are in a season of being homebound to care for your mother Carolyn? God is giving you space to write and publish, not for vanity, but for encouragement."

What Don did not realize was that on that very day, September 23, 2015, when he was once again for "the third time" (I write this number in jest) petitioning me to "Write, man, write," I was writing him a letter informing him that I had made a commitment to write and publish a book to share the Gospel.

Not as Spectacular, but Similar to Cedric's Miracle

On September 23, 2015, Don was writing his letter from Vacaville, California, beseeching to me to begin writing a book to be published; 2,300 miles away in Waikoloa, Hawaii, I was writing a letter to him relaying my intent to begin writing. A week later we would both find that we had been writing to each other on the same topic on that same day. May you the reader decide if God had a hand in the timing of the two letters being written at separate locations, thousands of nautical miles apart.

In Chapter Five, Don shared another "on that very day" incident which is more powerful than the one that took place on September 23, 2015. The "on that every day" miracle which Don disclosed involved a man named Cedric, a faithful servant of Christ. On the very day in 2002, Cedric's mother on the East Coast, 3,000 miles away from Cedric on the West Coast, was praying to God to send a Christian to strengthen and encourage her son. She could not be there to spiritually support him; it was then that Cedric and Don met and shared their faith in Jesus with each other and embarked upon a lasting brotherhood in Him. Would you conclude that the timing was purely coincidental, or would you conclude that it was divinely intentional that on the same day in which Cedric's mother was praying for Cedric to meet a supportive Christian, Cedric met Don Fortin? May your choice be the true one and may you share with the joy that Cedric's mother, Cedric and Don feel even today.

Don's First Advice: Treat Time as a Treasure

Five days after he wrote his September 23, 2015 letter to me, Don received my September 23, 2015 letter. Upon reading my commitment to begin writing a book, Don's first instructions to me dealt with the imperative matter of time. With the seriousness like that of the Old Testament prophet Jeremiah, tattooed with whip marks on his back or with the sternness of an eighteenth-century Bostonian whaler, branded with rope burns on his hands, Don lectured me, not even yet a neophyte writer,

"As Ben Franklin, every man's friend, once famously said in his Poor Richard's Almanac: 'There is no better time than the present to get a job done;' or, 'Don't put off until tomorrow what you can do today.' I believe when it comes to the spiritual gift of writing . . . Satan becomes gleeful when he hears us say: 'Tomorrow I'll do it.' It must give that serpent pure happiness when otherwise dutiful servants of God bury their talents."

A few pages after this valuable caveat, Don continued his lesson on valuing time:

"So, move boldly, Christian, and set aside all hesitation and put your book in motion. As the Scripture tells us: 'Work for the night is coming when men work no more.' What we do for Christ today is all that matters; there is no guarantee of the morrow."

Valuing Time: A Core Biblical Message

Don's words and actions pertaining to time reflect one of the essential values of Scripture: the stewardship of time. Don served for six years on Bethany Lutheran Church's Life Management Committee (LMC), a team of dedicated, committed, and compassionate managers of God's resources. As were all the disciplined and wise members on LMC, Don was blessed with the gift of skillfully managing gifts from God—all the physical and spiritual blessings we have received from Him. Management is another word for the Biblical word stewardship. As with his fellow stewards on the LMC, Don's behavior and speech reveal what righteous stewardship of God's blessings looks like.

Linked to the management and stewardship of time, Don's conduct and communication are in harmony with what the Bible teaches:

God gives micro-seasons of opportunities to everyone each day. For those who write, their miniature season of opportunity during the day may be a few minutes to write while on the go. It is shameful to waste these micro-seasons of harvest. "He who gathers crops in summer is a prudent son, but he who sleeps during harvest is a disgraceful son" (Prov. 10:5, New International Version).

When God gives us a miniature summer season during the day to harvest His blessings, even if it is only for a few minutes, we need to be like ants who do not squander the opportunity of having such a season. "Ants are creatures of little strength, yet they store up their food in the summer" (Prov. 30:25, New International Version).

Just as ants don't need anyone to tell them to make the most of the summer season, we would do well to not depend on any human to motivate us. We need to follow the directives of God just as ants innately do. "Go to the ant, you sluggard; consider its ways and be wise! It has no commander, no overseer or ruler, yet it stores its provisions in summer and gathers its food at harvest" (Prov. 6:6-8, New International Version).

We need proper rest, but excessive relaxation will result in a poverty of blessings, depriving people of benefits that God intended. For writers, avoiding the strenuous activity of communication results in a shortage of truthful statements from which people might have been enriched. "How long will you lie there, you sluggard? When will you get up from your sleep? A little sleep, a little slumber, a little folding of the hands to rest – and poverty will come on you like a thief and scarcity like an armed man" (Prov. 6:9-11, New International Version).

We need to joyfully jump at any opportunity to do productive work from which others will physically or spiritually profit. Jesus encourages us, "As long as it is day, we must do the works of him who sent me. Night is coming, when no one can work" (John 9:4, New International Version).

When Jesus returns, we want him to find us properly resting or busily at work. We don't know when He will come or when we will come to Him in our dying. All the more, we want to heed His words. "It will be good for those servants whose master finds them ready, even if he comes in the middle of the night or toward daybreak" (Luke 12:38, New International Version).

For those who have not yet received Jesus Christ as their Savior, take to heart the words of the Apostle Paul. "For he says, 'In the time of my favor I heard you, and in the day of salvation I helped you.' I tell you, now is the time of God's favor, now is the day of salvation" (2 Cor. 6:2, New International Version).

Because of the evil in the world today, even more does God want us to use the time He has given us to share the Good News of Christ's gift of eternal life to all who will receive Him. For Christians who are endowed with a gift of writing, the sharing of the Gospel through the printed word is needed. The Apostle Paul wrote, "Making the most of every opportunity, because the days are evil" (Eph. 5:16, New International Version).

When I realize that I am a sluggard in not working as an ant does in the summer season and after I sincerely confess my sin to God, He gives great comfort through verses such as, "Being confident of this, that he who began a good work in you will carry it on to completion until the day of Christ Jesus" (Phil. 1:6, New International Version).

Time: Our Fiend or Our Biggest Friend

Through his letters filled with energy and conviction, Don continually pointed out to me that time is one of the greatest opponents that a writer has. When we think we have plenty of it, we will procrastinate in writing. When we think we don't have enough of time, we will use the perceived lack of it as an excuse for not writing at all. Don perceptively acknowledged that Satan uses this deadly two-pronged attack on all Christians who are seeking to become writers. Satan wants Christian writers to give up either because they wrongly perceive that they have a lot of time or because they erroneously estimate that they have too little time.

Don expounded on the treasury found in the seconds, minutes and hours of every day. When managed righteously, time is not an opponent. Every second, minute and hour are opportunities to serve God. What an asset then is each second, minute, hour, day, week, month and year, opportunities in each segment of time to share the love of Christ so that many will be uplifted in spirit, some even to eternal life by the power of the Holy Spirit.

I pray that the Lord will grant everyone and me the kind of seriousness that Don has toward time. I ask the Lord to stop me from squandering the jewels found in each segment of time. I pray that God would impart in me the joy of Christ to embrace every crumb of time realizing Christ creates loaves even out of crumbs.

What the Holy Spirit has taught Don in using time, even bits of it, to the fullest is a lesson not only for writers, but more importantly for all Christians in being thankful and resourceful in making the most of the time God allots to us. All praise to our Father, His Son and the Holy Spirit, eternal for all time.

Chapter Seven

GATHERING AND FORMING YOUR OBJECTIVES

I am but a little boy and I cannot do the work of a prophet or so must young Samuel have thought when old Eli, the priest told him: "Go, lie down: and it shall be, if he call thee, that thou shalt say, Speak, LORD; for thy servant heareth." So Samuel went and lay down in his place (1 Sam. 3:9, King James Version).

Let the Holy Spirit Inform Your Life

Some may wonder among today's Christians, just as the boy Samuel thought: "How can God possibly use someone as dull, uninformed, naive and seemingly unimportant as me to do His work?" One might even ask: "Why doesn't God's servants hear His voice audibly anymore? Is it that God has stopped speaking?" We have read: "God will not always strive with men," from King James Version, in Genesis. Or is it, we as followers of Christ, we have become hard of hearing, deaf to the voice of Almighty God? His is a still, small voice.

Pastor and friend Les has told me these things in many words as he continued to engage me to follow through with Christ-centered things.

Among these are to act on my thoughts to develop a penmanship training (journaling class) with members of Bethany Lutheran here on South Orchard Drive in Vacaville, California. I'd taught miniature model car building projects for families for five years with Les's approval and staunch support. I'd also done after-school enrichment classes for elementary kids to learn how to draw cars and hot rods. My interest in racecars and models was a great outlet for a hobby with my younger kids and their church buddies. I'd drawn Bucket T '32 Duce roadsters for years as a kid.

Les gave a vote of confidence that I should not be dissuaded in my ideas to teach and even branch out to developing a journal writing class with senior citizens at Bethany Lutheran Church. I delight in teaching. I love writing. I may love teaching writing classes.

Les helped me regroup my ideas about "Sister Vina's Boy," my manuscript. Rather than giving up on my work I had invested 180 days in writing, Les suggested that perhaps I should take a second look at the work likening it to Walt Whitman's "Leaves of Grass." That book was a life-long revision process for Whitman. I am considering ways my mother's story of her spiritual character, could be accompanied by others' in Mother's orbit. This was a sincere verification from Les to me as a writer. I recall the adage my Grandmother Bessie liked to say: "Never put all your eggs in one basket." In modern parlance: diversify. I concluded that I was writing in a one-dimensional style.

Too often we prematurely view our book as all-encompassing; then a friend or associate of ours, takes a glimpse and tells us the obvious—we need to stand back and notice that our work may be lacking in detail; skittering along preventing the reader to follow our story, much like a leaf flipping willy-nilly down a gutter on a rain swept street. Sometimes it requires just a switch from quick and easy formulaic writing, to delving deeper into the 'story'.

Walt Whitman considered his fine book to be a Life's work for him. "Leaves of Grass" was an ever changing, enlarging tapestry that captured the immediacy of a 'right now' feeling of his adventures in Nature before and after the American Civil War (1861- '65). He spent decades, modifying and adding to this luxurious book of poetry. As with many writers Whitman wrote one great novel or poetry book and was absolutely critical and unrelenting in the editing until his finished product was a masterpiece.

There are other writers who continuously publish stories and poems so that each has become a prolific writer. Reverend John MacArthur immediately comes to mind. He seems to release a new book or Study Bible each year. Several wonderful writers are discussed in Mrs. Louise DeSalvo's Book, "The Art of Slow Writing," which Les has mentioned was a 'game changer' in his writing endeavors.

Seizing Your Day

Amy Carmichael is an example of a role model, one that my own evangelistic mother often quoted from. Who was this single, slender Irish woman who spent fifty-five unbroken years single handedly tackling what we call interdiction of female sex trafficking in India? Carmichael took no furlough or sabbatical nor did she take any change-of-scenery vacations. In her missionary work, she was blessed to pursue the 'call' to be a Christian writer ultimately publishing 35 titles. Her writings deal with a common theme of being an inspiration and trusting in God through years of adversity. In her books, Amy nearly always highlighted the journey of others, seldom making herself the center of attention. Her books though published anonymously, were about being a mother to the motherless of India's orphans. Rescued children numbering one thousand, former prostitute slaves came to Christ and were freed from enslavement.

Carmichael's books are written love letters that were meant to educate the unknowing public of the horrors of enslavement of India's lower caste children. Often the predators were the so-called religious community's inner-circle. These horrible deviants devised ways to force girls to service, these evil men who hid behind the guise of religion. Boys too, were routinely abused having no escape from privation and hunger and they became Temple children.

Temple children were the ones Amy set out to rescue. She built a Christian orphanage during her years of sacrifice from what was once her private privileged life. Perhaps Amy was a forerunner, a true Mother Teresa before that saint was known.

In her middle years, Amy sustained an injury from a fall, and a homemade wheel chair was fashioned so that Amy could move about. She was born in Belfast, Ireland in 1867 and after her life of dedication to others she passed away in 1951, at the age of 83. According to her biographer as recorded in Wikipedia, Amy requested that no stone be put over her grave at Dohnaver, the orphanage she founded. Instead, the children she had cared for put a birdbath over her grave with the single inscription "Amma," which means mother in the Tamil language.

In my reading of this, I began to understand why Sister Vina, my mother, had such an interest in Amy Carmichael. Mother had an aunt, Bonnie, who also served as a missionary to India for 20 years in the 1930's. I met her once on a travel trip to Aunt Bonnie's Rose Motel, outside of Terra Haute. In the motel office, Aunt Bonnie had small ivory elephants and sari dresses for sale. I remember the sales became donations to help the children of India. Perhaps it was the books of Amy Carmichael that first drew my great Aunt to follow in Amy's footsteps. If only Aunt Bonnie had written of her travels and experiences, today I would know about her life of commitment to children.

The theme of answering the 'call to serve' extended Amy's missionary work, even though she had become afflicted, nearly totally wheelchair bound. These handicapped conditions provided an unwanted blessing, necessary to evolve Amy into a superior life. Amy was able to express her inward spirit's sweetest feelings in her books.

You will say, who of us could imagine being so disciplined? To write when we are a harried as most of, we aspiring writers seem; to publish when our book is written but still seems uncertain; to serve God all the while in a foreign land...What?! To forsake comfort and to give God all the glory; Oh, that my little cost of discipleship could be permanently fixed on the bringing of honor to Jesus Christ. Yet it is possible to do this, as Les points out in this book and you don't have to be a bedridden missionary in India.

Les has blessed my family with some time spent in prayer. I can witness the abundant residual effects of his meditative calling on the Lord for me. Les has used the talents God ordained and has not shirked from his first love of Jesus Christ. This is self-evident in his writings. Les said in the previous chapter, that he has occasionally "offered excuses for tardiness to reply" to his correspondents. I have mentioned the time and motion survey conducted in the early 2000's. It was noted that Les worked an average of 270 hours each month to complete his duties as the senior and only pastor while at Bethany Lutheran, my home church in Vacaville, California. Compare these glaring survey results to the 160-hour working-month of an average employee. The commitment to the service of God requires a cast-iron constitution, a perpetual lack of sleep, and a tremendous prayer life.

'Tis a Treasure to Learn

When I was a correctional officer, I worked double shifts of sixteen hours inside the walls of a state penitentiary. I was healthy and hungry to make the overtime wages to feed and house our young family. I can attest that prison and emergency medical staff folks are sometimes fatigued and 'running on excess energy." The work of the correctional officer and religious cleric require dedication and unerring judgment—which, frankly, is not always possible to maintain in humans. Years of this requires keeping your wits about you, and grace under pressure as Ernest Hemingway once said. This line of work is not for the faint of heart.

The writing of tracts, short stories, books, non-fiction, and chapbooks of poetry is a treasure of our heart given to others. It is a therapeutic outlet, and a sure-fire remedy for 'sluggardly' conduct as Les chooses to call wasting time.

Such is the combatant who finds him or herself in the arena of battle called writing—it must be left foot, right foot, a regimen of daily devotion to the craft. Writer's block, the nemesis of all writers, is covered well by Mrs. Dorothea Brande's wonderful book about the time waster enemy. She writes about how we as writers undercut our own 'genius' to write with, as Brande refers to the unconscious mentation, the brain's best friend. Brande's book "Becoming A Writer," is a well-spent investment. I recommend you find a copy immediately, dear reader. After all, it is apparent that any book still being sold eighty odd years after it was first written in 1932, has staying power and Brande's work is appropriate in every way to today's world of writing.

Mrs. Brande wrote three bestselling books, conducted national correspondent writing classes, and may have been one of the first female authors to write million-selling books. Her treasury of thoughts skillfully researched from her years of experience in teaching, not only informs, but gently chastises and shows—not tells—how an average writer progresses to become what her titled book indicates: an accomplished author. You need to purchase, read, and follow Brande's prescribed roadmap to arrive at a pleasant destination. It is a treasure indeed!

Explore and you may find that there are many excellent teachers, such as a lady who I have had the pleasure to know. Her name is Mrs. Denny Johnson and she was my sophomore college writing teacher. She saw a tiny ember in her students and fanned the spark into a flame of desire to write. Denny was in her first year of teaching her writing classes in 1985. She invited students to get involved in a writing workshop held in our homes after class was over. She oversaw a publication of our short stories and poems by the students in her classes. We volunteered our efforts to collate our apprenticeship efforts at writing using the Solano College print shop to run copies for each class. I look back fondly at that manual of our writing and see how a gentle yet firm teacher, in tune with her students, can rally, and galvanized my first efforts into a published manuscript. Without Mrs. Johnson's hands on mentoring, I might never have had the courage to try my hand at publishing. That simple writing booklet made all the difference for me. I hope someday to emulate Ms. Johnson's love of writing and her style of 'can do' teaching.

I love writing, as does my co-author, Les Seto; however, I am not skilled in the art of listening. I am a gabber. I find that active listening to elementary students has been a godsend to me. I have learned to tell stories at the children's request and adlib some decent fairy tales. Still, the best are the original Bible stories that I recite from memory. Thank goodness I was blessed with a mother who loved to teach and share the many wonderful tales from Genesis to Revelations. When I say tales, I mean otherworldly heroic stories all of which are true, fascinating and easily understood by children. The kids have not become cynical and jaded; it was not long since they were babes being breathed the breath of life into their beings by their Creator. I learn from my weekly reading of one hour each Thursday to a second-grade class. I've been blessed to enjoy this activity for a dozen years.

Treasure is where you find it. If you love to be around kids; if you have a desire to enchant others with stories; and if you have a fondness to give back from what you have been taught, then by all means, find a willing teacher who will allow you to be a volunteer reader. A word of caution: teachers, by training, must follow all guidelines in allowing you to enter the classroom. I began volunteer work first to learn of schoolyard safety and control. I progressed to teach Sunday school which does not require a certificate. Upon demonstrating proficiency and with the Live Scan fingerprinting completed, I was asked to teach in the role of substitute instructor. These steps will often open doors to give a novice the training to move forward in the area of storytelling. Many senior citizens would be welcomed to come share their day with young students, who like to hear stories told by 'Mister Don' or you!

The Knack of Active Listening

I am learning to be a listener. I have noticed that in any line of work, as writer Studs (Louis) Terkel explained in his marvelous oral history book, "Working," people just naturally enjoy talking about what they know best—their hours spent on the job.

I've discovered that you can mine language for your book by being an interviewer of others. Find out what your subject enjoys most in his or her day. When you begin to truly listen to the interviewee's language, the idioms that they rely on to perform their work flawlessly, and his own peculiar insider lingo that outsiders rarely have heard—is brought forth for you. I do not take notes, but I do file these precious gems away for future use. As soon as possible,

I write out scripts of dialogue from what I had heard earlier that morning, writing them usually in letters to Les Seto. True language makes a believable character.

I discovered some of the children's comments to me show me the weak places and the best parts in my story telling. Then I can make revisions later. Children allow me to unobtrusively enter their world if I respond to their tender suggestions. Often, they want to act out the story into a play for my benefit. "Hooray!" I say: "Let's do that." A few of my better short stories were from the gem of the children's own fantasy make-believe world that they allowed me to enter each day. I wonder if that is how "Jabberwocky" by Lewis Carrol came to be?

You'll find that this 'out in the open hidden treasure' is like fine embroidery of silk and satin. The language and the color of the setting in which you hear the story unfold is a jewel to behold. I walk past a beautiful rose and never really notice its essence, its color, and its enjoyable beauty. Yet the rose is there all the while. The secret to skillful writing, you'll discover, is to hold onto everything in your mind's eye, examining it, and logging away its value and perfection. Little moments and ideas become meaningful and add rich dimension to your stories, poems, or novel. Just try it and see!

When interviewing others, remember fair-play. Praise from you will stimulate an outpouring of valuable information. To be a storyteller, requires a degree of respect for your audience. Again Mother's "Golden Rule applies here. "Do unto others as you would have them do unto you."

Imagine you want to write about a prisoner. You don't need to interview a felon. You can interview the person who holds the keys to the prison. If you were to ask me about my experiences and you wanted me to tell you what a typical day was like inside a prison, you simply tell me how important it is to try to rehabilitate offenders. You simply let me know how much you appreciate how the safety and security of the community relies on how secure we manage prisons and teach inmates to become responsible fathers and sons. You let me know that you value the work that I, the prison worker, does, because you know most offenders will someday be released back into our community. It's simple to see how this method matches up nicely with appreciation as an interviewer on your part.

We see veterans wearing their WWII or Vietnam caps in restaurants, gas stations or super markets. What an opportunity to show your appreciation. I will tell you that veterans adore telling you about their foreign service, how they survived, and what the outcome of their efforts have been to them as well as to our nation. Break the ice by extending your hand and thanking them for their service. WWII servicemen are now in their late 80's and 90's and few remain among us. They are the first-person observers of the world at war.

Last year our family laid to rest two wonderful veterans of the Pacific Campaign who served in President Roosevelt's era of the 1940's. Each was a relative and friend. Whenever I chose to ask Bob Mitchell and Bill Sheehan about the details of flying a seaplane with a crew of eleven airmen over Japanese held fortress islands, or operating behind the lines in occupied Japanese territory, both men were eager to finally tell their stories. They gave me details far beyond the usual funny anecdotes that most GIs share. They told me about the stacked casualties of war, bodies of young soldiers; not just casualties, but buddies, men who ate, slept, and served alongside them. They told me how they never saw their buddies again. These were hardcore stories I might not have heard, had I not been willing to listen, and let them delve into their own past.

Many servicemen and women have kept their harrowing adventure inside their private thoughts since they were in their early twenties. Initially, the veteran appears embarrassed to tell that story, as it may seem he is bragging, and he wants no glory for his service. "Hey, we were all just doing our duty," he will tell you. But there is a great need for the story to be spun out like the web that has been locked inside and haunting their thoughts for decades. As a writer you are free to shake a veteran's hand and ask them for a few minutes to talk. They served and fulfilled their duty then, so that you and I can live freely today in our nation of citizens.

As a writer, draw your ear close to hear a description of anyone's place of work; daily tasks; scheduled interaction with co-workers on the job site and you benefit as a writer. By observing with your eyes, listening with an actively attuned writer's ear, and compiling and sifting through the minutia, you will form your characters and scenes and bring it to life on the page. Tips like these are essential to your incursion into the world of the interviewee, who may even become a central character of your book. Details enhance your story. Remember the obvious: always put in the weather, as Ernest Hemingway said.

Management by Objectives (MBO)

This is a theme developed by business teachers in the 1980's when many books about the principles of success were widely read. There is some merit in visualizing what your goal is, writing it down, sharing it with other responsible parties in seeing that it gets done, on a certain time-line. It's called M.B.O. There is a visual picture in what Mrs. Brande suggests every writer do at the outset of publishing a book. You are to purchase a small picture frame to set on your desk. Include a short topic that will say what your goal is to be. My goal was to write "Sister Vina's Boy," a Memoir, to be published by April 15, 2016, by D. H. Fortin.

There you have it. Daily when I sat down to write my narrative, I looked at that small 4" x 4" framed goal and it became real, essential, and able to be mastered if I would persevere diligently in my writing. Whether you actually get the bloody thing published or not within that time frame, is not the immediate goal. It is the critical element of 'get going and write, man, write.' As Les has written to me in his letters, the goal is to get the words down on paper, revised, offered, and published either by your own device, as I did, or by a publishing house as is the choice for Les Seto's imminent book.

Les went a step further by writing a prospective of what his book will be. Les did a yeoman's job of setting down who might be his audience, and how his book will fill a certain void in the printing world. It was as though he'd done this a hundred times and I found his copy to be quite good. Practice makes perfect. I wish for Les that a good publishing firm will guide and promote his book. I feel any editor will embrace his effort. We shall see what the Lord has in store for Les's efforts.

In my second book "Sister Vina's Boy," I wrote about examples of the kind of up-close familiarity it takes to win the confidence and trust of the incarcerated man. Theirs is a posture of natural fear and self-survival fashion of keeping an arm's distance; but one can break through that veil of distrust by gentle and rational kindness, and you can be humble without appearing weak.

You can demonstrate a servant's heart without being considered a 'mule' or someone who could be 'set up' and lured into becoming a contraband carrier at the behest of a criminal plot. To walk this narrow high wire of conduct inside a state prison is a learned trait, not one to enter into unadvisedly. As I mentioned in an earlier chapter, those idioms or kernels of knowledge that I learned at San Quentin certainly served me well. Once again, I relied on God's mercy to carry out the almost impossible job in prison work of swimming against the current; being a 'good risk taker' and trusting my ability to be a logical, alert employee using established methods of getting a goal met. We shall examine the art of prison work, teaching college students, and corralling kindergartners later in this book.

Chapter Eight

ACTIONS OF RECORDING MEMORY

"Whatever you do, work at it with all your heart, as working for the Lord, not for human masters" (Col. 3:23, New International Version).

Memorialize the Day

In Chapter Seven, Don implored us to let the Holy Spirit immerse every minute of our day with fervor to do the work of the Lord. When the Holy Spirit baptizes us in such manner, we will seize opportunities to serve the Lord. No moment will be ever be squandered. Don's actions have been consistent with his words. He has walked the talk in doing what he has encouraged us to do.

As the daylight hours grew shorter with each day, Don's letters during the months of 2015 from September through Thanksgiving, chronicled many of his daily battles against obstacles which could have diverted him from doing God's will. Sometimes adverse circumstances did prevent him from accomplishing his daily God appointed tasks. But most of the time, by the power of the Holy

Spirit, Don achieved what the Lord had directed him to do. As Don daily read his Bible and prayed, the Holy Spirit propelled him to keep doing the work of the Lord. God's appointed labor for Don included helping family, friends and strangers, teaching children at Vacaville Christian School and Bethany Lutheran Sunday school and Elementary School, sharing the Gospel, and writing journal entries, inspirational letters, and memories about his dear mother Sister Vina Bonnie.

On Wednesday, November 4, 2015, a cold, rainy day in Northern California, Don concluded a letter to me with a mighty plea to "memorialize the day." Like the Roman poet Horace's verbal clarion blast of "carpe diem" (seize the day), Don's battle cry was to cherish each day. Remember the many blessings in it. Commit each day not only to memory but also to writing. Keep a record of God's abundant gifts in a journal or in letters (with copies on file) since our recall is so fleeting.

After exhorting me to "memorialize the day," Don passionately explained in that same paragraph,

"There is a necessity to write daily and to preserve your heritage for your children. Often, our memory of wonderful daily blessings devolves into folk tales unless you chronicle each important passage, of the daily blessings, of the families' journey."

Don makes a convincing case for putting into writing the gifts, which God pours upon us each day. As Don's faithful mother Sister Vina Bonnie often sang in the song "Count Your Blessings," when we log the many ways in which God is merciful to us each day, we will be ready to handle any difficulty by Christ's strength. By going back and reading about the Lord's marvelous kindness to us in the past as noted in our journals, we will be sturdy when conflicts try to overpower us.

Memorializing Christ's Healing Power

Remarkably, when Don declared, "Memorialize the day," in his November 4, 2015 letter, he was recovering from a severe bout of illness. After returning home from teaching Sunday school three days prior to writing his November 4, 2015 letter, he was stricken with agony. He recounted in his letter,

"Suddenly my stomach had unbearable pain and I believed it was a return of a month ago pain of diverticulosis. I prayed and remained bed ridden all of Monday as my wife plied me with soup and Metamucil. I asked God to deliver me from the pain, which swept over me in waves (like Pharaoh's army). Still I clung to God's unchanging hand. Recalled, also what a dry-cleaning lady . . . a dear Christian said to me last week: 'Don, a choir director spoke this truth to me . . . A fellow member of the choir had been diagnosed with an illness. Our director and the choir prayed over the woman, 'Do not claim the illness; claim only the healing.'"

Don did exactly that. He claimed the Lord's healing during the hours of his suffering. He described,

"So, I awoke in the early hours of Tuesday in a bath of night sweats and chills. I remembered what the Christian dry-cleaning lady had said to me. I did claim only the healing; praised God and magnified His holy name . . . Then I fell into a deep sleep. You know the end, Les; I awoke from two days of troubled sleep of 24 hours. The side effects were nearly gone, and the pain had diminished by the hour of my breakfast."

Upon being healed, Don immediately gave all thanks and glory to Christ when he exclaimed,

"Jesus is ever victorious over sickness, death, and sin. I, too, claim the healing. Thank you to the Christian dry-cleaning lady; thank you, Heavenly Father. What mercy Jesus shows us, we broken creatures lost in sin, soon to perish. Yet God sent His only beloved Son, Jesus to die for our transgressions."

Don memorialized God's day of healing by writing about this miracle in his November 4, 2015 letter, which also serves a dual purpose as a journal entry. Because the healing God marvelously granted Don is in writing, there is no way that this blessing will turn into a folk tale in the future due to faulty memory of the details, as Don alluded earlier in his letter. No, there will be no inaccurate rendering of what occurred on November 3, 2015, one day before Don wrote his letter to me. Instead there will be a truthful account of Christ's intervention of healing, which will give glory to him for generations to come. Don did well to memorialize Christ's might and mercy by preserving what occurred in writing.

Memorializing God's Promises and Fulfillments

On a clear but humid, early autumn, red moon Monday in an area where the dry winds of the California Central Valley meet the moist breezes of the Bay Area, Don reiterated in a letter dated September 28, 2015 that he was continuing to put together a portfolio of stories, essays, letters, and other documents related to his devoted-to-the-Lord mother Sister Vina Bonnie. Don's collection would serve as a pool of memories and insights for a biography about her. Don believed that the writing of her biography would be a fruition of blessings which dedicated servants of Christ had pronounced upon him a half a century prior:

"How clearly I recall those ministers of yesteryear laying their hands on me and anointing me with oil and reminding me as a lad, as David was anointed by Samuel as a lad; 'Donnie, God is going to use you in a mighty way.' I was given this great future as those words were spoken into my sensitive, youthful, uncorrupt ear. 'God has a plan and a future for you, and it is a good future.'"

The Lord had already fulfilled an exceedingly large portion of those promises from God which "Donnie's" ministers had voiced fifty years or so ago in the Old Dominion state of Virginia and the golden state of California. God raised up Don to indeed become mighty as an honorable husband, father, correctional officer and counselor, son and son-in-law, church member and leader, Sunday School and Christian School teacher, poet, and writer. Only a few bricks were needed to complete the strong structure of Don's blessed life here on earth. One of those bricks was the writing of a biography for his steadfast mother Sister Vina Bonnie who raised and nurtured him in the faith as righteous Eunice did for her son Timothy with the help of Timothy's grandmother Lois as recorded in 2 Timothy 1:5.

In his September 28th letter in the fall of 2015, Don commemorated both the promises God made to him when he was a child and the commitment he was making as an adult to fulfill those promises. He declared that he was going to complete a biography of his mother Sister Vina Bonnie. Don would thus be fulfilling one of the promises God made that Don would be mighty in spirit. For generations to come many would be strengthened and inspired to serve Christ by reading the annals of Sister Vina Bonnie's remarkable life of dedication to the Lord.

Don fully knew, of course, that he would succeed only by the resources, which God gave him. Don was well aware of the verse, "For it is God which worketh in you both to will and to do of his good pleasure" (Phil. 2:13, King James Version). Don was aware that he would need to rely on God to complete the magnificent task of chronicling his mother's extraordinary life of God's grace in Jesus.

In the months ahead with ardent focus, Don would complete a fitting homage to the Lord for blessing Don, his family and countless others with the gift of Sister Vina Bonnie. Don joyfully then dedicated his book to the Lord as the prophet and priest Samuel presented a stone to God for granting the Israelites a miraculous victory over the Philistines: "Then Samuel took a stone, and set it between Mizpeh and Shen, and called the name of it Ebenezer, saying, 'Hitherto hath the Lord helped us'" (1 Sam. 7:12, King James Version). As Samuel did, so did Don memorialize the Almighty God by presenting to Him an Ebenezer stone, an admirable biography of his mother, Sister Vina Bonnie.

Memorializing Where Christians Gather

Five weeks after his September 28, 2015 letter, Don sent the letter dated November 4th, which reverberated, "Memorialize the day." In that letter, Don included a copy of a church newsletter article, which he wrote, "The Timeless Joy of Bethany." As chairperson of Bethany Lutheran Church's Life Management Committee, Don composed this article in response to a request from the church newsletter editor. The editor felt that there was a need for a series of articles on the satisfaction and fulfillment, which comes when one serves the Lord. Don's article would be the first in that series. In his November 4th letter, Don explained the reason for the article he wrote:

"The idea behind the Joy of Bethany article is to invite others to describe their pleasant memories of the old Bethany even as we look forward to what may be the blessing of one congregation on Ulatis property [instead of the current status of two campuses: one on Orchard Avenue and the other on Ulatis Avenue]."

Don's article memorialized both the physical and the spiritual blessings of Bethany congregation, as experienced by those living in the last years of the twentieth century, and first years of the twenty-first century. If it be the will of our Lord, in the multi-centennial celebrations of Bethany Lutheran Church to come, members in those future eras will have Don's article to peruse, either on a faded yellow tinged, aged sheet of paper or on the screen of an electric device. Don's article will be one of the many memorial documents, which will be perused by readers in the centuries to come. Don's article will describe the delight, which members in the bygone year 2015 experienced in serving the Lord at Bethany Lutheran Church. As they read Don's article, they will visualize, hear, touch, smell and taste through Don's descriptive words and expressions what it was like to be a joyful servant of Christ in Vacaville, California in the ancient era of the 1950's to the 2020's.

Don painted these word pictures of the physical beauty of Bethany at its "old location" in the epoch after World War II up to the global Internet Revolution:

"Bethany's wooden cross, the spire and pews and the candles, balcony, stained glass, and altar are the sign posts of the physical feeling of what I know as the 'Blessed Assurance-Jesus is mine. Oh, what a foretaste of glory divine.' . . . To my eyes, the towering redwood trees (triune) planted 50 years ago and the portico, fellowship hall and kitchen; garden room, and preschool buildings on South Orchard remind me of past Americana when someone like Frank Lloyd Wright might have laid out our campus. For me, it is the thousands of visits and opportunity to come, be at peace, and return to our home."

The joys of serving at Bethany which Don noted in his article were performing as a "costumed actor" at many preschool and school pageants, chapel services and assemblies (Santa Claus, Easter Bunny, President Lincoln, FDR, JFK, RFK, John Adams and others), organizing many "model car workshops all in the Fellowship

Hall," teaching the sixth grade Sunday School class for "twelve fabulous years," "volunteering for cross walk duty on Azalea Street" for two years, and reading a Bible story at Bethany Elementary School each week for twelve years. In order to limit the article to one page, Don did not list other volunteer blessings he gave and received at Bethany, including starting a prison ministry involving Bethany staff, serving as a member and chairperson for the Life Management Committee, helping with countless school fundraisers, and steadfastly uplifting the morale of many Bethany staff including pastors, pastor interns called vicars, youth ministers called directors of Christian education, principals, preschool directors, teachers and teacher helpers.

In an honorable tribute, Don also eloquently reminisced in almost T.S. Eliot-like manner,

"Today as I walk the sidewalk beneath the redwood trees and look at the church and playground, there comes that familiar feeling of those events in our lives – today I saw the architecture, the furnishing and sensed the attitude of longtime friends, some departed, some remaining with us."

In concluding his motivating article, Don wrote this stirring appeal,

"With church renewal and expansion plans, this modernization will bring change as we progress to one location on Ulatis campus. We must embrace this change. As I set aside this inner scrapbook of memories, I recall Jesus commanded us to 'Go into all the world and make disciples of the Nations (for Jesus)'. As these plans unfold for our growth and new Bethany church happens, let us follow Joshua's lead as it was, he who said: 'Who among you is on the Lord's side?' Let us march uniformly forward remembering Whom our victorious Leader will be."

Memorializing Our Families

In that November 4, 2015 letter which included a copy of his article on the joy of serving, Don also paid tribute to some of his and Liz's family members. In almost all of his letters, Don highlights different family members and expresses his appreciation and awe to

God for their support, skills, and accomplishments. In his November 4th letter, Don recognized the outstanding achievements of his wife Liz, her sisters, and their mother. Again, to prevent hurt feelings from the many remarkably and exceptional women and men in Don and Liz's family who may be reading this chapter and may feel slighted that they were not mentioned in Don's November 4, 2015 letter, it must be emphasized that in many other letters Don exudes admiration and respect for them. It is not possible for Don to include every family member each month in a monthly eight-page letter, and so Don allocates space almost every month for different family members to be memorialized.

Don inscribed in his November 4th letter how much he respected the sacrifice and unselfishness of his wife Liz. He noted that from the time Liz was a child, she had the great responsibility of caring for her three younger siblings since she was "the eldest of four children with both parents (Dr. Robert and Dr. Dace Mitchell) hard at work for the University of California San Francisco Medical fields in which they were employed."

When Liz married Don, she willingly and lovingly accompanied Don in visiting, as they were able, Don's mother Vina Bonnie who lived in Sacramento near Don's sister Esther who provided almost full-time care for their mother. Liz also supported Don in helping Vina Bonnie and her husband (Don's stepfather) Russell with "clothing, money and gifts."

Years later, Liz and her sister Annie, the two siblings living closest to their retired parents, Dr. Robert and Dr. Dace Mitchell, would both partner with each other in caring for the elderly Mitchells. Don commented with esteem for Liz and Annie, "Clearly it takes great patience and love for Liz . . . and Annie . . . to care for their parents. I greatly admire both women."

Don also gave a glimpse of the extraordinary adversity which Liz's mother, Dr. Dace Mitchell, had to overcome in her life. Don notated, "She certainly came from little beginnings having been rescued from Herzegovina Yugoslavia as a young pre-teen and raised as an adopted child in Alaska." Don also mentioned how Dr. Dace Mitchell and her husband, Dr. Robert Mitchell raised all four children to attend some of the best universities in the nation and rise to prominent positions in their careers.

Liz retired as a high-level administrator, having had positions such as Inspector General and Associate Warden in the California Department of Corrections and Rehabilitation. Dr. Robert Mitchell, Liz's brother, is a cardiologist at Montana's "famed White Fish Hospital." Cathy, a Harvard graduate, "heads up a Special Education program for all of Vermont School system." "Annie . . . is a high-profile Apple Inc. manager and travels the world for Apple."

The Lord has greatly blessed the Mitchell family. How important it is that Don has recorded these blessings from God. Don and others pray that these impressive deeds of God in the lives of the Mitchell family members will be recognized for generations to come. May the Lord then be exalted for His goodness. Don has done his part in memorializing the blessings God has bestowed upon families. Might we do the same, too?

Memorializing Our Veterans

As a one who served in the navy reserves, Don has an enormous regard for the men and women who have served America. On a cold, wet, 39-degree Fahrenheit, Veteran's Day holiday, November 11, 2015, Don began a letter with this noble and stately paragraph, cadenced and poetic, fitting enough to be read by a president at a solemn gathering:

"For he shall give his angels charge over thee, to keep thee in all thy ways" (Ps. 91:11, King James Version). What a verse – in fact the entire 16 verses, commonly referred to as the Soldier's prayer. Millions have read this Davidic poem in hooch's, tents, on the battlefields and beaches of Normandy, Iwo Jima, Saigon, and Bagdad and in all the points of the globe where God's soldiers have fought for truth. So today and every day we honor the United States of America and our Veterans and their families whom they must leave behind to go to foreign fields to fight for liberty around the whole entire world. "

Don then went on to etch with nouns, verbs, and other words, how just one out of a thousand or so Veteran's Day week commemorations took place across the U.S.A.:

"Les, on Sunday, 64 Bethany Lutheran Church members came after Pastor Ted Zimmerman's service to honor our military active, retired, and deceased. Patty Pratt and Sandy served a bountiful buffet of spam, S.O.S., military style with toast and beef chip gravy and coffee. Patty put forth a flower arrangement and five or six photos of service men. Medals, boxed ribbons for combat and service, were elegantly displayed for all to see and remember. . ."

More was written in the November 11th letter about the August luncheon at Bethany Lutheran Church, a sample of America at its best, on the Sunday before Veteran's Day in 2015. By preserving this one honorable event in writing, Don was providing the opportunity for many in the distant future to see, feel, smell, touch, and hear through his words how God had blessed a country named America with unselfish soldiers and grateful citizens around the turn of the second millennium A.D.

Depictions of reverential events such as what took place at Bethany Lutheran Church play an important role in restoring our faith in God. We often only remember the vile and abhorrent acts of humans. Many conclude that God, therefore, does not exist because if there were a God, He would not let the disgusting acts of humans prevail. However, when we read of incidents such as Don described on the Sunday before Veteran's Day 2015, God affirms to us that He is real and that He continues to bless us with human decency through Jesus Christ, Son of God and Son of Man.

Don's recording of acts of human and divine kindness in Christ is crucial to preserving our reliance upon God. May we do our part in inscribing for people today and tomorrow that God not only exists but that He continues to instill dignity into His creation.

Memorializing Everyday Miracles at McDonalds

Not only did his 2015 Veteran's Day letter praise God for America's women and men in the military, but Don's letter also magnified God for miracles that abound every day in common gathering places such as McDonald's. With great enthusiasm Don followed up his coverage of the luncheon for veterans with the following extraordinary occurrence at an ordinary location:

"Yesterday I had a half hour to myself and I sat on a high table and stool at McDonald's restaurant. This was a rare luxury for me. I had my authorized King James Bible before me as I turned the pages . . . a well-dressed smiling lady . . . tapped me gently on my left shoulder. She said, "We're Jehovah's Witnesses, and we're walking around the neighborhood . . ."

Don then recounted the cordial conversation that followed between him and the Jehovah's Witnesses. Even when one of the women quoted a verse from Isaiah implying that Don was a "vain man," Don kept his composure intact by the power of the Holy Spirit. He could have gotten curt with the witnesses, but he treated them with the highest courtesy. Because the love of Christ guided Don to be civil and well mannered, an amazing result took place.

After Don and the women completed their dialogue and as Don was walking to clean his tray, a couple at a nearby table greeted Don, introduced themselves, and mentioned how impressed they were that Don had been reading his Bible in public. The man's name was Randy and the woman's name, Prince Marie. Randy shared with Don that he was a Christian and how the Lord had miraculously saved him from drug abuse, homelessness, and from a near-death experience while in a hospital in Vallejo, California. Randy also testified of a vision he had of his parents in heaven, and of an encounter he had of an angel.

Don urged Randy to write down his testimony in a journal so that many people for years to come would read about how the Lord rescued him to life here on earth and to life eternal in heaven. Randy said he would strongly consider doing that.

With a keen spiritual perspective, Don realized the connection between the kindness, which God imparted to him in conversing with the Jehovah's Witnesses and the blessing Don received in fellowshipping with Randy and Prince Marie immediately thereafter. Don explained,

"Suppose I had been abrupt with the first (Jehovah's Witness) lady and dismissive to her overture of friendship, only because she was a Jehovah's Witness? What then would Randy have thought? As he had unburdened his soul to me, earlier, I remembered how he had that, obvious to me, urgent desire to tell someone of his spiritual experience!"

Because Don took the effort to jot down the sequence of events that took place at McDonald's on that week of Veteran's Day, 2015, it is possible that readers in the next century and even the next millennium will be greatly blessed. The events at that McDonald's may touch the hearts of many people so that they will be led to read the Bible and then be saved by Christ or will be further strengthened in faith through the work of the Holy Spirit.

As Don pleaded with Randy and Prince Marie to write down how God had tremendously blessed them, so does Don beg us to do the same, so that many even in eras to come may benefit.

Memorializing Instead of Forgetting

In his autumn of 2015 letters, Don made it emphatically clear that unless we memorialize the day (write down the blessings God grants us each day), we will forget the impact and the important details of the gifts God gave us. By writing down what occurred, however, we will have a much higher degree of retention. We shall remember the power, kindness, and majesty of God. We shall not be overwhelmed by the evil in this world. We shall always know that God is stronger than any person, any power, and any predicament.

As the Word of the Lord declares, "I will remember the works of the Lord: surely I will remember thy wonders of old" (Ps. 77:11, King James Version).

Chapter Nine

SAY WHAT YOU MEAN, MEAN WHAT YOU SAY

"Suffer little children, and forbid them not, to come unto me; for of such is the kingdom of heaven" (Matt. 19:14, King James Version). In the wonderful book that Saint Matthew gives us, its 28 chapters are chock full of the beauty of Jesus' stories of love. Matthew uses this scripture to show the unending love of Jesus for all of us, His children. To Jesus, there is no such thing as a stepchild; we are all equal heirs to the kingdom of God. God makes no distinction between race, color or sex. We are all His precious children for we are His creation, as mentioned in Romans 8:17.

When I speak of books and letters, this is any form of communication in writing that is designed to inform, ask and verify questions. The highest form of knowledge we can receive is probably the most readily available book. The Holy Bible is an exquisite love letter to the people of earth. It is commonly known as a road map to life. Others refer to it as God's instructional booklet on how to be a happy husband or wife, a loving mother or father and an obedient, kind, son or daughter. With that in mind, when Les Seto and I mapped out our plan for this book, we wanted it to be gentle, informative, and to try and straightforwardly ask questions of the reader.

As first-time collaborating writers, we wanted to show, not tell, how to praise God for what He has provided through His Son, Jesus Christ. We wanted to show how you can do this in the middle of personal distressful battles in life. Lastly, by inculcation of ideas, based on our own lessons learned, we suppose we wanted to teach you, dear reader how simple, yet exquisite life can be when one humbles himself before his Creator, placing his own stubborn willful self under the control of a loving God. Both being 68 years of age, Les and I felt that now, not later, was the opportune time.

People, it is said, do not want to be governed, do not want to be subjected to authority. You have probably heard the comment, whether in a college class or just among friends: "Exercise your freedom of speech and actions. Do not be enslaved to the past (morals)." What remarkably foolish thinking. All of us are subject to the laws established by and for society. Still, we each have freedom to choose whom and what we will serve. It is free will given by God who made us free moral agents—so that we have the choice to do what we please, guaranteed in the rights of the Constitution given to all Americans. But have we gone too far with these rights? Have we thought of the consequences of our actions?

Christians have a tough time hearing course, vile language in movies and books. Vulgarity in writing, I know, is hard to define and censor because it must pass a test of free speech. But the common man with ears can easily detect what is appropriate and what is vulgar. I wrote about prison work in "Sister Vina's Boy," specifically about unprofessional prison workers. My vignette was about a conversation that a new manager, Tim, had with the staff under his supervision. Tim called the officers, supervisors, counselors and captains into the chapel giving instructions on how to meet his goal to maintain decorum in the prison.

After speaking about dress code for uniformed staff and proper telephone demeanor, Tim made an interesting comment: "Never use idle talk (with cursing), especially around the inmates. If you are unsure, don't use language you would not use if your mother was present." We received Tim's message, and by speaking plainly, we realized there was a self-governing agent of respect. I believe the violence level in prisons dramatically decreases when people control their language. After years of seeing violence, Tim impressed us of a first step to civility; to treat people as we would want to be treated. The resultant improvement was noticeable.

What has foul language got to do with writing books or letters? It has everything to do with your future posterity. Writers will tell you, whatever you write, always imagine the greatest audience of your letter. Although John Steinbeck wrote his novel notes to only Editor Pat Covici, he may not have known that future analysts of his works would read his diary notes. But we know this is what happened to not only Steinbeck but to many writers who have written private letters or diaries.

I use my writings as an example to underscore the importance of writing truthfully without unnecessary ornamentation. "Say what you mean, and mean what you say," was one of those kernels of truth I learned as a documentation employee. When I wrote a departmental report on any matter, it became a legal document. I recall in a report-writing class I attended, our instructor, Lieutenant Lowe enlarged a handwritten police report with the aid of a projector. We students could easily see smudges, poor spelling, a lack of coordinating sentences, and the use of improper grammar.

After the students stopped snickering and laughing, Lieutenant Lowe made a pithy statement: "Officers, that's what you may be subjected to in a courtroom presided over by a judge. Make sure your report says what you mean and that you mean what you say." Soon after the class, I made it a quest to print a carbon copy of each report I wrote (hundreds of reports and reviews of prisoner misconduct and their readiness for parole). I proofread everything I submitted to my superior to ensure compliance to the four W's of report writing: each had to contain When (time), Where (location of activity), What (subject matter details) and Why (evaluative opinion when available). The remaining How was carefully included to ensure that releasing authorities, i.e., judges, juries and attorneys would know precisely what my language was imparting.

Les mentioned the handwriting style of letters including one-inch margins left and right, as well as three-quarter inch top and bottom spacing. This underscores the training I received over several decades of working inside State prisons. Your report, including rough copy, we were taught, should stand on its own, absent the scribe who covered the action.

Les and I believe you should write truthfully in everything you publish, if your intention is to honor God with your work. This isn't easy to do when reaching back into the past and pulling forward memories. The human mind is a wonderful computer from which to retrieve events, but it is also colored by nuance and emotions as to what you did or said. Getting it right is dependent on thorough proofreading and having a reviewer audit your work. Les once wrote that he prepared and delivered sermons over 3,808 times while he pastored Bethany Lutheran Church for sixteen years. No course language or vulgarity appeared in any of those sermons. So, it can be done!

When in court responding to my official reports, I was given a copy moments before being called to the witness stand. I would read the report to recall what had happened on a particular day, sometimes months or even years earlier. What had I been doing at the prison that day? Was the time and date correct? What had I been doing before the action mentioned took place? What had my day been like? All these things, the opposing attorney could be expected to ask me under oath. So, if I couldn't recall, the State attorney cautioned State witnesses to 'pause to give Counsel an opportunity to ask for clarification as to the crux of the question.' It was then that prior review when writing my report paid dividends for me. I could be assured of my testimony to be accurate.

The truth is expected from witnesses in court. You must raise your right hand and affirm that what you are about to give is the truth, the whole truth, and nothing but the truth. It (truth) goes to ensuring that there is no miscarriage of justice in court as to whether a witness' testimony is reliable. Liberty, a precious commodity, is in the balance of what you may have written. In a courtroom, it can be assumed that an inmate already serving a term for crime will be evasive and state things that will enable him to evade responsibility, including entering a plea of not guilty. Conversely, the assumption with a peace officer, is that you are a paid employee representing the people of the state and that you are trained in the processes of observing, and reporting detailed facts, not falsehoods. You are sworn to uphold the law including the Constitutional Rights of

Prisoners. Therefore, you are assumed to be telling the truth. An unwitting, ill-prepared witness can blunder into making erroneous statements that undermine the district attorney's effort to present a felony case before a jury.

To preserve standards of professional behavior on the part of corrections workers, our managers insisted that we follow department rules pertaining to the employee (both on duty and off duty). This thick rulebook served us well as reporters of criminal misconduct. Our training was to write descriptively, truthfully, and to use easily understood language. In our training, we were reminded that city newspapers contain articles written at a sixth-grade education level so that the varying audience can grasp the content and meaning. The use of 'fifty-cent' words can derail the story or article unless it is clearly written. I avoid using words that don't describe the intent of my thoughts. Able writers (like Saint Matthew) use plain language. The story moves seamlessly, is interesting and understood, even two thousand years from the day it was first written. That is one reason why the Holy Bible in its many languages and versions is still the most widely purchased book of all time.

A well-equipped writer gets her thoughts perfectly into a cohesive story and this has to do with writing with clarity. How clear is the narrative, after all, must be the overriding objective? Differing styles and manner of writing may be negotiable. Dorothea Brande, wrote about these objectives in one of her best seller books, "Wake Up and Live!" She wrote:

"Having taken all these things into consideration, having formulated as clearly as possible the idea towards which your own work should tend, before launching it into the world [your writing] you should check it against a set of questions which arise logically from the possession of well-defined standards. Each line of activity will have a different set, each individual worker will alter the emphasis, or have his own idea of the proper order for these critical questions, but roughly the finished work should be measured in somewhat this way:

Is what I have done as good as the best in its field?

Has it everything necessary for all ordinary purposes?

Have I added any special values by way of an original contribution?

Have I made it as attractive and convenient as possible for those who are its logical users? (Or audience, or clients.)

Have I considered whether there is another group to which it might also be made to appeal?

What more can I do before I release it from myself and send it out to make its own way?"

Mrs. Brande went on further to ask these concise questions that relate to any job well done, but particularly in the art of writing;

She wrote:

Have I conveyed what I thought?

Have I conveyed what I felt?

Is it as clear as I can make it?

Is it as distinguished or beautiful as its matter permits?"

Having done all that, you may rely on your best work having been done. (Brande pp. 124-126)

A Parable of the Two Brothers

Les and I have discussed in email format what has been an aggregate of writing to other interested would-be writers. One such apprentice to the art, is my younger brother James Fortin, a deacon in his church in Syracuse, New York. My brother is 'a jack-of-all-trades;' he is handy in remodeling stain glass windows; proficient in the hanging of doors; adept at automotive repairs; and he is superior in indoor carpentry of cabinet and wall painting. James certainly received his mechanical inclination from our dad, Norman, an engineman in the navy for twenty years. Norman's job was to help ensure that his vessel, a heavy cruiser was always in tiptop shape, diesel engines humming, ready for any action.

On the other hand, Mother trained me in skillful writing. It was she who enjoyed writing hymns and constructing beautiful letters to mail to her correspondents. Mother passed on her love of the printed word to her eager eldest child.

Unlike James, I am barely able to change a car's flat tire or jump a dead car battery. I am limited in my domestic home repairs, so that my incompetence often drives my wife to distraction with my amateur approach to chores. Somewhat to compensate, in my letters with James, I can become preachy and a know-it-all type of heavy-handed instructor. I try to guard against this. My brother bears it well, knowing I am the elder and the keeper of a repository of family history. Older brothers do doubtlessly hold the upper hand.

Sometimes to help James in his pursuit of clear writing of letters, I give him examples of style and content by comparing it to painting a kitchen, of which he is the abler of the two of us. I write about selecting paint, primer, masking tape, drop clothes, brushes, and the value of the ambience of music to 'soothe and eliminate rushing of painting." With much of this, he agrees.

I compare tools for painting to the tools of writing. I use a certain bond of paper and a type of ink-pen that is comfortable. I talk about margins and page numbers relating it to the taping of a surface to be painted in a kitchen. I compare selecting paintbrushes and the art of paint strokes to the way in which I organize and inventory my thoughts when I first sit down to write. Whether I write indoors or outdoors, with noise or quiet, I can perform with minimal distraction. But as I allow a release of my muse and turn my daydream to reality, I explain that I first use broad swathes of words to describe the overall story, and then I go back with a smaller brushing of details, with words to convey time, weather, emotions (a coloring of the story) is included.

James considers suggestions when I juxtapose it in a language he is familiar with, the use of equipment, and physical dexterity in completing a job to his satisfaction. Currently, James works as a 'maintenance super' for his apartment complex and is called on to keep the buildings from becoming uninhabitable. After a job, James stands back and squints happily at his repair work with an eye to improvement, just as I sit back and review my choppy paragraphs and run-on sentences, with their florid purple prose wording. Then I tell James, that next comes the cleansing and redacting as I touch-up my work to make my narrative endurable if only simply readable. James takes pride in the cleanup and care and use of tools. In his bi-monthly letters, he gives me the details of his workmanship. It's these things that broaden the bond between brothers and that shrinks 3,000 miles that separate us.

What a Friend We Have in Jesus

As we go through our life, we recall childhood adventures and if our keen will to remember allows, we think back on the times Jesus befriended us. It was like this for me being brought up in a God-fearing family of six, including Beth, Esther, James and me. We were so like little stallions and mares, running hither and fro in our many adventures. In a letter dated Sunday, November 6, 2016, at 11:05 PM as the quarter moon and Orion in the eastern sky provided light, my friend, Les wrote a thirty-page letter to recap the fall days of which I had earlier written. Even now as I re-read this lengthy letter, I am amazed to think that Pastor Les had just finished a full Sabbath day of preaching, singing, and praying with his congregation. But loyal friend that Les is to so many, he set words to paper. His words were far ranging, and real benefits did I receive from his message. He said this:

"When you wrote about your 12:30 pm "breakfast at the Valley Café as you viewed the "plowed-over fields" nearby, I thought for a moment that I was reading John Steinbeck's "Of Mice and Men" as he [John] described the Salinas farm lands and orchards, so dignified was your style.

"I read with much interest about your childhood experiences of picking tomatoes for twenty-three cents a lug in Elmira with Robert Self and your sister Beth and Esther. You vividly described the trauma that Beth experienced when she jumped into a drainage ditch and a hidden broken bottle cut her foot. How painful and harrowing that must have been for her, for you, and Esther who were close in proximity to Beth.

"Then as she so often did, your stalwart mother Vina Bonnie came to the rescue. She rendered first aid to Beth and drove her to Travis Hospital. As you eloquently summarized, "On that late sweltering summer day in 1966, fifty years ago...we learned things that remained with us; the value of a dollar earned; the lush fresh taste of a hand-picked tomato; the intense power of a mother's prayer, and the testimony of God's enduring love for us." Well stated, Don."

I was gladdened by Les's appreciation for my writing. I wondered how he would fill thirty pages. I know he is excellent at restating the contents of a letter he receives, and he shows such wonderful appreciation for communication. I suppose Waikoloa is a small community and not like the bustle and hustle of some of the other more luxurious islands, so he enjoys what goes on in his former community of the sleepy, yet vibrant town of Vacaville. Les continued writing something very near and dear to his heart, having just lost his mother.

"You cited "What a Friend We Have in Jesus." What timing. This Saturday, November 12, 2016, at my mother's celebration of life service, the first hymn to be sung is "What A Friend...." It was one of my mother's dearest hymns. How amazing that you would mention this hymn even without knowing that my Mom loved it. Yes, as you properly assessed, there is power in those old, traditional, beloved hymns that Sister Vina Bonnie sang exuberantly."

Les is a very private person, loath to speak to others about the events that cause discomfort in Les's family life. I knew Les is predisposed to be a good listener to the problems of others and to provide counseling. I had never heard him speak about tragedy and sad things, so I read with great interest, as the letter continued. I knew also that Les was about half way through a very detailed, lengthy, biographical book containing his research into the life of King David and other Israelite leaders found in the Bible's Old Testament. He had spent those precious little free hours late at night and early in the morning typing out his manuscript.

But instead of elaborating on the funeral service of which he himself had conducted for Mrs. Seto, his mother, Les went in another direction to provide encouragement to me in my pursuit of writing two books. To let me know about the service rendered for his mother, Les had opted to economically and sweetly enclose with this letter, the order of service. I could visualize and perhaps glimpse what had just happened 2,300 miles away from my home in California. One can sometimes fail to be aware of the events that shape the life and daily struggles of one's friends when they are so far away. I knew the importance of keeping in touch with Les, because of my writing campaign to my brother in Syracuse. Letters of encouragement are so vitally important among brothers (Christian and biological).

Les continued to extol Biblical quotations, both conveying the importance of our voice and our mouth, in testifying to others about the greatness of the Lord and His salvation through His Messiah.

Les seemed to realize that I needed to hear "I'm ok; you're ok" as it applied to my writing endeavor. Sometimes, we just do not feel our work is vital and we assume in the absence of any supportive comments from editors, that we are not truly gifted to write. You'll recall John Steinbeck's hopelessness when that ever-present evil thought enters the brain. So how to remedy this? Les simply did some comparative compliments to shore up my lagging confidence in a temporary period of self-doubt. I hadn't said anything that would have revealed this; but I realize that pastors in general and Les Seto are astute and have spiritual discernment in their souls.

He continued:

"...You shared your testimony about how the Lord has motivated you to tell others of His love and gift of eternal life. You truly have carried out Christ's Great Commission, and because of your enthusiasm to share the life of Christ with others, I, too am motivated to do the same and write a book. Thank you, Don, for exhorting me to do what you are doing, proclaiming Jesus to others with our voices and mouths. Yes, as you wrote, I, too, "want to be in that number; "Oh, When the Saints Go Marching In." I know that your mom, my mom, Bill [Sheehan, a mutual friend who had recently passed in this same time period], Dr. Mitchell, [my father in-law], Dave Van Bemmel, Lt. Col. Warren, and many other sincere Christians will be in that number too."

Les stoked my ego and gave what every budding writer desires, a comparison to an established writer. Les tells me that my narratives are reminiscent of Hemingway! Steinbeck...not everything, but just little phrases, and colorings that are my attempt to discover the elusive writer's voice. He wrote:

"Regarding your letter on September 29th, your charming description of the fall season sun rays made me think of the opening pages of William Faulkner's "A Light in August." In which he observed that the August sun rays in Mississippi were a tad softer and suppler than the glaring rays in July and June. Your reference, of course, was to the waning days of October, but you wrote with a similar cadence and dignity of Faulkner. Very effective."

He added:

"Your narrative of your conversation with your waitress at Valley Café dealt with a significant topic, the metamorphosis of a landscape. What a happy surprise it must have been when you found out that your waitress, Miss Dillman, was the granddaughter of a former principal of your alma mater Armijo Joint Union High School. I was impressed how Miss Dillman loved the Suisun Valley countryside, and how she lamented that big homes would one day invade the landscape, and fields would be few or would be gone. As you added that not only large homes, but shopping centers and dealerships would also descend upon the fields, I could not help but think about the opening chapters of "The Grapes of Wrath," in which John Steinbeck wrote about the farms in rural Oklahoma being gobbled up by big corporations (banks) back East and ferocious bulldozers were smashing and leveling farm houses and barns across the plains. Your paragraph on the changing vista of Suisun Valley had the solemnity and grace of the Salinas laureate."

I was so pleased to read these comments. I was still struggling mightily with grief over our mutual friend, Mr. Sheehan's passing. Bill Sheehan had just celebrated his 95th birthday and had been my constant friend and mentor for the past twelve years since my retirement from the state of California. Bill and I shared breakfast fellowship with prayer and pancakes and coffee at our local Waffle Shop restaurant. I don't believe we missed many Friday mornings over a ten-year period. Those hours were significant to me, as Bill leisurely told me of his World War II experiences as a navigator on an eleven-man PBM airship assigned to the Navy. He and my dad shared similar experiences, both entering the Navy in 1944-45. Both spoke with a certain élan about their exploits and their tours of duty. Both were twenty-year men who had remarkable stories to share. Upon Bill's passing, I knew I would be subdued and feel a profound sense of loss.

Months before, our family lost its patriarch, Dr. Robert Mitchell, a true American who also served in WWII and went on to great accomplishments in the field of medicine. I had the privilege of spending years in consultation about life, husband behavior, and child rearing. Now both were gone leaving a void in my life. I was soon to lose another decade long companion, our family canine, Jake, a wonderful apricot colored Labra-doodle. If you have read the book "Marley and Me," you can almost interchange the dog, Marley for Jake. The loss of all these friends was weighing my mind down to a place, where only daily prayer, writing my book, and keeping my Bible near to me, would be the prescription to get past this period of sadness. All the while, I was continuing working with high school students at our local campus, as their teacher. But I think it was Les's kindness and generous comments in his letters which strengthened me, and gave a sense of boldness, 'can do' resolve. No matter how you cut it, the loss of loved ones so close together is difficult and is draining to the conscious efforts it takes to do your daily tasks.

So, it was a blessing to read what Les wrote next in this thirty-page document:

"Thank you once again for your comforting and uplifting words about my mother Carolyn. Over the past ten years since relocating from Vacaville to Hawaii, you consistently took the time to ask about how my mom was doing and how you were praying for her. I am deeply grateful for your kindness. You have truly supported me during those ten years. Your caring helped me greatly in carrying on in Christ." ...

"...Enthralling was my reaction to the revelation which God unveiled to you on Sunday, October 23, 2016 at 1:30 P.M. As God gave to Paul a vision of the third heaven, so did our marvelous Lord give you a glimpse into His heavenly realm. Ten seconds to view his eternal Kingdom, the Celestial City itself. You must have felt like Christian whose eyes beheld the Celestial City the first time when he stood upon Mount Clear. I am very excited that God unfolded to you a vision which included my mother Carolyn singing in a choir with other Christians there. How comforting that is to me. How blessed are you to have received that privilege to view heaven and how blessed am I that you have shared with me what you saw?"

Les remembered that the song that choir was singing was "Peace, Peace, Wonderful Peace."

There will be more on this beautiful revelation as we continue forward in a future chapter. Suffice it to say, I appreciated the resultant up-tick in my mood and outlook after reading what my friend had to write in his most generous way. In an age of mean tweets, horrific Hollywood bruhaha and relentless political sleazy behavior, it is so refreshing to have conversations and letters that put God first in its design and follow-through.

Chapter Ten

MINISTER BEGINS A WRITING CAREER

"But showing love to a thousand generations of those who love me and keep my commandments" (Ex. 20:6, New International Version).

Our Family and The World Were Changed Forever

On Sunday morning, December 7, 1941, my grandfather Taichiro Seto, an early riser, woke at dawn to begin his daily routine, a cup of coffee, a piece of toast, and a stroll around his property, picking up fallen leaves and plucking a few weeds. Though the setting was peaceful, my grandfather's soul was troubled. It had not been a happy fifty-fifth birthday for him three days prior. He was still mourning the loss of his wife Masano who at the age of forty-four had passed away just twenty-six days prior on Armistice day, November 11th, a world peace holiday. As my grandfather strolled along his Asian orange and lemon trees, laden with their ripening green and yellow fruit, he was pondering how he was going to care for his five children, now without a mother. In a few hours, however, his sadness over the loss of Masano wouldn't be the dominant emotion in his heart. Other feelings would drastically replace it. Fear, shock, horror, shame and trauma would overcome him and millions of others around the world. The hopes of Armistice day, the day Masano died, had been shattered.

Don's Invitation to Me

In prior chapters including Chapter Nine, Don has described many noteworthy events in the lives of his parents and of recent generations before them. I also have referenced incidents in the lives of my parents and my grandparents, but Don asked if I would write more about the family into which God placed me. Don was very gracious in offering me this delightful opportunity, and so I gladly consented. In this chapter, I shall share about my father and his parents and great grandparents. In later chapters I shall recount occurrences which took place on my mother's side of the family. I am sharing these incidents in the lives of my father's and mother's families for only one purpose: To give glory to the Lord of all generations.

"The counsel of the Lord standeth forever, the thoughts of his heart to all generations" (Ps. 33:11, King James Version). Even before the first persons in my father's (Seto) and mother's (Ishikuro) clans came to faith in Jesus Christ, the God of all nations and time had been pouring out His mercy upon hundreds of their prior generations. Such is the infinite kindness of our Lord. He extends His mercy on earth to even families whose first converts to Christianity are yet centuries even millennia away in the future.

Jesus proclaimed on His Sermon on the Mount, "For he maketh his sun to rise on the evil and on the good, and sendeth rain on the just and on the unjust" (Matt. 5:45, King James Version). Even though hundreds, likely thousands, of Setos prior to my father and the same with my mother's family, thousands of Ishikuros prior to my mother were not Christians, our Heavenly Father sent the sun and the rain upon them just as He did to the people of Israel and to the Christians. The blessings of course for those without Jesus are just for this earth; nevertheless, those blessings are still precious because they all come from the Lord. The God of all nations, the Lord of all time, sent his sunshine and his rain upon my father's and my mother's families knowing that one day, some of their descendants would receive Jesus as their Savior.

The Seto Clan Was Restless

At the end of the 1800's, thousands of people, especially young and middle age men, from southeast Japan were boarding ships and sailing to China, Hawaii, North America and South America. From the records of ship manifests of that era, twelve of these emigrants had the last name of Seto, all from the same region. They apparently were related to each other from areas near the coastal cities of Wakayama and Yokohama. They were among the hungry laborers who emigrated out of Japan due to harsh economic conditions and who were seeking the sweetness of opportunity wherever they might find it; Peking, Hong Kong, Hawaii, California, Brazil, or Peru. Making ten dollars a month in Hawaii, for example, was better than being unemployed in Japan.

My dad's grandfather, Tarokichi Seto, around thirty years old, was one of the twelve Setos who ventured out of southern Japan. His destination was Hawaii where sugar plantations were anxious to hire field laborers. Tarokichi and his wife Amaya talked about him going to Hawaii, and they agreed that that it would be best for their family for him to do so. Tarokichi then signed up to work for three years at a sugar plantation on the island of Hawaii. Tarokichi pledged to his wife and children that he would send them back money from the wages he would make during his three years in Hawaii. With sadness, Tarokichi and Amaya parted, looking forward to the day when Tarokichi would return.

The Resilience of Tarokichi and Amaya

Ship manifests from those years are difficult to discern. Sometimes the English speaking and writing recorder of the manifests would simply write the first letter of the Japanese passenger's first name such as "T. Seto" which could stand for Tarokichi or possibly not. Other times the spellings of the first names of the passengers are so close. One manifest shows "Tarakichi" and another shows "Torakichi." Scribal error referring to the same person or different persons entirely? A challenge to determine.

To the best of our family's knowledge, Tarokichi left Yokohama, Japan on January 26, 1899, and sailed on the S.S. Coptic, a steam ship, to the island of Hawaii. For two weeks he would travel among the huddled masses in steerage (economy) class where the ship crew served simple but at least familiar food to the passengers, a bowl of rice with pickled vegetables and a sparse ounce or two of meat.

Upon arriving in Hawaii, he began his arduous labor on a sugar cane plantation. Up every morning before sunrise. Working ten hours a day under the scorching tropical sun or in the drenching torrential rain. Choosing whether to wear heavy protective clothing but then boil in perspiration or expose one's skin to the fresh air but be tortured by the almost microscopic, glasslike hair fibers of the sugar cane plant or be slit by its razor sharp, serrated leaf edges. Six days of work a week. Two holidays a year. Fourth of July and New Year's. Historians write that thousands of laborers in Hawaii broke their contracts by fleeing to California to escape the backbreaking work. If they made it to San Francisco or Long Beach, no authorities would seek them out. Tarokichi must have considered that desperate option, but he chose to remain in Hawaii to fulfill his contractual commitment. That was the right thing to do.

While Tarokichi was weeding, hoeing, planting, and harvesting in the orange brown, muddy soil in Hawaii, Amaya was in Yokohama disciplining their children, cooking, serving and cleaning up after every meal, washing their kimonos and linens, sweeping their rice mat covered floors, shopping at the outdoor and indoor markets for necessities, balancing the budget, nursing children who were ill and sometimes staying up all night to attend to their needs. Amiya was essentially a single parent trying to keep the household together.

Through it all, however, she remained loyal to her husband and supported his decision to go where the best opportunity was offered for the sake of their children. Though she encouraged Tarokichi to go to Hawaii, Amaya still experienced loneliness just as her husband did, too.

My grandfather and father never explained the details, but communication between Tarokichi and his family in Japan stopped after Tarokichi had been in Hawaii for a while. Did Tarokichi at least keep sending money back to his family through the Japanese Consulate or Japanese bank even though communication had been halted? Most likely so. No one in my family ever mentioned that he was derelict. Was he having an affair over in Hawaii? Again, my family did not even hint that he had been unfaithful to Amaya. Did Tarokichi write letters to his family but his letters never made it across the Pacific? Possibly. In any event, Tarokichi's wife and other relatives in Japan were worried about him because they had not received word from or about him in months.

My grandfather Taichiro who was fourteen years old took it upon himself to travel to Hawaii to find his father or to find out what had happened to him. Today people would have looked upon Taichiro as a middle school student. Would a parent today allow her or his fourteen-year-old son to travel across Pacific on a steam boat unsupervised and then to search through unknown villages in Hawaii for a missing person with no cell phone or any kind of phone to communicate with anyone?

Taichiro traversed the Pacific Ocean for fourteen days, landed in Hawaii and began the search for his father. My father said that Taichiro walked from one plantation village to the next, an average distance of twenty miles, asking if anyone knew Tarokichi Seto and his whereabouts. He may have even had a photograph of his father and may have shown it to people asking them if they recognized the face on the photo. My father shared that his father finally found Tarokichi one night sitting around a camp fire, drinking sake, and having a jolly time with other plantation laborers. No doubt, Tarokichi was shocked to see his son, and Taichiro was elated to find his father healthy and happy, maybe too happy. My father's family never explained why Tarokichi's communication with Amaya had gone silent, but after my grandfather found him, Amaya received regular correspondence, probably written by their son Taichiro, a more faithful correspondent than his father.

The exact information becomes hazy, but in 1900 the United States annexed Hawaii and one of the results was that all indentured contracts between sugar plantation employers and their foreign laborers were voided. The U.S. declaration was like an Emancipation Act for all the contracted workers. They could voluntarily remain as laborers for the same wages they had been receiving, or they could return to their homeland without any penalty. Thousands of workers opted to return to their families overseas to free themselves from the almost slave-like existence on the plantation. Many laborers, however, chose to stay and keep working for their employer. Tarokichi may have stayed to complete his contract with the plantation voluntarily or he might have taken the route of leaving before the end of his three-year obligation. Either way, Tarokichi eventually returned to Japan to be reunited with his family. Surprisingly, his son Taichiro, decided to stay in Hawaii. He was already there. He was single. He was young and energetic. He saw the advantages of trying to make a go of it in Hawaii rather than to return to Japan.

And so Taichiro and his father said, "Sayonara," to each other at the dock on the day that Tarokichi boarded his ship back to Yokohama. They most likely consoled each other with the reassurance to see each other again. That, however, was not to be. Taichiro would never see his father and mother again and would never return to the country of his birth.

Though Tarokichi and Taichiro did not physically connect with each other in the years that followed, Taichiro wrote letters to his father, mother and family. As mentioned in an earlier chapter, Taichiro was a lifelong, faithful correspondent to his family in Japan. I recall as a child seeing dozens of envelopes, both white four-by-nine-inch ones and larger pale brown colored manila ones, sent out weekly by my grandfather. Each envelope had hand written to-and-from addresses, in both English and Japanese, and many colorful stamps which with the handwritten addresses took up almost all of the envelope's face.

Though absent from his son Taichiro for the remainder of his life, Tarokichi left these enduring values imprinted upon his son: a spirit of adventure to travel overseas if necessary, a courage to embrace situations outside one's comfort zone, a willingness to do whatever it takes to survive and thrive, an open-door policy to hard work, challenges, and adversity, and a durability to cope with the harshest of conditions. My grandfather and father acquired these traits from Tarokichi, and I continue to ask the Lord to grant me these qualities every day in my pilgrimage on earth.

The Dignity of Taichiro and Masano

Quiet, soft spoken, his eye brows thick. Narrow nose, circular black framed glasses, coffee and cream complexion. Clean shaven. Slow, measured, smooth pace in his movements. Never in a hurry. Hours a day at his desk, fountain pen in hand, writing in a journal or on a sheet of paper, a letter. Sitting in his rocking chair every afternoon on his front porch reading the Japanese newspaper received daily in the mail delivered to his house. Seldom if ever laughing. Just occasionally expressing a restrained smile. Working long hours during the day in the yard, wearing a long-sleeved khaki shirt, khaki shorts, olive drab woolen socks up to his knees, brown leather shoes, and a British safari hard hat. Such are the memories I have of my grandfather.

My grandmother Masano died eight years before I was born. From the air-bleached brown and white photos of her, adorning the walls of my grandfather's house or carefully positioned in family albums, Masano had a soft eggshell white complexion. A face that was the shape of an apple. Almond outline eyes, black button pupils. Wide nose, plump lips. Straight ebony hair; level, horizontally cut across her mid forehead and along her ears and back. Light colored, cotton, long sleeved, full-length dresses, often wearing an apron. Black leather shoes.

Many single Japanese men in Hawaii purchased the services of mail order bride agencies to find a wife. My grandfather, however, was blessed to find a wife who was already living with her parents in the town of Hilo where he lived. Her name was Masano Enoki and she was eleven years younger than Taichiro.

As was the custom of that time, my grandfather most likely asked Masano's parents, Masanoru and Tsumayo Enoki for permission to marry their eighteen-year old daughter. How grateful my grandfather must have been when Masano's parents consented. From what my father, mother, aunts and uncles spoke about Masano, she was nurturing, warm, encouraging, and supportive of her family and friends. While Taichiro had a more serious and reserved temperament, Masano was more spontaneous and outgoing. Masano gave birth to five children and devoted her whole life to caring for them.

Before and while Taichiro was married to Masano, he occupied himself with many jobs. He taught Japanese language classes to children. He helped immigrants fill out required Japanese government forms. He wrote letters to the Japanese embassy and other government departments on behalf of immigrants in Hawaii.

Taichiro also started a wholesale fish company in which he bought fish from the fishers and then sold the catch to retail stores and restaurants. My father, however, said that Taichiro purchased the catches of the fishermen at a price higher than his competitors and sold the fish to retail outlets at a price lower than other wholesalers. "He had too big a heart," my father said, and so Taichiro eventually got out of the wholesaling profession.

One of the activities which Taichiro and Masano devoted much time together was to host in their home the officers of Japanese naval training on wind-powered schooners which would dock at the port in Hilo once or twice a year. I recall seeing in photo albums my grandparent's living room filled with Japanese sailors in their thick woolen, black jackets with white buttons and stripes and bleached white slacks. They would be sitting, cross-legged, on both sides of a fifteen-foot pine wood table, a foot and a half high. The table displayed serving bowls of rice and platters of sushi, stir fried vegetables, various cabbage, cucumber, and eggplant pickles; strips of beef, and slender porcelain jars with tiny cups for sake.

Perhaps dozens of the officers who stepped into my grandparents' home and hundreds of the midshipmen whom they trained on their clippers would be assigned to metal warships, and five or ten years later at Midway, Guadalcanal and the Coral Sea. They would be battling against sailors in ships from the U.S. Maybe some of the officers and sailors would also be on the ships in the fleet that attacked Pearl Harbor. A chilling thought. Future enemies of the

U.S. in the home of my grandparents, the same house in which I grew up. But during the 1930s these gatherings at the Seto residence with officers from the Japanese navy were jovial, innocent occasions.

With each birth of their five children, Masano and Taichiro celebrated. Taichiro's dream was being fulfilled. To earn a living in Hawaii, to send money home to his aging parents in Japan, and to provide for his wife and children. How devastating it was then on Armistice Day, November 11, 1941. When people in Hawaii and all over the world were remembering the war that would end all wars, the honorable and nurturing Masano died from a severe illness. She was forty-four years old. In the family albums, I remember the somber photo of the hundreds of people who attended Masano's funeral. The men were dressed in dark suits and ties, the women in their formal three-quarter length black dresses, and the children in their short sleeve white shirts and coal dyed trousers. All of them were gathered around Masano's polished coffin laden with floral bouquets. Everyone had stunned, blank and empty stares conveying piercing grief and disbelief that Masano would no longer be among them.

My nineteen-year old father Ellsworth was the oldest and only adult child of Masano's and Taichiro's children. He willingly discontinued his education at a business college on the island of Oahu and returned to Hilo to help his father care for my father's siblings Hiroshi, Yasushi, Mona and two-year old Jane.

How insurmountable it must have seemed to my grandfather and my father that they now would be responsible for raising a family without a mother. They had no way of knowing that very soon their daunting challenge would become a thousand times more difficult.

Having the same sturdy outlook as Tarokichi and Amaya, my grandfather and father made the best of an adverse situation. They were resolved to work together to care for Hiroshi, Yasushi, Mona and Jane. They were confident that they would get through this ordeal. After all, if my grandfather's mother Amaya raised her and Tarokichi's children with Tarokichi working thousands of miles away, so could Taichiro care for his four children with my father's assistance.

As the weeks passed, my grandfather and father gradually gained more confidence that everyone in their family would gradually adjust to Masano's absence. Then on December 7, 1941, an attack by the Japanese Navy two hundred miles away from the Seto's residence shattered the lives of my father's family and all the world. How ashamed were Taichiro, his family and the thousands of Japanese Americans in the U.S. The Japanese had killed 2,403 Americans and wounded 1,178 others. Six Japanese Imperial carriers spewed out 353-armed aircraft which destroyed or damaged 350 U.S. aircraft and 49 vessels including all eight of the battleships in the U.S. Pacific fleet.

Were some of the Japanese sailors on the aircraft carriers and escorting ships guests in Taichiro's and Masano's home in the years prior to the assault? Were some of the Japanese midshipmen on the training schooners that docked in the port of Hilo also in the disreputable fleet that snuck its way across the Pacific? After spending time in my grandparent's home, did these sailors then go on to Pearl Harbor and later provide logistical information that abetted the Japanese commanders in their sinister attack? These agonizing questions must have been running through Taichiro's mind.

Besides dealing with the outrage and trauma of Japan's attack upon Pearl Harbor, Taichiro and his family's lives would become unhinged not only emotionally but physically as well. A few months after December 7, 1941, U.S. military men abruptly knocked on the door of Taichiro's residence and took him away giving very little information to my father and his two brothers and two sisters. If we had been neighbors to Taichiro, we would have undoubtedly heard unnerving wailing from the children in his home. The crying might have been reminiscent of what had occurred on Armistice Day some months prior when Masano had passed away.

My father's role in the family immediately became more challenging with the departure of Taichiro. My father had some very agonizing decisions to make. He assessed the situation. He would need to work to provide for his four younger siblings and to pay the loan for my grandparent's home and for any other outstanding debt which my grandparents had. When his grandmother Amaya took care of her and Tarokichi's children, she at least had income coming in overseas from Tarokichi. With my dad, however, there was no Tarokichi to be sending monetary support, and so my dad realized that he could not be both the breadwinner and child care provider for his four younger siblings. He could fulfill one, but not two roles. He needed help.

Though none in the Seto household were yet Christian, God still had mercy upon them. Friends of my grandparents stepped up and offered to take in my father's siblings so that he could work and receive an income. My father humbly and gratefully accepted the help of his parents' friends. When he started earning an income, my father, of course, would contribute money to his parents' friends for the expenses they would incur in caring for his siblings even though they did not expect any payment. And so, the two boys, Hiroshi and Yasushi, went to stay with a family, and their six- year old sister Mona went with another family.

But there was one child left. The youngest child Jane was only two years old, and a family who lived just one block away from the Setos pleaded with my father to let them care for Jane. However, there was one condition. They wanted to adopt her, meaning they would keep her even if Taichiro should one day return home. They also added another stipulation. No one, including those in the Seto family, would ever mention to anyone, especially to Jane, that she was adopted. The family would tell Jane that she was their biological daughter. Maybe out of desperation or more likely because my grandparents had a very close relationship with the family making the request, my father consented, and the toddler Jane was given up for adoption to the family who lived a block from the Seto home. Fifty years later when both parents of the family who adopted Jane had passed away, Jane found out that she was a Seto and that she had been adopted. Jane was understandably shocked, but over time she appreciated knowing the truth. Once Jane's brothers and sister knew that Jane was aware of her adoption, both Jane and her siblings mutually reached out to each other and became very close. My father, his two brothers and sister shared with Jane how badly they felt as children when they would see Jane walking or playing in the neighborhood. They always knew she was their sister, but they could not reveal to her of their relationship.

And so, with his younger siblings all being taken care of, my father could then begin earning money in order to contribute to the families taking care of his two brothers Hiroshi and Yasushi and their sister Mona. My father and his two brothers Hiroshi and Yasushi were old enough to ask the question of why, was their father taken away and confined while all their Japanese friends' fathers were not.

My father and his brothers gradually learned that my grandfather had three strikes against him in contrast to their Japanese friends' fathers who may have had only one or no strikes on them. One, my grandfather was a Japanese language instructor, not a common profession in the town of Hilo, and so he was considered as a high security risk. Two, he had a history of corresponding with the Japanese government even though he was helping people take care of mundane issues such as visas, citizenship, taxes, and immigration. Three, he entertained Japanese Navy personnel in his home. For those reasons, he was understandably identified as a threat to national security.

My grandfather spoke very little about his years in detention. All family members know is that he was detained first on the island of Oahu, then at Sharp Point in Pacifica, California and finally in New Mexico until the war ended. My grandfather never mentioned that he was treated unfairly. The message he communicated through his silence was that the United States needed to take measures to protect its citizens. The United States did not have the luxury of spending years vetting every Japanese citizen to see if they were loyal to America. The U.S. had a massive war to fight, and so all resources had to go into that effort. Sometimes the rights of citizens are put on hold temporarily until a crisis is over. My grandfather grasped this reality.

What few words my grandfather did share about his experience behind barbed wire was that the guards and personnel of the camps were always fair, respectful and thoughtful to him and the others who were interned. He did not go hungry, was never tortured, and was always treated humanely.

Even though Taichiro did not profess Christ to be his Savior, the Lord was merciful to Taichiro. God blessed him with kind sentries in the internment camps and eventually brought him home, once again reunited with his family. Both Taichiro and his wife Masano demonstrated dignity in handling difficulties. They were not complainers or blamers. If they were in rough waters, they quietly rode out the storm. They always hoped for the best.

I am saddened that Tarokichi and Amaya and Taichiro and Masano did not know Jesus as their Redeemer. I am thankful, however, that at least while they were on this earth, the Lord was still merciful upon them and implanted in them honorable traits.

Ellsworth Seto, Resilient as His Parents and Grandparents

"Bam!" was the sound my father and the waitresses heard. They immediately realized that the thud was caused by an irate customer flinging his twelve-ounce steak against the swinging door into the kitchen.

"Go learn how to cook a decent steak, you foreigner!" screamed the inebriated patron.

"Yeah! Go get some training, you bum!" chimed his intoxicated friends at the table.

While most of the clientele were cordial and satisfied, my father had to put up with some very hard to please diners at the steak house he opened. He converted his father's house into a restaurant to generate income to provide for his brothers and sisters. Taichiro's home had become a steak house, "The Service Inn." When I was a child growing up in my grandfather's house, I often wondered why his house had a swinging door leading from the living room into the kitchen. None of my friends' homes had a door like that. Later I learned that my grandfather's house had been a restaurant during the war, and the swinging door was left hinged to the frame as a reminder of how the family had made it through desperate times. The needs were so dire, that their home had to be transformed into a steak house.

After President Franklin D. Roosevelt declared war upon Japan, soldiers on their way to Iwo Jima, Tarawa, Guam, the Philippines, and other western Pacific Islands often stopped in Hawaii to receive further training while waiting for their orders to deploy. There were many military camps among the islands. One such camp was quickly established one block away from Taichiro's home in Hilo. The camp site was on a county ball park and horse race track. The camp remained operational throughout the war. My father saw the need for a steak house especially for the soldiers who may at times want a break from eating at their mess hall. My father worked rapidly to acquire the necessary permits to open a restaurant. He also did some speedy low-cost renovations to the house to make it adequate as a dining place. Many soldiers patronized the steak house. Almost all the servicemen were appreciative that there was a steak house within walking distance from their barracks. My dad consistently thanked the soldiers who ate at his restaurant and thanked them for their service to America. Even though my father had no training in being a cook or in running a restaurant, like his grandparents and parents, he saw an opportunity and ran with it even if conditions were not perfect and he was completely out of his element. As his grandparents and parents did, he would take risks to climb above adversity.

The Service Inn steak house brought in sufficient income for my father and his three siblings to stay afloat during Taichiro's confinement in New Mexico. When the war thankfully ended, the troops stopped passing through Hawaii, and many camps in Hawaii were closed including the one near my grandfather's home. There was no need for the restaurant anymore. Taichiro would be coming home soon, and he would return and help in bringing in income for my father's brothers and sister. My father could then shut down the restaurant and reconvert it back to a home except for the swinging door to the kitchen. My father would also be able to return to business college to get his degree.

Unlike his grandfather Tarokichi or his father Taichiro, my father didn't board a steam ship and travel for two weeks to an unfamiliar land. My father spent his whole life, except for his years at business college, in the same home he was born, his father's house. Yet in his emotional realm, what my father did in his young adult life was as courageous as leaving Japan and living in a totally different culture and region. My father's daring voyage was becoming a father to his younger siblings, handling the adoption of his infant sister, and opening and operating a restaurant, a business in which he had no experience. He took on challenges with composure. My father had his grandparents' and parents' tenacity to grab hold of opportunities and to not let go and to make long voyages in his soul.

In the decades after World War II, my father would continue to validate in his life the quality of persistence which his grandparents and parents had. The post-war years for my father would include meeting my mother Carolyn. She would share with my father the God given attributes which she received from her parents and family. Together they would be a mighty team in serving the Lord.

More about my father's and mother's life together will be shared in upcoming chapters of this book. For now, it would be sufficed to say that up to this point, the end of World War II, on my father's side of the family, no one in his family history, to my knowledge, had relied on Christ for his or her salvation. About two decades after the end of World War II, however, this pattern would change. By the intervention of God, my father would become the first Seto to be baptized in Christ. In my father's direct line of genealogy, covering hundreds of generations, going all the way back to Adam and Noah, no Seto had ever made a public profession of Jesus. Was God merciful to the generations spanning many millennia before my father because God knew that in 1962 my father would publicly testify that Jesus was his Lord and Savior?

And not only my father, but my father's two brothers, Hiroshi and Yasushi, and my father's two sisters, Mona and Jane who was given up for adoption would all testify that Jesus is their Savior. All five of Taichiro's and Masano's children, the grandchildren of Tarokichi and Amaya, placed their trust in Jesus as their Savior. Had God been gracious to all the preceding generations of my father's family because He foresaw the conversion of all five of Taichiro's and Masano's children and many of their children, grandchildren and great grandchildren, too?

As the psalmist declares, "Lord, thou hast been our dwelling place in all generations" (Ps. 90:1, King James Version). Even to the thousands in the Seto family who did not know the true God the Father or His Son Jesus Christ, God was still kind to them during their life on this earth and consigned to them calmness to curtail calamity, composure to confront catastrophe, and resources to rebuild ruins. By the generous kindness of God, these qualities were passed on to each generation after them. By the work of the Holy Spirit, may I also learn these skills and hand them over to my children and grandchildren.

"For the Lord is good; his mercy is everlasting; and his truth endureth to all generations" (Ps. 100:5, King James Version).

"Thy faithfulness is unto all generations; thou hast established the earth, and it abideth," (Ps. 119:90, King James Version).

"The Lord shall reign forever, even thy God, O Zion, unto all generations. Praise ye the Lord" (Ps. 146:10, King James Version).

Lester Seto's Father

Ellsworth Futoshi Seto (1922-2006)

Brother: Hiroshi Seto
Brother: Yasushi Seto
Sister: Mona Seto Byrnes
Sister: Jane Seto Amasaki Nakano

llsworth's Mother: Masano Enoki Seto	Ellsworth's Father: Taichiro Seto
(1897 - 1941)	(1886 - 1970)
No Record of Brothers or Sisters	No Record of Brothers or Sisters
Ellsworth's Maternal Grandfather:	Ellsworth's Paternal Grandfather:
Masanoru Enoki	Tarokichi Seto
(? -?)	(ca. 1856 -?)
No Record of Brothers or Sisters	No Record of Brothers or Sisters
Ellsworth's Maternal Grandmother:	Ellsworth's Paternal Grandmother:
Tsumayo Enoki	Amaya Seto
(? -?)	(? -?)
No Record of Brothers or Sisters	No Record of Brothers or Sisters

Chapter Eleven

WONDERS OF LETTER WRITING

"Peace, peace, wonderful peace; coming down from the Father above! Sweep over my spirit, forever, I pray. In fathomless billows of love!" (From Peace, Peace, Wonderful Peace by Warren D. Cornell)

As Pastor and writing partner, Les Seto has written, the letter is a valuable tool readily at hand to aid us in many ways. We can reach out to our loved ones and lift them up with encouraging words, and we can memorialize the blessings we receive from our heavenly Father God.

Les enjoyed telling us a back-story of the Seto Family. I was surprised at the in-depth review Les shared, on Ellsworth, his father and the struggles his dad faced and overcame. This was a few days before the Pearl Harbor attacks when Ellsworth Seto had lost his loving, kind mother. Her passing in late November 1941 left eighteen-year-old Ellsworth responsible for his four orphaned siblings. I had not known of these things before Les shared them.

The burden of taking care of his family as well as the Imperial Japanese raid on Oahu made for a terrible new set of circumstances, including, as we have read, the imprisonment of the chief breadwinner and provider, Ellsworth's father.

Saddened beyond belief, Ellsworth's gentle, patriotic father was interned in wartime captivity leaving his family destitute. Les's dad, Ellsworth, was forced to drop out of college and convert the family residence into a steakhouse (The Service Inn).

The almost unbearable element of this catastrophe is the part where Ellsworth had to allow his sister Jane, to be adopted by a caring neighbor family. Les wrote that Ellsworth and his siblings would see her playing or at their school, but could not speak to her or acknowledge Jane, as terms of the adoption contract dictated in those years.

From the reading of Chapter Ten, one could certainly feel the nearly palpable pain that event had caused the Seto family. Had I not asked Les, we would not have this beautifully told story. The difficulties of those events were: internment; adoption; and a loss of their income causing the Seto family to convert their modest home into a restaurant. These things the Seto family learned to rise above, such was their strength of purpose from their cohesive family ties to one another. Yet this had never before been captured in writing.

I had a belief that the culture of Asian-American families included that they put generational family members first, refusing to abandon the aging parents in convalescent homes. This belief I had somewhat understood, but I now know it is true. When Carolyn Seto became bedridden with end stage Alzheimer's disease, Les and his wife Bernadette as well as Les's brother, Emmett had, with much love, taken care of their mother in their homes in Waikoloa. This required Les to forsake the income a pastor receives from his church for one year or more, and to tighten his home life activities in order to provide 24/7 care for his mother for many months. In spite of the hardships this imposed, Les's letters conveyed only that his family was indeed blessed to return Carolyn's love by caring for her in her golden years, in spite of the disease of Alzheimer.

Les said in his letters, that often Carolyn did not recognize family members, yet her face would brighten at the sight of the family dog. How sorrowful this made Bernadette feel not to be recognized by her mother-in-law in her own home. When Jesus took Carolyn home to be with Ellsworth and the saints of God gathering by the crystal-clear river of life, there was much rejoicing that Carolyn would be clothed with a new body and never be sick again in her longed-for heaven. Pastor Les was able to conduct his mother's funeral and arrange for her favorite song, What a Friend We Have in Jesus, to be sung by the church choir.

These things were occurring as Les steadfastly worked on his book, Gentleness in the Old Testament. What a paradox this must have seemed to Les. But you, dear reader, can quickly ascertain that God had a purpose for having Les write such a profoundly tender and embracing book at such a time in his family's life. We see once more, the good and proper decorum that the writing of letters in easy and lighthearted times can be advantageous in difficult, even heavy-laden times when we trust in God to provide his comfort.

Whenever I thought of Hawaii, my impression was of beautiful islands in posters in the window of the local travel agency in our village of Vacaville. I would see the advertisements of a sunny pristine beach, a Polynesian luau, and the glamorous hotels. I'd dream of the pampering I'd receive from the local islanders while on vacation.

It is true that I did not understand the gap between the lifestyle I was enjoying while visiting Hawaii and the hard life that those wonderful Hawaiian people were bearing up under in this Pacific paradise. I did become aware after Les told me in one letter he had no right to complain about his care giving to his mother Carolyn. Les reasoned, that in another season of his life, he had worked at a hotel and knew that some of the employees managed to labor on two jobs, with no days off to support their families.

I recognize that I had been a typical mainlander coming for seven glorious days to enjoy the hospitality of the islanders. Wretchedly, I hadn't embraced the idea of generously tipping the efficient servers and housekeepers in the hotel and restaurants. The tavern maids or janitorial staff had made sure each evening I had pleasant drinks and a freshly made bed and clean room to enjoy. I had winced when I paid my bill of fare at the concierge counter, feeling as if I was owed an upgrade or other special service. I always looked at it as if others were 'in my way' when I stood in the car rental agency or any of Maui's many courtesy outlets. I think now as I read Les's heartfelt recap of all that his family endured on Hilo and now Waikoloa. Indeed, I was the ugly American abroad.

Definitely, I needed to understand that the people of our fiftieth State of Hawaii are gentle, kindhearted and long suffering which, according to the Holy Bible, are some of the fruits of the Spirit. I needed to know about their modest homes and they must work diligently to provide each of their wonderful families with a standard of living so different than I enjoy back home stateside. I am thankful that my eyes were opened by just the few innocent comments Les had shared with me about his islander acquaintances. Now his riveting history of his family made me see that I was clueless about many things.

It pleases me that we share in our letters, growing in God's amazing grace.

The Wonders of Letter Writing

On August 6th, 2012, five years to the day of this writing, on a Monday, I had written a caring letter to one of my daughters, Rachael Michelle. Follows is that letter as recorded in my August journal:

"Arriving back at Chris' home, Rachael's brother, I brought in tuna casserole Liz had made for us. At around 5:30 p.m., the Suisun City marine layer finally brought in mild afternoon breezes. We had just returned from the dialysis hospital.

"I made biscuits and heated Liz's main dish along with salad and milk. We ate our meal and Chris offered prayer. 2012 was the movie we selected...one half hour into the movie, Chris, exhausted, went upstairs to bed. I wrote an eight-page letter to my eldest child, Rachael Michelle. The kitchen had a delicious smell and I finally thoroughly enjoyed the quiet time to correspond with Rachael. Excerpts of this letter follow:

"Dear Rachael: As promised, I decided to write...I did not want another day to pass without putting my thoughts on paper.

"It was nice hearing your voice; of course, you were busy clearing and organizing your pantry as we spoke. Rachael and her husband Bo lived in Texas, and my grandson, Beau Oliver had just joined the Navy leaving them in an 'empty nest'. I could hear the joy in your words while you, my eldest child, were collecting your home, putting things in order.

"Rachael, you can come organize our home if you have the energy. Only two closets, one garage, and an upstairs room that is a catchall room for everything we can't seem to part with. We are very pleased to have a comfortable home with a back yard, a three-car garage, and I haven't always been a good steward of this gift of our home. My intentions were honorable; however, the road to hell is paved with good intentions not followed through on. Here, I drew a happy face emoji.

I began to summarize the shortness of life, drawing a connection to the plans of most Americans to get control of their lives freeing themselves from the rubble of debris that make Americans somewhat uptight than they might be in an orderly home. I continued:

John Lennon had an inspiring life. At 40 when John died, he had achieved all that the world could give—early stardom worldwide; a wife; two sons; great music albums; published books; and he was revered among old and young alike. John was one of my working-class heroes when I was twenty-one. In fact, your middle name, Rachael, I took from John's beautiful song with Sir Paul McCartney, Michelle.

A Little About Your Father

"My words about are based on decades of writing. Since turning thirty-five, I wrote a chapbook of poetry, Unveiling Liberty, and at age 55, a ninety-page autobiography, Faith Beyond Doubt an Allegory plus approximately ninety journals of daily observations.

"Writing has opened a window to my inner thoughts, my soul and therefore my life, one that you and others are free to experience once a book of it is in print. Like your life, the reality is I wrote daily in my law enforcement career for thirty-three years—what we would call voluminous government non-Sicilia.

Knowing my daughter is a theology graduate with her degree in religious studies, I offered her this insight:

The Stimulation to Write

"Reading great authors truly shapes a wordsmith's talent, (if in fact she has a skill). Let me describe for you my take on the daily regimen that I follow. You'll quickly see my role models are widely divergent: Moses, who was over 80 at the time, wrote the first five books of the Old Testament. It's a resource of particularly brilliant phrasing. How Moses succeeded in such a wide-ranging colossal work defies description...except we know it was divinely inspired.

"Reading Genesis almost compels you to document your origins: "In the beginning, Rachael Michelle was created in the image of God, who made her a little lower than the angels. God looked, and He said, 'It is good.'

"Rachael, as I began journal number one, it was the gradually focusing goal to bring honesty to my words. I began each daily entry, 'Dear Heavenly Father' as my opening salutation. Obviously, any writer, in this situation, is compelled to write with sincerity. Truth is as he or she knows it to be.

"A writer is compelled with that opening addressee, to write without deception, neither to use modern, transient slang or fall into the trap of self-aggrandizement. I am by nature a self-serving person. I soon realized a fault in my character is portrayed in my sentences. So, I amended this practice by avoiding constant usage of the first-person tense.

"My writing is not always based on my own thoughts; I love quoting wonderful Bible passages, and it is always fully put down, date and time noted, with my right hand. This method enables you to learn a trait of conversational writing as well. How this occurs, I cannot explain to you, dear Daughter. I do know that some other entity, to my relief, is channeling words 'from their thoughts', not mine. I don't imply here that I'm guilty of cheating, and I give credit to direct quotations such as hymns—by author, lyricist, and if known, publisher.

You'll soon see dear Reader that I had hoped Rachael to be able to grasp by example how some of my favorite authors produced their magnificent books.

Where Lessons Are Taught

"Along with Moses, I include other stellar writers of past centuries: most of them were native to America soil: John Bunyan, author of Pilgrims' Progress, (a must read for fledgling authors); Benjamin Franklin's autobiography; President U.S. Grant's Memoir, still the longest, largest selling book by an American author who wrote of his own life; Mark Twain / Samuel Clemens's personal bio and his book: The Adventures of Huckleberry Finn (1888); Hemingway's A Moveable Feast (1964) and Hemingway spelled moveable in that specific way.

"Returning to the Bible, I found superb writing styles in the 150 psalms, many by King David, son of Jesse of Nazareth. I love the power and rhythm of the boy prophet Isaiah's work. His great minister's call to a nation to repentance is the source of many of today's Sunday sermons...one by an American president John F. Kennedy in a national speech. "But they that wait upon the Lord shall renew their strength; they shall mount up with wings as eagles; they shall run, and not be weary; and they shall walk, and not faint" (Isa. 40:31, King James Version).

Knowing that Rachael has a poet's heart and wanderlust for travel and adventure (she has since sold her gated-community home and purchased a fifth-wheeler home; she and Bo and their hound dog, Bo, are traveling the USA seeking a place to buy and build their dream home), I wrote:

Everything Old is New Again

"I discovered in the New Testament the skillful language of Dr. Luke to be a wonderment of brevity, always scholarly, with whom, what, where, how, when and why, always contained in Dr. Luke's prose. Luke, the physician was not one of the twelve disciples, but was an understudy of Saint Paul (formerly Saul of Tarsus). When you read Paul's letters to Timothy, or to Corinth, Ephesus, Rome, Thessalonica, Philippi, the early churches in Asia Minor, you'll see his clear mastery that has no equal in authorship. Complex themes are readily grasped, faith being the underpinning."

Rachael has knowledge of spiritual things, so I continued in this vein:

Better to Great Writing

"That which required, for me, spiritual training since 1998... constantly reading from these sources, I am hopefully providing a digest in these pages...I assure you that the world with all its book-reading people, are hungry to know things that are of true value. A good writer spills out his thoughts as though he or she has discovered an open window to release the imprisoned ideas and events from their day dreaming."

Then I continued knowing Rachael's prowess as a communicator:

"A great writer carefully crafts a story in such a way as to provide comfort, encouragement, humor and goodwill amongst her sisters and brothers, the readers. You see that this is not a time waster either for the author or reader. You can do no worse thing than to waste time.

"God's people are peculiar, but not weird. I have found, curiously, that in my nearness to God through prayers, He recognizes, befriends and became my companion. To believers of Jesus Christ—that statement is no deep secret. To the uninitiated (however, someday every knee will bow, and every tongue confess that Christ is Lord), for them it is a mere rattletrap thought of a deluded mind; "He drank the Kool Aid," they might say of Christians. But God is not mocked and neither does His Word, the scriptures in the Holy Bible, return void. He has given us freely His Word and it is a roadmap to successfully navigate this life."

Any father who is physically apart from his children has intrusive worrisome thoughts about the welfare of his family. He feels like his primary purpose is to guide and properly influence his sons and daughters to make good decisions. I rarely had to concern myself with Rachael. She graduated from Armijo High School, (my alma mater) and enlisted immediately into the Navy. She then made it three generations of navy sailors and her son; Beau Oliver made it four generations of navy sailors. She graduated from the Defense Language Institute in Monterey, California. One of her duty stations was in Hawaii with

Chinese language skills as an interpreter. I had a twinge that dictates that I must advise her of matters of goodness. So, I continued:

"In the confusing days in which we live, we feel we're insignificant beings in the great universe—and we should not blame God for our distractions. We know who the culprit is. When we come to those crossroads of decisions, it is this master of confusion, the serpent, who is waiting. We rebuke Satan without delay. When we are set on by his temptation and our spirit is vexed, we can recall the time that Jesus was tempted.

"Jesus was in the desert at the hour of his temptation having been on a fast for forty days. We read that Jesus fought fire with fire. When Satan tempted Him by quoting from scripture, Jesus conquered Satan by using scripture appropriately. "Thou shalt not tempt the Lord thy God" (Luke 4:12, King James Version).

"Daily, most of we humans have thousands of uncalled, intrusive thoughts, all ours. These are not Godly thoughts but are provocations of Satan. Again, consider Jesus; He is the only man who was sinless, and His example in times of temptation is invaluable...and it works. "But he turned, and said unto Peter, "Get thee behind me, Satan: thou art an offence unto me" (Matt. 16:23, King James Version)

"Simply upon the name of Jesus, these intrusive thoughts will diminish. Whenever you silently (or aloud) invoke the name, Jesus, Satan's work is done, and the serpent cannot remain present in the Holy presence of Jesus' name.

"I know this almost sounds Harry Potter-ish. But consider that the Holy Bible predates Harry Potter books by twenty centuries.

"I don't know about you, Rachael, but when my faith lags, as it will do from time to time, I simply ask Jesus to take that burden from me. The Bible tells us that Christ will not give us any burden too hard to bear. "With man, many things are impossible, but with God, all things are possible—only believe."

It seemed fun to share these things with you, about my need to communicate. Dear reader, know that Rachael donated a kidney to her brother Chris, and she has become, as all organ donors, a champion to her Aunt Esther, my sister. This is my conscious thought as I finished this portion. By sharing the contents our brief letter, other parents may find encouragement to write to their daughter or son. If you agree, proceed with zest.

Chapter Twelve

FROM BUDDHIST TO CHRISTIAN

"Strength and honour are her clothing; and she shall rejoice in time to come. She openeth her mouth with wisdom; and in her tongue is the law of kindness. She looketh well to the ways of her household, and eateth not the bread of idleness. Her children arise up, and call her blessed; her husband also, and he praiseth her" (Prov. 31:25-28, King James Version).

Remarkable Rachael and Other Inspiring Christians

Don's words were articulate in Chapter Eleven and in prior chapters about the uplifting power, which Christians transmit to others through both their words and actions generated by Jesus. In Chapter Eleven, Don highlighted his remarkable daughter Rachael and how the Holy Spirit has energized her to live every day in service to Christ and to even ascend to lofty heights of compassion as in becoming a courageous organ donor.

As the Apostle Paul wrote,

"We give thanks to God and the Father of our Lord Jesus Christ, praying always for you, since we heard of your faith in Christ Jesus, and of the love which ye have to all the saints" (Col. 1:3-4, King James Version).

When we hear (or read) about the faith and love which fellow Christians convey through their words and deeds, we, too, give thanks to the Lord, and are strengthened to serve Him with more zeal.

Sometimes the faith and love about which we hear, read or see come from Christians like Rachael who are still serving Jesus here on earth. Other times the faith and love which inspire us to carry Christ's cross come from pilgrims of Christ who have already entered the Celestial City, our Heavenly Jerusalem, such as Don's father-in-law Dr. Robert Mitchell, Don's and my dear friend Bill Sheehan, and my mother Carolyn Seto, all three who passed away in 2015 and 2016 while Don and I were corresponding to each other.

As mentioned previously, Don asked if I would share about the faith of my parents as he had done with his parents. In Chapter Ten, I related how the Lord was kind to over a hundred generations of Setos who preceded my father but who did not know Christ. With great gratitude, I expressed how the Lord brought my father and his four siblings to faith in Jesus, the first Setos to my knowledge who received Jesus as their Savior. In completing Don's request, I shall now introduce my mother's family, who like my father's family, had over a hundred generations who did not have a relationship with Jesus.

The Ishikuro Clan: Blessed with a Solid Work Ethic

Unlike my father's family who endured harrowing experiences, my mother's family had a more peaceful transition from Japan to Hawaii. My mother's family traveled to Hawaii around 1900, toward the end of the great emigration era when thousands left Japan. Plantations in Hawaii in 1900 had become more accommodating to married couples in contrast to the early days of the immigration era. Unlike most of the earlier Japanese sugar plantation laborers who traveled alone to Hawaii without their spouses, my mother's parents Tazo and Fuyo Ishikuro migrated together as a married couple from Japan to Hawaii.

Also, when Hawaii became a U.S. Territory in 1898, working conditions on plantations were not as brutal as in earlier years. One reason was that all contracts that forced laborers to remain with their employers for a specific period became illegal. Hence, life on the sugar cane plantations became more humane so that employers could retain more of their laborers. The work, however, on the sugar plantations was still strenuous. My mother's father Tazo labored hard in the sun and the rain, and his fellow workers and employers recognized his love of agriculture and his work ethic.

One of Tazo's fellow field workers, Kango Yamato, left the sugar plantation where he was employed and purchased agricultural land. Yamato soon discovered that he could not use all his land, and so he sought to lease about twenty acres of it to someone who would be a good steward of his property. Yamato immediately thought of his friend Tazo Ishikuro who worked with him when Yamato was employed at the sugar plantation. And so, Yamato asked my mother's father if he would be interested in leasing some of his agricultural land.

My mother's father jumped at the offer. He left the plantation and leased Yamato's land. Tazo built a humble, single wall, pine lumber home which had a tin, corrugated roof and which rested on stilts, four to six feet tall, conforming to the uneven contour below. Tazo then cleared most of the twenty acres leased to him and planted lettuce, cabbage, tomatillo, turnip, carrots, beans, corn and other vegetables.

Though my mother's father was not a Christian, the Lord mercifully retained in him the value that He imprinted in the first human. Adam states,

"The Lord God took the man and put him in the Garden of Eden to work it and take care of it" (Gen. 2:15, New International Version).

For Tazo, the twenty acres of land he leased became his verdant Garden of Eden.

Tazo's wife Fuyo was also a diligent worker on the farm. Before she gave birth to her children, she worked many hours of the day helping Tazo, washing and sorting vegetables and hoeing weeds. When Fuyo, however, started having children, her time with farm work diminished while her time in taking care of Tazo's and her children increased.

Tazo and Fuyo went on to have seven children of whom my mother was the third youngest. God had given to my grandmother Fuyo many of the traits of the virtuous woman described in Proverbs 31:10-31 though Fuyo never became a Christian. In this life on earth, Fuyo received the satisfaction, dispensed by God that comes from working diligently and being an asset to one's family:

"Who can find a virtuous woman? for her price is far above rubies. The heart of her husband doth safely trust in her, so that he shall have no need of spoil. She will do him good and not evil all the days of her life" (Prov. 31:10-12, King James Version).

The Lord would also bless my mother Carolyn with these same precious attributes.

Long before trusting in Jesus as her Savior, my mother as a child was embracing, by the grace of God, Christian values such as the love of honest work. As an elementary school aged child, on many mornings before the sun rose, under the light from kerosene lanterns, my mother Carolyn was washing cucumbers or celery before going to school. When she got home in the afternoon, she would wash turnips or carrots until evening. The Lord was preparing my mother for the time when she would serve Jesus as her Lord and Savior and do what the Apostle Paul instructed his fellow Christians, "And whatsoever ye do, do it heartily, as to the Lord, and not unto men" (Col. 3:23, King James Version).

Tazo's and Fuyo's children including my mother learned to find fulfillment in productive labor in God's Eden. As a child, I would occasionally visit my Ishikuro aunts' and uncle's homes, located in places like San Jose and Redwood City, California and in towns in Hawaii. Each had a tidy garden or a well-landscaped yard that they personally kept up. Even when my mother was in her eighties, she would spend at least a half hour watering her plants, picking low hanging avocados, oranges or tangerines, or weeding around her dozen pineapple plants. She would tell her family and friends that her time with her plants gave her an opportunity to thank God for His many blessings including the food and beauty which the Lord's plants provided.

Who Is This Holy Ghost?

The Lord was kind to Tazo, Fuyo, and their children though none of them knew Jesus until my mother Carolyn and one of her sisters Judy became Christians as adults. I asked my mother when she first learned or thought about Christianity. I expected her to say at Christmas or at Easter when many non-Christians learn at least a little about Jesus' birth and resurrection. My mother said the first time she ever had an awareness of Christianity was as a child. She witnessed an elaborate, annual parade sponsored by her Portuguese immigrant friends and their families, specifically those Portuguese from the Azores Islands in the Atlantic Ocean. The Azorean Portuguese residents called their procession the Holy Ghost Parade.

When I lived in Northern California, I noticed that there were many communities with a significant Azorean Portuguese population such as in Santa Cruz, San Jose, Half Moon Bay and Sausalito. I learned that in each of these cities and towns, the Azorean Portuguese also held Holy Ghost processions like the one my mother mentioned. The marchers honor the Holy Spirit to whom Queen Isabella of Portugal gave credit when a ship laden with bread, water and supplies brought relief to the residents of the Azores Islands who were experiencing a severe drought and famine. The Queen is said to have led a procession through the streets of Lisbon and then left her crown as a thanksgiving memorial at the cathedral.

As in all Holy Ghost Parades, the organizers in my mother's hometown selected a queen in memory of Queen Isabella and two maids to accompany the queen during the procession. The festive event was held in the late spring, close to, but not on the Sunday that many Christians call Pentecost, the Feast of the Holy Spirit. The Holy Ghost Parade was a jovial procession, almost like Mardi Gras but without the glitzy costumes or boisterous dancing.

Those in the long Holy Ghost procession were dressed in their formal attire, men in suits and ties, boys in white shirts with dark slacks, and women and girls in full length white dresses. Some of the marchers in the parade carried baskets of bread on their heads, probably symbolizing both Jesus the bread of life and the bread delivered to the drought and famine victims in the Azores Islands during Queen Isabella's reign. Decorations included large crowns with doves above, the crowns signifying God the Father, Jesus His Son and Queen Isabella; and the doves, the Holy Spirit.

My mother was fascinated by the annual parade and wanted to know more about the Holy Ghost. "Who is this Holy Ghost?" she asked. God was using an Azorean Portuguese parade to catch my mother's attention so that she would want to learn more about the true God. By asking about the Holy Ghost, my mother would later more importantly learn about whom the Holy Ghost served. As an adult, she would discover that the Holy Ghost gives honor to God our Heavenly Father and His Son Jesus, the One who saves us from sin and everlasting punishment. My mother also learned in a mystifying way the Holy Ghost is also divine and one of the magnificent Three Persons of the Holy Trinity.

Bodhisattvas Can't Save Us

My mother's parents were Buddhists just as their ancestors had been for centuries. My mother and her family worshiped at a Buddhist temple in the town where they lived. The temple contained many gold colored statues and paintings of a man to whom they referred to as Buddha and of other men called Bodhisattvas whom they believed were reincarnated righteous persons, almost but not quite as pure as Buddha, but who nevertheless were enlightened enough to save people from the recurring pain of reincarnation.

There are hundreds of denominations in Buddhism. Many contradict the teachings of the others. But in general, most Buddhists teach that countless enlightened, reincarnated humans known as Buddhas have lived on earth throughout history, and countless more Buddhas will be reincarnated and live on earth in the future.

Many Buddhists believe that the most recent Buddha is a man named Siddhartha Gautama who lived in Nepal and India around the same time as the Biblical prophets Daniel and Ezekiel, circa 600 B.C. Until a new Buddha comes upon the scene, most Buddhists honor Siddhartha Gautama as their current Buddha.

The ethical life, which the Buddhists teach are like Christianity: don't be greedy and materialistic; be humble, honest, and peaceful. However, the spiritual teachings of Buddhism conflict with the Bible. Most Buddhists teach reincarnation. The Bible, however, declares,

"And as it is appointed unto men once to die, but after this the judgment" (Heb. 9:27, King James Version).

Many Buddhists don't believe in the existence of God. When pressed as to who then created them and the universe, many Buddhists will answer, "That is not a question that I consider to be important. Nor am I interested in answering that question. The more important question is 'How can I live a more harmonious life?" The Bible, however, proclaims,

"The fool hath said in his heart, "There is no God" (Ps. 14:1, King James Version).

Some Buddhists teach that there are very kind reincarnated humans called Bodhisattvas who can save people by removing them from the curse of being reincarnated every time they die. Many who are not Buddhists think that Buddhists look upon reincarnation as a completely good outcome because an animal or a human never really dies. That should be good, right? But that is not so to a Buddhist. A Buddhist believes that reincarnation is also a torture because a human or an animal must continually come back to earth and suffer the horrific process of dying a thousand or a billion times. That's not a blessing or a comforting thought to a Buddhist or to anyone.

A Buddhist would like to get off the eternal roller coaster ride of reincarnation. Many Buddhists trust in a bodhisattva, a really altruistic human, not quite Buddha but close to becoming one, to save them from the weariness and torment of reincarnation. But in Acts, Peter asserts,

"Neither is there salvation in any other: for there is none other name under heaven given among men, whereby we must be saved" (Acts 4:12, King James Version).

The Bible makes it clear that the only one who can save us is Jesus, not a bodhisattva.

Not all Buddhists believe in Bodhisattvas who can save people from the tormenting cycle of reincarnation. These Buddhists teach that a person must save herself or himself if she or he wants to get off the never stopping train ride of reincarnation. A person must not seek the help of anyone. How does one do this? These Buddhists teach that a person can give up all desires completely, including the desire to sin and the desire to have even good things like health and love. When a person can be perfectly content with whatever the situation may be, then he or she will have lived the spotless, pure life and can then hop off the reincarnation treadmill.

At doughnut shops or manicure places owned by people of Asian descent, customers will sometimes see a counter top, ceramic figure of a jolly fellow with a big smile on his face. That kind of statue is an ideal of Buddha who is perfectly content whether he has a severe headache or has just sold his house for a favorable price. He has no desire to sin and no desire to have good health. He is perfectly satisfied with reality as it is. Many Buddhists define this condition to be perfection. When one reaches this state of perfection, he or she will have earned for themselves the ticket go get off the reincarnation rail train.

The Bible, however, says,

"As it is written, There is none righteous, no, not one: There is none that understandeth, there is none that seeketh after God. They are all gone out of the way, they are together become unprofitable: there is none that doeth good, no, not one" (Rom. 3:10-12, King James Version).

No human, except one, namely Jesus has ever achieved perfection.

The Apostle Paul also laments,

"I find then a law, that, when I would do good, evil is present with me. For I delight in the law of God after the inward man: But I see another law in my members, warring against the law of my mind, and bringing me into captivity to the law of sin which is in my members. O wretched man that I am! who shall deliver me from the body of this death?" (Rom. 7:21-24, King James Version).

While we live on earth, our sinful human nature, Satan, and temptations from the world will get the best of us, sometimes less frequently, other times more frequently, and so we all need Christ to save us from this wretched condition. And He will save us as He did my mother Carolyn when the Holy Spirit turned her life over to Jesus.

The day would come in my mother's life when she would learn that there is a condition more horrid than reincarnation, namely, suffering in hell. But she would also learn that God does not want anyone to go there and has sent a Savior to rescue us from the path to hell. His Savior is not a Bodhisattva, but God's own Son Jesus Christ. Christ lived the perfect life that no Buddha or any human has ever lived. He truly has the qualifications and the divine power to save us. My mother would learn those truths in God's merciful time.

Learning to Be A Servant

After graduating from high school, my mother could have gone to the city of Honolulu on the island of Oahu where there were many job opportunities such as a bank teller, a retail clerk in a big department store, a secretary in a business office or a civil servant in a government department. She, however, decided to stay on the island of Hawaii which was still very rural and where job opportunities were limited. It was more important for my mother to keep close to her family rather than to venture out into the commercial world.

My mother found a job as a live-in domestic worker for a medical doctor and his wife who lived about 30 miles from where my mother's parents lived. Since the doctor worked long hours and since the couple had no children, my mother's attention was mostly devoted to helping the doctor's wife. My mother's duties included housekeeping, cooking, laundering and other tasks. Since my mother had been responsible for these chores at her home since she was a girl, she smoothly transitioned into the routine that her employer established.

The woman and her husband whom my mother helped were appreciative of my mother's labor and were very kind to her. My mother was very happy with her job and was not in a hurry to find a job in an office or in a business. She was at peace in serving the couple that had taken her in to be their helper. The couple treated her as if she were in the family.

She would have been satisfied working for the couple for many years, but God had other plans for her. She would be carrying out similar tasks to what she was doing at the couple's house, but it would be in a different setting.

What God Has Joined Together

On September 2, 1945, a few hours after Japan officially surrendered on the deck of the U.S.S. Missouri in Tokyo Bay, General Douglas Macarthur delivered a radio address to the world. He began by solemnly saying, "Today the guns are silent. A great tragedy has ended. A great victory has been won."

The nightmarish war, which started with the diabolical sinking of American battleships and other vessels in a U.S. Territory harbor ended with a civil submission on an American battleship in a Japanese harbor. The end of World War II brought long awaited relief to millions including my family. My grandfather Taichiro returned from his internment in New Mexico, relieving my father Ellsworth of his duties in being totally responsible for the care for his three younger siblings. Now that responsibility could be shared between his father Taichiro and him.

My father then resumed his studies on the island of Oahu at the business college where he had been enrolled when the war broke out. He completed his course work and returned to Hilo, pondering what kind of career he would pursue.

When the Japanese attacked Pearl Harbor, my father was twenty years old. When Emperor Hirohito signed the peace treaty on the U.S.S. Missouri, my father was twenty-four. During those four years, my father, as with millions of others impacted by the war, had little if any time for recreation with his friends and for dating. The years after the war gave Ellsworth the opportunity to enjoy some of the informal pastimes for which he as a young single adult had been denied during the war.

One of the ways in which my father would relax would be to take one-day drives on weekends to different parts of the island of Hawaii with two of his good friends. One day my father and his two friends drove to the northern part of the island, a seventy-mile drive one way, and as they were driving home, they saw two women, about their same age, standing on the two-lane highway, apparently waiting for a ride.

As many young single men would have innocently done, my father and his friends slowed down and pulled up alongside the two women and congenially asked if they needed a ride. The two women were my mother Carolyn and her younger sister, by two years, Judy. They were standing in a forested area just on the edge of their parent's farm.

Carolyn replied, "No thank you. We appreciate the offer, but I'm waiting for the county bus. My sister is just keeping me company." Carolyn had been visiting her parents on the farm and on that afternoon needed to return to the home of the couple where she worked as a housekeeper and cook.

Carol's sister Judy instantly assessed that they three men in the car were trustworthy. They were casually well dressed, neatly groomed, and looked like genuine gentlemen. She quickly urged Carolyn to reconsider her decision and accept the men's offer. Carolyn disagreed, and so the two women continued to discuss the matter while my father and his two friends observed in polite amusement.

Finally, Carolyn gave in to Judy's pleading and let the gentlemen know that she would gratefully accept their offer to give her a ride. Carolyn got into the sedan and drove off waving good-bye to her sister.

Of the three friends in the car, my father Ellsworth was the one most interested in getting to know Carolyn, and so his friends let him freely converse with her. Carolyn and Ellsworth were comfortable in their dialogue with each other, and Carolyn appreciated the company of Ellsworth's friends, too. Carolyn and

Ellsworth exchanged contact information with each other, and both shared that they would like to keep in touch in the future. When the vehicle they were in arrived at the home of Carolyn's employers, she thanked the three men, and they bid a cheerful adieu, ending a most pleasant day.

What if Carolyn had stuck to her initial response and had refused to catch a ride with Ellsworth and his two friends? God would have still extended His grace to them. That's for sure. They might never have met again, but each would have been blessed in their separate lives. Or the Lord might have brought them into contact and into a relationship with each other again. Either sequel could have occurred.

How wonderful it was, however, that the Lord had urged Carolyn's sister Judy to persuade her sister to accept the three gentlemen's invitation to drive Carolyn to the home where she was employed. That one "yes or no" answer to the three men had outcomes that would last forever. How grateful were Carolyn, Ellsworth and others, including me, that Carolyn consented to Judy's pleas according to God's extraordinary plan. The Bible asserts,

"And we know that all things work together for good to them that love God, to them who are the called according to his purpose" (Rom. 8:28, King James Version).

Without Carolyn, Ellsworth and Judy knowing it, the Lord was working out His purpose on that weekend afternoon next to the farm where Carolyn and Judy's family lived.

For the next year, Carolyn and Ellsworth saw each other often, and their relationship grew closer. Carolyn continued to work for the couple that had been so gracious to her. After about a year of courtship, Ellsworth proposed to Carolyn, and she enthusiastically said, "Yes!" They were engaged and soon married. With sadness, Carolyn let the couple who had employed her know that she had become engaged and would not be able to work for them once she became married. She moved into the home of her new husband and began taking care of Ellsworth's household. First, she thanked her affectionate employers for the generosity that they had extended to her at a time when she needed employment, and the couple expressed gratitude for Carolyn's faithfulness in carrying out her duties.

The Lord brought together Carolyn and Ellsworth, two persons who had no relationship with Jesus and from families who had never trusted in Christ as their Savior. Yet the Lord had compassion upon them. He knew in advance that He would send His Holy Spirit upon Carolyn first and then Ellsworth. They would then both rely on Jesus and receive the everlasting life, peace and joy that can only be found in Him.

A New Role with Similar Noble Duties

After Carolyn and Ellsworth were married, Carolyn moved into Ellsworth's father's home. Since Ellsworth's father Taichiro did not have a spouse to help care for my father's two brothers, both in high school, and my father's sister in middle school, Carolyn gladly took on the role of being a full-time homemaker, cook, and foster mother for Taichiro's and Ellsworth's household.

Carolyn struggled somewhat in her relationship with Ellsworth's father Taichiro. Unlike her parents who were inclined to be cheerful, Carolyn's new father in law Taichiro was serious. He expressed criticism if he didn't like the way Carolyn cooked a dish or cleaned a certain area of the house. Yet he seldom if ever complimented her when he liked a meal she prepared or a shirt that she had ironed. It is possible that he didn't approve of anything that Carolyn did; however, that would be unlikely. He just did not comment in a positive manner if Carolyn had done something right in his eyes.

Despite the complex personality of Ellsworth's father Taichiro, Carolyn continued to pour her heart out in sweeping and mopping floors, washing and hanging clothes on a line, preparing three meals a day for all six persons in the home, and doing whatever chores were needed. The Lord was continuing to give Carolyn a servant's heart with His foreknowledge that she would later serve Jesus who said,

"Even as the Son of man came not to be ministered unto, but to minister, and to give his life a ransom for many" (Matt. 20:28, King James Version).

While Carolyn was attending to the domestic needs of Ellsworth, his father, her two high school aged brothers-in-law and middle school aged sister-in-law, Carolyn became pregnant and give birth to a son, me, in 1949. My mother Carolyn then had an infant to nurture in addition to her many other homemaker and kitchen duties. By the strength given to her from Almighty God, she managed to carry out her responsibilities with dignity and steadfastness.

With a child to feed in addition to financially helping his siblings and aging father Taichiro, my father Ellsworth was feeling the pressure to generate more income. Though he had a business college degree, he hadn't yet been able to find a job or start a business that satisfied him.

My father Ellsworth told me that after I was born, he was so worried about needing to bring home more income for the family that he borrowed money to purchase an order of men's shoes that would fill up the trunk and interior of his sedan. He parked his car on a vacant lot in the town of Hilo and sold the shoes out of the trunk and interior of his sedan. He said he somehow sold his entire inventory, paid back the loan, and made a modest profit to provide a few months' worth of food and clothing for his younger siblings, my mother, his father and me, his son.

Sometime later the Lord blessed my father, not yet a believer in Jesus, with an excellent opportunity to receive training to become an agent for Transamerica Occidental Life Insurance, a company affiliated with the corporation which later built the famous pyramid in San Francisco. My father signed up for the training and successfully completed his orientation with Transamerica Occidental Insurance. He did moderately well in selling policies and servicing clients, enough to bring financial stability to raise a family that added another child named Emmett, born five years after me. My father's days of selling shoes out of his car had mercifully passed.

The Ultimate Blessing

Our gracious God had blessed my mother, father, and their families with tremendous blessings including protection for the patriarchs and matriarchs of the family when they immigrated by steamship to Hawaii, safety during World War II; provision of health, food, shelter and clothing; and citizenship in the United States. Jesus' words that God takes care of both believers and unbelievers, the righteous and unrighteous, in this life on earth, rang true for the Seto and Ishikuro families:

"That ye may be the children of your Father which is in heaven: for he maketh his sun to rise on the evil and on the good, and sendeth rain on the just and on the unjust" (Matt. 5:45, King James Version).

The crown of all the blessings, however, took place in 1954 when the Lutheran Church Missouri Synod sent a missionary, Pastor Norman Abbott, who had been serving a congregation in Iowa, to the town of Hilo, Hawaii. Pastor Abbott's assignment was to share the Gospel and to start a church there.

Pastor Abbott often recounted to fellow pastors and church members what the mission board staff of the Lutheran Church Missouri Synod first told him about the town of Hilo. The mission board essentially said to Pastor Abbott, "We are sending you to the U.S. Territory of Hawaii, specifically to a town with a population of about 25,000. You will be sharing the Gospel with native Polynesians and with first and second-generation immigrants from Japan, China, the Philippines, Puerto Rico, and the Azores Islands. Though Hawaii is a territory of the United States, consider this assignment to be an overseas mission to a foreign country, the only difference being, that you will not need to learn a foreign language. You will be able to communicate in English."

Shortly after Pastor Abbott, his wife, and their six children arrived in Hilo in 1954 he began to canvass neighborhoods there. He kept meticulous records of each door upon which he knocked. Thirty years later in an eight and a half by eleven inch, spiral bound, soft covered, eighty-page autobiography, Pastor Abbott noted that he knocked on the doors of over two thousand homes in Hilo. Out of those calls, only two persons invited him into their home to talk about the Gospel. Not a high percentage to say the least. One of those two persons was my mother Carolyn.

She graciously asked Pastor Abbott to come into her home, offered him a glass of water, and listened to what Pastor Abbott said about the Gospel. Pastor Abbott invited my mother and the Seto family members to the church services that he conducted in a former motel. He also encouraged my mother to sign up for a class, which would explain the Gospel of Jesus and then to consider becoming baptized. My mother was open to both invitations. She began worshiping every Sunday in the former motel and attended mid-week evening classes to learn about the Bible. A few months later, she was baptized along with her two children, my infant brother and me, a five-year-old.

Dr. Luke recorded,

"And a certain woman named Lydia, a seller of purple, of the city of Thyatira, which worshipped God, heard us: whose heart the Lord opened, that she attended unto the things which were spoken of Paul. And when she was baptized, and her household, she besought us, saying, if ye have judged me to be faithful to the Lord, come into my house, and abide there" (Acts 16:14-15, King James Version).

My mother Carolyn was a Lydia to my brother and me. My brother and I were of the household who were baptized with our mother. About five years later, our father Ellsworth would be baptized. And so, the whole household, the immediate family of Ellsworth and Carolyn Seto eventually became baptized as Lydia and her household were.

How different our lives would have been if my mother had not let Pastor Abbot into our home to learn more about Jesus. If she had brushed Pastor Abbott off as many did in our town, would my parents, my brother and I later have become Christian? We might have, but such a scenario is uncertain. But all thanks be to God, the fact is that the Lord softened my mother's heart to welcome His messenger, Pastor Abbott, into our home and our lives.

How wonderful that the Holy Ghost, of whom my mother first inquired as a child, tugged at my mother's heart to listen to the Gospel that Pastor Abbott explained. The Holy Ghost. of whom my mother was curious when she was a child, led her to God the Father and to Jesus His Son. My mother would then proclaim Jesus to be her Savior and the Savior of all who would trust in Him. So true are the words of St. Paul:

"But as it is written, Eye hath not seen, nor ear heard, neither have entered into the heart of man, the things which God hath prepared for them that love him" (1 Cor. 2:9, King James Version).

By the Providence of God, my mother became the first person in the Ishikuro clan, as far as I am aware, who received the gift of salvation through Christ which God the Father offers. Going as far back as Adam and Noah, no one in the Tazo and Fuyo Ishikuro direct line of genealogy had depended upon Christ to save them from eternal death. How sad it is that it took so long for someone in that direct line of genealogy to be saved. Nevertheless, how joyful it is that my mother Carolyn and her sister Judy became the first in their direct line of genealogy to know the love of Christ and the eternal life He gives.

The Holy Ghost would continue to breathe life into my father, mother, brother and me in the years after our conversions into Christ. More of the Lord's loving intervention into our lives will be shared in later chapters including how my mother did not allow a despicable teenager and young adult as I to skip Sunday school, worship services and church youth group activities. I shall also recount how she was the greatest human inspiration, directed by God, to influence me, a wretched sinner, to become a pastor.

My mother led others to Christ, including my father, brother and me, by her example, through her genuine love of Christ in her words and deeds, just as Don described in Chapter Eleven of how his daughter Rachael has inspired others by her example. In previous chapters, Don has catalogued how his mother Vina Bonnie, how Rev. Earl Self, how Bill Sheehan, how his wife Liz, their children Alison and Will, and other Christians have inspired others to know more about Jesus through their actions as well as words.

To Rachael, Carolyn, Sister Vina Bonnie, Liz, Bernadette and all the virtuous women filled with the Holy Spirit, the Lord commends you for your faithfulness in Christ in these words from Proverbs:

"Favour is deceitful, and beauty is vain: but a woman that feareth the LORD, she shall be praised. Give her the fruit of her hands; and let her own works praise her in the gates" (Prov. 31:30-31, King James Version).

As well, to all virtuous men, boys, girls, teenagers and senior citizens in Christ, may you be praised for the example you are, in pointing people to Jesus through your words and actions.

Chapter Thirteen

A TEACHER SPARKS THE WRITER'S HEART

"Isn't He wonderful, wonderful, wonderful. Isn't Jesus my Lord wonderful; eyes have seen, ears have heard, what's recorded in God's Word. Isn't Jesus my Lord wonderful?"

(S. Jones and Homer Hammontree.)

You have just read that Les Seto's family was blessed long before his mother and father Ellsworth and Carolyn came into the greater family of Christ. No doubt, you could feel the marvel in Les's words as he exclaimed this spiritual truth about his family. Through Carolyn Seto son's words, we now have an appreciation of her morals and her stick-to-it-tiveness that she carried through ninety years of her long life. Certainly, Carolyn's faith impacted her husband; her sons; her grandchildren and now, great-grandchildren. Perhaps by the telling of her story about a woman who embraced and loved Christ, all those in her sphere of influence will come to know the loving Savior.

What's taken from this story of the Seto matriarch is that the things done for Christ have a pre-ordained, chartered journey of its own that cannot yet be seen while we are living on Earth. But someday, as Pastor Abbott perhaps has discovered in heaven, the seeds sown in his attempt to plant God's Word in the 2,000 home visits the pastor made—he did not reap only two converts to Christ. The fact is when one of those congregants, Carolyn first agreed to come Pastor Abbott's Lutheran Church, five years later Ellsworth followed his wife's example and after her first step out on faith, came her son, Les Seto. He became an ordained minister bringing a message to hear about and become acquainted with Jesus, the Prince of Peace.

Who is this Prince of Peace?

During the formative period of our attempt to write and publish, a key element was on the mind of we writers; how can we give God praise, honor and glory through our words? Clearly, a sermon on Sunday can bring forth good fruit (words and message), and the evangelist who has dedicated his life to sharing the blessing of the knowledge of God can reap rewards both for the speaker and the hearer. There are ways the non-clergy can perform work for the Lord. God has many ways available of harvesting the tender blades of grass that we think of as souls. It may be through the language of music in Christian songs. It may be the poetry of messages from the heart that will help others to overcome their immobility of spirit. It may reveal itself through the book that you now hold in your hands or are reading on an electronic device.

Letters are a way to issue a centrifugal ripple effect upon the waters of the world. Scripture reveals: "Cast thy bread upon the waters: for thou shalt find it after many days" (Eccles 11:1, King James Version). In earlier chapters, you have seen how inmates came to understand the impact of writing. Their encouraging words to their children reaped successful family reunification and a reentry into good society for the ex-prisoners. You have read how children being taught to write about their day to their father overseas, provided a contact with distant America from his children. You've read that many writers shared their victory through Christ around the world as with the missionary, Amy Carmichael in her books. You may already know that a blind woman, Francis (Fanny) Jane

Crosby wrote the words to thousands of spiritual songs (Blessed Assurance; Rescue the Perishing) that are sung today in churches many years since Crosby passed on to heaven.

Each of these stories is included to show that like the murderous, once evil Saul of Tarsus, God can use anyone to carry His message to lost and suffering humanity. God greatly used the latter, giving Saul the new name of Apostle Paul. Paul, we know, wrote a substantial portion of the New Testament and his letters helped guide the churches of The Way, which was early Christianity.

None of this would have been possible, if not for the enduring love of Christ. This is revealed in the direct command Christ gave to His first followers: "Thou shalt love thy neighbour as thyself" (Matt. 22:39, King James Version). Jesus said this would fulfill all the commandments if we loved God with a full measure as well as each other. The prime guiding rule of most formal religions is: "Do unto others as you would have them do unto you." My mother called it the Golden Rule. This seems foreign today to many who have mistakenly taken another path. Even young people who were raised in Bible-centered families can lose their way, becoming seduced into a far-flung chase after the excitement which the world offers; this is not Godly at all. We think of these children, now young adults, as wandering stars. Some Millennials have no set course or destination in mind but are simply looking for the next big thrill. Fortunately, for them, Jesus is still at the door of their heart. He is the Good Shepherd and is waiting to be invited in.

Christians, who have discovered the joy and lightness of knowing Jesus, realize there is no peace without Christ. Letting Christ into your heart is to invite the Prince of Peace to dwell within and alongside you. The joy of knowing Christ is limitless. Telling someone else of this amazing discovery is equally a beautiful thing to do. This passage is from the wisest man who ever lived, King Solomon. He speaks of giving a blessing to others, such as writing a letter to a loved one or friend. He wrote: "Cast thy bread upon the waters; for thou shalt find it after many days."

(Eccles. 11:1, King James Version).

Perhaps this was my thought as I wrote to my friend, Les, and encouraged him to read a beautifully written book I'd discovered in a used bookstore. The writer within me, admired Les's ability to convey his message without sounding preachy. Being that I am fond of all the American Presidents, it seemed important to talk about one who helped fashion our American way of life. I knew that Les would enjoy reading something thoughtful, provoking him. This was a topic we wrote about to one another.

Letter Writing at Its Finest

You too, may find the book, Thomas Jefferson, The Art of Power, by Presidential Historian, Jon Meacham enjoyable to read. My copy is currently on my bed from where I write the sequential odd numbered chapters of this book. Since school days in the tidewater area of Virginia, I have enjoyed reading of American leaders who were the designers of our government. "T.J.", as his closest friends called him, had many virtues beyond being the third US President, a Vice President, a Minister to France, a governor of Virginia and one of the creators of our country's government. He led an interesting life as it was, he who was the architect of Monticello and a writer of over twenty thousand letters to men and women, many with equally great minds. Our memory today of Jefferson, is as a symbolic watchman in his writings, carefully, intelligently laying out what he perceived to be blueprints for the protection of our democratic way of life. Yet not all was a bed of roses for this tall, handsome auburn-haired Virginian.

Jefferson served as President from 1801 to 1809. Federalists often roused public opinion against Jefferson using a tactic of marginalizing him because of his outspoken stance against elected government officials using their power to promote one's own religion over another. For example, Jefferson did not follow Washington and Adam's tradition of proclaiming national days of religious fasting nor observing Thanksgiving. He felt it was each citizen's choice.

It wasn't until the mid-civil war days that Lincoln, the first so-called Republican president, declared a Thursday in November, Thanksgiving Day. It was a burden for Jefferson to support only one of the established religions in America: Episcopal, Catholic, Baptist, Presbyterian, Quaker or Methodist. It was his argument to insure no church such as Great Britain's Episcopal Church ever became the sole Church of America. Some scholars debate that Jefferson was the chief cause of the dissention in modern day religious expression, yet that was not his intention. Yes, Jefferson believed in separation between state and church, but it was in a document that he wrote to a Baptist Association that many legalistic minds have seized on to try to banish prayer in schools, remove our Ten Commandments and of an icon, the cross of Christ, from public view.

As the newly sworn president, Jefferson received a congratulatory letter from the Baptist Association and he responded on January 1, 1802. He wrote to the leadership assuring them that his intentions were not to violate the Constitution and what his administration would pursue in terms of religious tolerance. His written response was intended to serve a two-fold objective. He wanted to be clear that he had no desire to alter the freedom of religious expression nor to gratify public opinion in Republican strongholds like Virginia, "being seasoned to the Southern tastes only." By this he meant to "issue a condemnation of the alliance between church and state."

Four years later came the Bill of Rights. Its First Article reads:

"Congress shall make no law respecting an establishment of religion or prohibiting the free exercise thereof; or abridging the freedom of speech or of the press; or of the right of the people peaceably to assemble, and to petition the Government for a redress of grievances."

There is much written given to this argument, as to Jefferson's meaning, so we will not proceed further in this area. Suffice it to say I encourage you to read Jon Meacham's book.

The lost expression in the writing of letters will have a crippling effect on future generations. We read in the Bible, that fathers should speak about God 'when sitting down with their children, when lying down at night, when taking a meal and whenever the occasion offers.' In other words, fathers should be constantly expressing the teachings of Christ. This needed voice of authority is often silent and, in the void, caused by a lack of instructing children's hearts and minds, the sensual things of the world will seep into their once spiritual minds unnoticed. When hearts are hardened against good teaching and the father falls into general apathy, they all reap the wind as a harvest. So easily then 'the tares are sown by Satan into the wheat.'

Jefferson's Letters and What We Can Learn from Them

Thomas Jefferson continues to loom large in our memory as a subject of historic proportion. He was a botanist, editor, architect of his home, Monticello, and the university he loved in Charlottesville, Virginia. Avidly writing letters, he managed to write 20,000, all with quill and inkbottle. This defies imagination. We know Jefferson's mind was full of curiosity with an interest in all things, writing letters to scientists around the world. One of his many interests was in horticulture, growing vegetables, fruit and flowers in his gardens at his home at Monticello. He was a violinist and greatly enjoyed music.

Jefferson was frequently surrounded with other men and their wives who seemed to capture his love of fellowship. As a writer of so many letters, he is remembered as a man of great arresting phrases. It is evident, the range of his interests beyond political things. Letters to and from Jefferson were urgently needed; he professed he 'felt chained to the writing desk' all the years he labored on the correspondence that would eventually insure his posterity in the world's pantheon of writers. Read the Declaration of Independence and you readily feel the gentlemanly, yet torturous pain Jefferson felt at the divorcing of his 'country', Virginia, from Great Britain's rule. Here, he listed the intolerable acts of King George III and Parliament toward the thirteen American colonies.

Jefferson had a previous duty-laden chore of developing the Virginia Assembly governance statement and later as Vice President, he'd write congressional rules for the Senate that are still followed by today's House of Representatives.

You can see in Jefferson's letters, whether he was responding to a personal bill of expense or to a grieving husband, James Madison upon the death of Dolley, Madison's wife, his magnitude of comfort and gentleness. These were key elements of America's early presidents' letters. His fellow men loved him because his behavior embraced high morals through which a reasonable approach to governing was the outcome. Americans knew well the rule of monarchs so by the time this third president took office, there was wrangling and opposition to any changes in the early ruling of our country. Jefferson trusted his compatriots, unlike Alexander Hamilton, who expressed that he did not trust his countrymen. Conversely, supposedly Hamilton's intellect did not feel comfortable with the common man.

Jon Meacham reveals that he found in many of Jefferson's letters, remarkable comments. It is evident that Jefferson's astute mind mulled over a given idea examining every side and angle drawing finally to a proper conclusion. Here is a well-known comment in consideration of Jefferson' knowledge:

"I think this is the most extraordinary collection of talent, of human knowledge, that has ever been gathered together at the White House, with the possible exception of when Thomas Jefferson dined alone." (Meacham pp.308).

President John F. Kennedy said this at a dinner in honor of all living recipients of the Nobel Prize, 1962.

There are some elements of the lifestyle and habits of Jefferson that I disagree with. I disagree with Jefferson's violation of the passage that states:

"For I testify unto every man that heareth the words of the prophesy of this book, If any man shall add unto these things, God shall add unto him the plagues that are written in this book: And if any man shall take away from the words of the book of this prophesy, God shall take away his part out of the book of life, and out of the holy city, and from the things which are written in this book" (Rev. 22: 18-19 King James Version).

That should be alarming to anyone reading these words. This scripture, however, seems to have been a perfunctory challenge to the intellect of Jefferson's mind to set down the life of Jesus Christ as he, Jefferson, thought it should be.

According to author Jon Meacham, Jefferson deleted the supernatural acts in the Bible. Meacham does not entirely tell us why Jefferson chose to create his own version of the Bible with deleted passages, only that he was predisposed to write out a differing version of this most beloved book in giving his account of as he believed it. Some at the time, cursed Jefferson, calling him an atheist and despising him for doing this.

Thomas Jefferson's life was controversial. Much has been written about Sally Hemings, Jefferson's concubine slave who bore children to Jefferson, her slave master after the death of Mrs. Jefferson. Author Meacham does an excellent job of addressing the foibles in his subject's life and Meacham reveals that from an early age, Jefferson looked and observed that slavery was wrong. In the last years of his life, Jefferson kept a promise to Sally and by proclamation freed his children whom he fathered and were born into slavery with Sally. Thomas Jefferson was a man of his time and to judge him harshly would do nothing to change the culture of his day.

In the greatest of all the documents co-written by Jefferson, the Continental Congress framed the Declaration of Independence. We read it and see its author, Jefferson's true heart:

"We hold these truths to be self-evident; that all men are created equal: that among these are life, liberty, and the pursuit of happiness: that to secure these rights, governments are instituted among men, deriving their just powers from the consent of the governed..."

Legacy Large and Small

Jefferson the letter writer, once wrote this admonishment to his grandson:

"Take pains at the same time to write a neat round, plain hand, and you will find it a great convenience through life to write a small and compact hand as a fair & legible one."

Today, we see honor and laurels placed upon heroes, and statues and monuments are erected that are viewed by millions of people from around the world. We have in our wallet and in cash registers, President Jefferson's visage on two-dollar bills and on the nickel coin. The $2 (two-dollar bill) has on the front, Jefferson's facial features that portray a youthful energetic leader and the reverse side has a famous portrait of the signing of the Declaration of Independence. The $2 bill is seldom seen in circulation mostly because it is very low in demand. The two-dollar bill is, however, still printed by the United States Mint.

When Thomas Jefferson helped to draw up the Declaration, he may not have known the outcome of the American Revolution; he could not have known the acceleration to power he would experience, and he could not have known the Jefferson Memorial statue in Washington, District of Columbia, would be visited daily by thousands all these years later. He certainly could not have known his face would be magnificently portrayed on America's currency.

The legacy we will have from each of our own letter writing that perhaps, future students may study is difficult to comprehend. However, the careful, temperate letters we write are as Jefferson said to his grandson "you will find it a great convenience in life…".

Begin today; do not postpone your writing, dear Reader. Benjamin Franklin once wrote in his Poor Richard's Almanac, "Never put off until tomorrow what you can do today". You may not always write the most sublime words, but you can bring comfort and put a troubled soul at peace with your encouraging, truthful letter. Winston Churchill once said:

"The short words are best, and the old words are best of all."

Remember to ask God's blessings on even your thoughts, your words and your actions before you proceed just as the blind lyricist, Fanny Crosby did before writing each of her 9,000 songs.

Chapter Fourteen

GRAPPLING AND TESTING FOR A WRITER

"Since my youth, God, you have taught me, and to this day I declare your marvelous deeds" (Ps. 71:17, New International Version).

Letters: Declarations of God's Grace

What fascinating information Don shared in Chapter Thirteen about how Thomas Jefferson positively influenced our nation and the lives of countless persons then and now through his powerful letters. How many persons do we know have written twenty thousand letters as President Jefferson did? We may be acquainted with someone who has written twenty thousand emails or tweets, but usually those take less time and effort to compose than even a one-page handwritten letter.

As I write this chapter during the first week of October 2017, there is a wind advisory in the village of Waikoloa, Hawaii where I live. The howling thirty miles an hour wind outside, however, is nothing compared to the winds of destruction that have recently struck parts of our United States and our neighbors in Mexico and the Caribbean. Certain regions in our nation and in neighboring countries are still physically and emotionally recovering from a series of devastations caused by nature and a human: Hurricane Irma flooded southern Texas and Louisiana, an earthquake crushed Mexico City, Hurricane Maria pummeled the Caribbean and Florida, Hurricane Maria tore apart Puerto Rico and surrounding islands, and a diabolical mass murderer killed close to sixty people and wounded or caused injuries to over five hundred others in Las Vegas. What would President Jefferson have written about the hurricanes, the earthquake or the mass murders? What comfort or insights would his big heart and his genius mind have shared?

Like President Jefferson, Don is also a prolific letter writer. Undoubtedly in some of his upcoming letters to his family and friends, he will be giving encouragement and hope from God as he comments about the hurricanes, the earthquake and the senseless mass shooting in Las Vegas.

Don has penned over two hundred hand written letters to me over the past ten years. His many letters to me, however, are just a few kernels in contrast to the giant silo of letters from which he has sent to others. He has written thousands of letters, handwritten and typed, to family, friends and State of California coworkers and supervisors, going all the way back to his elementary school days in Portsmouth, Virginia, when he was corresponding with his father away from home on a Navy ship. Don may well be on his way to match President Jefferson's twenty thousand letters. That would be a phenomenal accomplishment.

As Don underscored in Chapter Thirteen, every letter he has written or continues to write gives glory to the Lord either by directly referencing Him or by exemplifying His values such as courtesy, honor and respect towards all. Every person who receives a letter from Don will either read a direct reference to God or will experience the Lord's dignity through Don's thoughtful words.

A Wandering Star 1.0

In prompting others to give glory to the Lord through letters, Don often asks those with whom he corresponds a question similar to this: "How did the Lord influence you to serve Him as you are doing now?" In reply to Don's question, I shall relate in this chapter how the Lord led me, a prodigal, to become a pastor.

In Chapter Twelve, I recounted how the Holy Spirit converted my mother from Buddhism into a living relationship with Jesus Christ. Five years later my father came to faith in Christ, but my mother remained the primary parent who made sure that my brother and I learned the Bible, served the Lord, and worshiped Him regularly.

In Chapter Thirteen, Don solemnly wrote,

"Even young people who were raised in Bible-centered families can lose their way, becoming seduced into a far-flung chase after the excitement which the world offers; this is not Godly at all. We think of these children . . . as wandering stars."

I was one of those wandering stars whom Don accurately described. As a teenager I often rebelled against my mother by refusing to go to worship services, Sunday school, Confirmation Class, youth service projects, and Sunday night youth group fellowship. I complained to my mother, "It's not cool to go to these activities. None of my friends go to boring church activities. Why do I have to go?"

My mother Carolyn, however, ignored my complaints. At times she literally dragged me by the arm out of the house into our family car, a white Volkswagen Beetle. She then drove me to church. She never forced me to play sports or a musical instrument, but when it came to attending church functions, she imposed her will upon me. Skipping worship services and other church activities were never an option.

I grumbled about going to church all through my middle school, freshman and sophomore years. My mother, however, never gave in to my resistance. With the Holy Spirit on her side, she somehow always got me to church. The Lord finally granted my mother a breakthrough in breaking the defiant streak in me during the summer after my sophomore year in high school. As mentioned in Chapter Two, that was the summer of 1965 when I attended a Youth Gathering in Squaw Valley, California with thousands of other Lutheran Church Missouri Synod teenagers. There in the Winter Olympics Village built in 1964, the Lord brought me back to the faith He created in me when Pastor Norman Abbott baptized me as a kindergartener. By interacting at Squaw Valley with committed Christian teenagers from all over the United States and by listening to inspirational Christian speakers, the Holy Spirit changed my attitude toward worshiping and serving Jesus. I looked forward to returning home to Hilo, Hawaii and going to church to praise God, to learn more about the Bible, and to serve Jesus.

Back in God's Orbit 1.0

Also, as detailed in Chapter Two of this book, in the two weeks after the Squaw Valley Youth Gathering, God continued to shower His grace upon me when a group of us from Hawaii who attended the gathering, traveled around California in a Volkswagen van. We stayed in the homes of church members in places like Sacramento, San Luis Obispo, Terra Bella, Los Angeles, and Daly City. In each of those homes were teenagers who were enthused about worshiping at church, attending Sunday school, participating in youth group activities and volunteering for community service projects. Their excitement in actively praising and serving Christ further melted my defiant spirit and replaced it with a repentant heart. I then returned to Hawaii, a changed teenager, wanting to worship God and study His Word rather than detesting the Sabbath Day and the Holy Scriptures. Though I deserved His wrath for the years I had resisted His grace, God poured His mercy upon a hardened sinner like me.

After returning from that spiritually cleansing trip to California, my mother was elated. She was experiencing the fruit of her often-frustrating labor in raising me in the way of the Lord. For the remainder of my high school and college years, she would no longer need to grab me by the arm and pull me into our family Volkswagen Beetle to go to church. When it was time to leave for church on Sunday mornings, I would be ready to go. I gladly got into the car that would take our family to glorify the Lord and learn more about the Bible.

Preparing to be a Pastor 1.0

During my senior year in high school, my pastor, Dennis Kastens, born and raised in Kansas, encouraged me to enroll at a Lutheran college to prepare to become a pastor. I listened to Pastor Kastens' advice and attended Lutheran colleges in Portland, Oregon and Fort Wayne, Indiana until the end of my junior year. However, during the summer after my junior year, I was not certain if I wanted to serve the Lord as a pastor. My faith was intact, and I still wanted to dedicate my life to the Lord, but I was not sure if serving as a pastor would be the way that I would serve Him. I did not want to become a pastor unless I was completely convinced to do so.

And so, I took a break from college for a half year and worked as a construction worker near Waikiki Beach in Honolulu. All during those six months, I attended Bible studies and worship services, still desiring to serve Jesus. The Lord then placed a peace in my heart to return to college to complete my senior year. I would not be studying to become a pastor. I placed into God's hands my plans to earn a bachelor's degree in sociology and then wait upon His lead as to what job He would provide.

The Lord led me to Portland State University in Oregon and blessed me with an opportunity to volunteer as an adult leader of a high school youth group at a church there. I taught the high school Sunday school class and chaperoned the youth on camping trips, retreats, bringing meals to migrant farm workers, movie nights, ice-skating, pizza parties, and other activities. Many of the high school youth grew in their love for Jesus through the activities of the youth group. That year was one of the most joyful in my life.

After graduating from college, I felt that the Lord was prompting me to return to Hilo, Hawaii to find employment and to continue to serve Him in a career that He had planned for me. The Lord, however, would first strengthen my faith through adversity before revealing His plans.

Finding work with a bachelor's degree in sociology was difficult. I applied for a jailer position but was denied. I was almost hired by the State of Hawaii for a social services intake worker on Maui, a job I would have enjoyed. But another person got the job. Though disappointed, I was very thankful to the Lord that He provided me with a substitute teacher position for the public schools during the months that I was searching for permanent employment. Without that job as a substitute teacher, I would have been unemployed for three months. I thoroughly enjoyed teaching the middle school and high school students to whom I was assigned just as Don has shared about his fulfilling assignment from God to serve Him as a reliable, well-informed and respected substitute teacher in Vacaville, California.

A Wandering Star 2.0

Finally, the Lord endowed a full-time job position to me. I applied for a youth coordinator position at a nonprofit organization helping low-income persons. I did not think that I would get the job because there were twenty-five other applicants who seemed much more qualified than I. How thankful and elated I was when I learned that I had been hired. I poured my heart into that job and felt that I was serving Christ as I worked with high-risk youth who were on the fringe of getting in trouble with the law. I planned youth activities, counseled teenagers, chaperoned their events, drove students on outings, and visited their homes. Because most of the youth activities took place when school was not in session, I worked almost every night and every weekend including Sundays. There were stretches where I did not attend a worship service or Bible Study for six or seven straight months. I carried on with this schedule for five years.

I found fulfillment and delight in working with youth from low-income families. I truly felt that I was serving the Lord. However, at times, I yearned to have a more stable schedule where I could worship on Sundays, be in a Bible class, teach Sunday school or help with other church ministries.

A Turning Point: A Not So Merry Christmas

A disturbing event took place on Christmas Eve, 1976 which exposed how far I had drifted from fellowshipping with God and with fellow Christians. The youth and adult leaders with whom I worked wanted to have a dance on Christmas Eve with the theme "You Ought to Be Having Fun" (a song recorded by a band out of Oakland, California). I pleaded with the adult leaders and youth to not have a dance on Christmas Eve because that should be a night in which youth need to be spending time with their families and more importantly going to church.

The adult leaders and youth, however, insisted that the dance be held on Christmas Eve because most of the troubled youth we served did not have families who would be celebrating Christmas or going to church. And so, a dance with their friends' present would be the only family time they would experience on Christmas Eve. Even though I had wandered far from fellowshipping with other Christians, the thought of a dance on a night set aside to remember the birth of the Messiah still disturbed me. As the youth coordinator, I had the authority to override the recommendations of the adult leaders and youth, but I caved in and gave them permission to have the dance. After all, I rationalized, it was our duty to provide supervised activities for high-risk youth to keep them out of trouble even if an activity were held on Christmas Eve.

When Christmas Eve arrived, I was already feeling agitated as I drove up to the gym to help chaperone the dance. I saw teenagers in the parking lot trying to hide in brown paper bags what appeared to be bottles of alcohol. There was a large crowd of youth gathered outside the gym anxious to get in. As soon as the chaperones and I opened the doors and let youth enter, some teenage boys immediately headed for the shower room and began smoking marijuana there. I then herded them out of the shower room. After about an hour later, while the gym floor was crowded with teens dancing, two high school boys got into a fight, and other boys immediately joined in. Instantly, about fifteen boys were slugging it out with each other in the middle of the dance floor. I jumped in to try to break up the fight. In the tussle, someone tore off my glasses and other teens in the crowd unknowingly stepped on the glasses and smashed them. It was all out chaos, punching and screaming for about fifteen minutes. It was not a "Silent Night, Holy Night" to say the least.

By God's benevolence, the chaperones were able to eventually break up the brawl, and it seemed that they had restored order. However, just when the DJ was going to play a song to re-start the dance, one of the boys who had been beaten up in the fracas yelled as he stomped out of the gym, "I'm coming back with my gun. I'll get even with every one of you." I followed the embittered teen out the gym and watched as he jumped into a car that screeched out of the parking lot. At that point, I unilaterally made the decision to call the police and shut down the dance. The adult leaders and youth protested my decision, but I said that we had to take precautions. Though the angry teen was most likely spewing an empty threat, there was a one per cent probability that he could come back with a gun. We could not take that one per cent risk.

The police came quickly and were ready to respond if the teen did return with a weapon. The chaperones and youth were very thankful that the teen did not come back. In about an hour all the teens there safely left the premises. When the last youth walked out of the gym, I turned off the lights in the gym and walked to my car with the crumpled wire-rim, frame of my glasses tucked in a pocket of my blue jeans. That night was one of the bleakest Christmas Eves I had ever experienced.

In my despair following the dance, I realized that my life was out of control as the Christmas Eve dance had been. I had an addiction. It was not an addiction to drugs, alcohol or smoking. I was addicted to my work. One of the consequences of my addiction was that I had broken God's command. "Not giving up meeting together, as some are in the habit of doing, but encouraging one another – and all the more as you see the Day approaching" (Heb.10:25, New International Version).

I had become so obsessed with my work to help at risk teens that I had neglected to fellowship with Christians in worship and service to God. I had made my job more important than God. I was worshiping an idol, my work. No one told me that I had to work seven days and nights a week. My director did not require that I put more than a hundred hours a week in my job. Yes, I did need to work on many Sundays and many nights during the week, but there were also many Sundays when I could have adjusted my schedule to be free. The truth was that I had chosen to work. No one forced me.

As with many who have an addiction, however, I did not make immediate changes to my life even after experiencing that Christmas Eve crash. Even the gnarled wire rim frame of my glasses did not induce me to reform my life. Pathetically I continued to work longer hours than I was required. I continued to neglect worshiping and serving with fellow Christians. I continued to defy God by not heeding His command in Hebrews 10:25. It would take an intervention from God to heal me. Because of His compassion and not because of any merit in me, the Lord did intervene.

Back in God's Orbit 2.0

A Woman Again Tugs Me Back to Christ

Just as God had assigned my mother to lead me back to Jesus when I was a defiant teenager, so did the Lord choose another woman to lead me back to Christ when I was a hopeless addict to my work. God sent into my life a woman named Bernadette Yung who would help in reconnecting me with Christian brothers and sisters.

Bernadette and I were classmates from the seventh grade on through high school. However, because we never had any classes together and because the middle school and high school, we attended had high enrollments, we did not know each other. We "met" at a ten-year class reunion planning committee meeting. We both had volunteered to serve on that committee, and for the next year leading up to the reunion, we became friends as we conversed at the monthly meetings.

I learned that Bernadette had two young children from a previous marriage. The name of the older child, a two-year old boy was Kili. The name of the younger child, a one-year old girl, was MewLan. I looked forward to one-day meeting Bernadette's children. After working for one year on the planning committee for the reunion, Bernadette and I had our first date at the ten-year class reunion in the summer of 1977. I picked her up at her parents' house in my 1975 eight passenger avocado Chevy van, and we went to the reunion together.

During the week after our first date, I met Kili and MewLan for the first time. They were adorable children and was thrilled to get to know them. In months that followed, Bernadette and I got together frequently. In one of our early conversations, we talked about our faith. Bernadette shared that as a young child until about middle school, she was very active in a Christian church where her grandmother Rose Kuamoo was an organist. Her grandmother Rose and her husband Philip were surrogate parents to Bernadette and her older brother. Though Bernadette's parents were happily married and financially stable, it was a custom among many Native Hawaiian families to have grandparents raise some of their grandchildren. Such was the case for Bernadette and her brother. They lived with their grandparents Rose and Philip. Since their grandmother Rose played the organ every Sunday at church, Bernadette and her brother went to church with her and attended Sunday School.

Sadly, Bernadette's grandmother Rose died when Bernadette was almost in middle school. There was no one else in Bernadette's immediate family who was active in church. Bernadette and her brother returned to live with their parents and had an enjoyable and smooth upbringing. Bernadette, however, no longer had any connection with a Christian church.

As we became closer friends, I confided to Bernadette that I had once been very dedicated in worshiping and serving God with fellow Christians but had not been connected to any church for five years. She then surprised me when she said, "I want to take my children to church, and we want to go to your church. Will you take us?" Her words stunned me. Here was a person who desired not only to have fellowship with other Christians, but she also wanted to do so in the church in which I grew up. I did not deserve to have the blessing that God had granted when Bernadette spoke those magnificent words.

"Of course, I'll take you," I quickly replied. "Let's go this Sunday." I spoke those words without any hesitation and without glancing at my calendar. I was immediately resolved to cancel any commitment I had on that coming Sunday. Even in the bondage of my addiction to my work, God gave me the presence of mind to not squander that rarest of opportunities, to take someone to church who not only was willing to go but who asked to go.

Bernadette, her two children Kili and Mew, and I then attended on that coming Sunday a worship service at Christ Lutheran Church. My mother who, of course, was worshiping at church was thrilled to see Bernadette and her two children and welcomed them with much gladness. My mother was also pleased to see her wayward son who had not been in church for months.

Having been content with what she experienced at her first visit to Christ Lutheran Church, Bernadette wanted to return the following Sunday. She wanted to enroll Kili and MewLan in Sunday school and wanted to attend the Sunday morning Bible Class that was held at the same time as Sunday school. In the weeks that followed, Bernadette, Kili, and MewLan and I attended Sunday almost every week.

With my priority now in spending Sunday mornings at church, I let the workers and volunteers of the youth program that I coordinated know that I would not be able to work on Sundays and that activities for that time would-be put-on hold. Prior to attending church on Sundays with Bernadette, Kili and MewLan, I would have never thought of cancelling work-related activities on Sundays. My heart still went out to youth in turmoil, but the Lord would address their needs. For the time being, I knew that the Lord wanted me to be with Bernadette, MewLan and Kili in church on Sundays.

In the months that followed, Bernadette, Kili, Mew and I continued to worship, study God's Word, and volunteer for some of the ministries that Christ Lutheran Church sponsored. Bernadette signed up to chair a Fourth of July Weekend yard sale in which proceeds were given to programs for the needy. Bernadette also went on a women's retreat with my mother in which the Holy Spirit refreshed the faith that Bernadette had as a child attending Sunday School and worship services with her grandmother Rose. I carved out time from my work schedule to serve on the church preschool board and on the church council of leaders. In addition to attending Sunday school, Kili and MewLan participated in many of the events for children such as a fall festival and a Christmas drama.

Through Bernadette, the Lord had brought me back into fellowship with Christians as the Lord encourages us to do in

Hebrews 10:25. By bringing Bernadette into my life, God had also intervened to stifle my addiction to my work that had blocked me from meeting, worshiping and serving with fellow brothers and sisters in Christ. By connecting me with Bernadette, Christ had brought back a lost sheep into the flock.

The Lord also relieved me of my duties as a youth coordinator by leading me to a new job which would allow me to devote more time to Bernadette, Kili and Mew and to serving Christ through our church's ministries. A position became open for a Head Start Director and some of my colleagues at the non-profit organization where I worked urged me to apply. I followed up on their advice and the Lord kindly granted me the position. Though I had ignored God's plea in Hebrews 10:25 for five years when I neglected meeting with fellow Christians to worship and serve, God handed to me a new job which allowed me to be in fellowship with my family and our church. As the Apostle Paul wrote, "But God demonstrates his own love for us in this: While we were still sinners, Christ died for us" (Rom. 5:8, New International Version). While I was willfully avoiding fellow Christian brothers and sisters because of my addiction to my job, God did not avoid me because Christ died for all sinners including me.

Preparing to be a Pastor 2.0

As Bernadette, Kili, MewLan and I were becoming more immersed in worshiping, learning and serving at Christ Lutheran Church, I shared with her about my past endeavor to become a pastor. I related how I did not feel a pull from the Lord to become a pastor, but that in the future the Lord might make it clear for me to become one. Bernadette said that she would support me if the Lord ever made it known that I should once again train to become a pastor. Her affirmation gave me much reassurance that if the Lord would make it certain that I should study to become a pastor, Bernadette would support me.

After a year of growing together in faith, Bernadette and I felt that the Lord was softly nudging us to become married. Being grateful that the Lord would bless our union, I proposed to Bernadette in the spring of 1978 and we were married on a sunny afternoon, September 9, 1978, with about fifty family and friends present, at Christ Lutheran Church in Hilo, Hawaii. The Lord proclaims, "A wife of noble character is her husband's crown" (Proverbs 12:4, New International Version). A crown is a king's most precious possession, symbolically more valuable than a king's signet ring, his throne, and even his palace. While Bernadette as my wife and my crown is was not a possession by any means, she is my most treasured blessing from God. Her noble character has many dimensions. God used her faithfulness to bring me, a wandering soul, back into fellowship with Christian brothers and sisters in Christ. The Lord has blessed Bernadette with an enduring love for our children Kili and MewLan. She cares for them as only a mother with noble character can. The Holy Spirit has also given to Bernadette the fruit of joy that brightens the hearts of those in her presence. Christ has given her a measure of His generous spirit. Hardly is there a day at her place of employment when she hasn't gladly donated, above the minimum, to a charity fund drive solicited by her co-workers. As the Word of God explains, Bernadette is my crown, God's most precious gift to me.

After getting married, Bernadette and I continued to be in close fellowship with the Christians at our church. Several members who knew me when I was in high school and college said that I should consider returning to my aspiration to become a pastor. One member said, "You and Bernadette are here at church almost every day of the week. You might as well be a pastor, and Bernadette might as well be the wife of a pastor."

The supportive words of the members at Christ Lutheran Church triggered me to once again consider becoming a pastor. This time I felt that the Lord was surely beckoning me to serve him as a pastor. The biggest obstacles I sensed was that I would have to take a lot of college courses in theology to be eligible to enroll at Concordia Seminary in St. Louis, the seminary that I wanted to attend. Also, when I had first studied to become a pastor, Concordia Seminary in St. Louis at that time allowed but did not welcome married students especially married students with children. Concordia Seminary in St. Louis wanted their students to be focused upon their studies. The Seminary understood that if married students especially with children were welcomed, the students would be distracted from their studies because rightly, so they would need to concentrate on providing for their family's spiritual, financial, emotional and psychological needs.

As I was wrestling with these concerns, I was surprised to receive a letter from Pastor Dennis Kastens, my pastor in high school, the one who originally encouraged me to become a pastor. I had not received a letter from him in years. Pastor Kastens was serving a church in Illinois. He had learned from letters sent to him by members of Christ Lutheran Church that I was interested in possibly studying for the ministry once again. He wrote how thrilled he was to find out about my interest.

Pastor Kastens then wrote about the major changes that Concordia Seminary in St. Louis had made in accepting students. He said that Concordia Seminary was accepting students who did not have all the theological classes that once were required. Concordia Seminary had begun to offer those required pre-seminary courses on its campus. The Seminary did not require students to take those courses before arriving there. Also, Concordia Seminary was welcoming married students including those with children. No longer would married students with children feel out of place there.

Upon reading Pastor Kastens' letter, the door appeared wide open for me to return to my studies as a pastor. As Bernadette had divulged when we were in the early stages of our relationship, she, Kili and MewLan were ready to accompany me. Bernadette's willingness to stay beside me was like that of Ruth in the Bible. Ruth vowed to her mother in law Naomi, "Where you go, I will go and where you stay, I will stay. Your people will be my people and your God my God" (Ruth 1:16, New International Version). I was overcome with gratitude for the devotion that Bernadette had to the Lord. Bernadette was ready to embrace major changes to the cozy lifestyle to which we had become accustomed.

After Bernadette affirmed my intent to become a pastor, I applied to Concordia Seminary in St. Louis, Missouri. I did not expect major challenges, but I was too over. The Lord needed to humble me. The Lord allowed obstacles to occur in the admissions process. Not only did these difficulties humble me, but also these adversities were like barbells to strengthen Bernadette's and my spiritual muscles. The workouts for the soul that God led us through would prepare us for the rigorous experiences we would face as a pastor and a pastor's wife. Humility and strength from the Lord would be required, and the Lord would provide them through painful struggles.

One of the ordeals which Bernadette and I experienced in the admission process was to explain to the Admissions Committee why Bernadette and her first husband had a divorce and why I married her, a divorced woman, which many Christians including many Lutherans consider to be adultery. Bernadette and I painfully wrestled with our answers which we would submit to the Admissions Committee.

Bernadette humbly related how her first husband was not putting his whole heart into their marriage that then led to their divorce. She confessed to the committee and to God that she could have done more to improve her relationship with her first husband just as all husbands and wives could do more to improve their marriages.

I wrote that I took seriously Jesus' words in Matt. 5:31-32, Mark 10:11,12; and Luke 16:18 that marrying a divorced woman is an act of adultery. I appealed to the Admissions Committee, however, that the Bible also teaches that every sin is forgivable except the sin against the Holy Spirit (Matt. 12:31-32 and Mark 3:28-29). I married Bernadette knowing that her first husband was not putting his whole effort into their marriage and that Bernadette had asked God for forgiveness for all her sins including not working harder to salvage her first marriage.

I also conveyed to the Admissions Committee that if I had sinned in marrying Bernadette because she had been divorced, then I confess my sin. I stated, however, that if I divorced her, then I would be committing another sin, which God expressly hates (Mal. 2:16). I stated to the Admissions Committee that if they did not see me fit to be a pastor, I would accept their decision and would not hold any bitterness toward anyone. Such a decision would be a sign that God did not choose for me to be a pastor or that God was leading me to apply to another seminary.

By the kindness of the Lord, the Admissions Committee was satisfied with Bernadette's and my response to the issue of her divorce and my marriage to her. The Admissions Committee later notified us that its members had approved my application to be enrolled at Concordia Seminary in St. Louis, Missouri. Bernadette and I were overcome with thankfulness to our forgiving God and His Son who hate sin and yet love the sinner. In the summer of 1981, Bernadette, Kili, MewLan and I left Hilo, Hawaii and moved to St. Louis, Missouri area to begin a new chapter in our lives.

Throughout our four years at Concordia Seminary, the issue of Bernadette's divorce and my marriage to her, a divorced woman, arose on several occasions, but the Lord sustained us through the controversy. Bernadette and I placed the matter into the Lord's hands. If He decided that I should not be a pastor, Bernadette and I would accept His will and do what He would reveal to us, forgiven servants of Jesus.

In the spring of 1985, my father and mother flew from Hilo, Hawaii to St. Louis for my graduation from seminary. It was the longest trip that my mother had made in her life. My father had traveled to New York City for a convention when he worked for Transamerica Occidental Life Insurance. But for my mother it was the first time she had flown over five time zones. My mother never mentioned the years in which she pulled me by the arm to get into our family Volkswagen Beetle to go to church. During the commencement ceremony, she might have remembered those incidents and thanked God for changing her son's heart and carrying him to that day when he received his diploma from Concordia Seminary.

At my graduation from Concordia Seminary were the two women who had each brought a wayward soul back into the fellowship of Christians, fulfilling God's plan stated in Hebrews 10:25. Each in their own God appointed time, my mother Carolyn and my wife Bernadette, had pulled me back to a setting of peace where Christ's servants meet to worship, study, and serve. My mother and Bernadette also brought me back to a place of encouragement where God uplifts His sons and daughters with the love of Christ as they uplift one another with that same love received from Him.

Might It Be Your Turn?

Through the writing of letters with Don and upon his invitation to recount how a stray sinner like me became a pastor, I was given the privilege to share about our faithful God who never gives up on us unless we reach His appointed time to depart from this life.

My story, however, cannot compare to the story of grace which you, Dear Reader, have. I urge you to tell how Christ has worked wonders of mercy in your life and in the lives of your children, parents, grandparents, great grandparents and ancestors. As Don has implored you throughout this book, please unveil the marvelous blessings which God has poured out upon you and your family and friends, past and present. Please share with us and others Christ's story in your life in a letter, a notebook, or a book. The Lord will bring much joy to all who will read His story in your story.

We may not write twenty thousand letters as President Thomas Jefferson did or as Don may well do, but even our few letters will still be priceless in their own unique way.

"I will give thanks to you, Lord, with all my heart; I will tell of all your wonderful deeds" (Psalm 9:1, New International Version)

Chapter Fifteen

EVENTFUL MATERIAL FOR A WRITER

A legacy is important to writers; we want to leave a written acknowledgement of sorts; to proclaim, 'I was here;" and how my life proceeded.

When the reader sees the history of the world accompanied by Scripture, he or she understands their own beginning and hidden within the scope of the Holy Bible's genealogy from Genesis to Revelations, there is a Roadmap to Life to follow.

Superior Grace Under Pressure

As with pilgrim Christian in "The Pilgrim's Progress" neatly shows us, the travel of the earthbound mortal is an ever-rising path to heaven. The road is narrow, and it is straight, though our man, Christian had to pass by and through many detours and overcome obstacles in this wonderful tale by John Bunyan. Some critics today prefer to call it a dull allegorical writing, yet it was and continues to hold the fascination of many—America's great leader, George Washington and so many others counted "The Pilgrim's Progress" as a must read. And so, it goes today, as many pastors who once entered the seminary will tell us, it was a remarkable picture of Emanuel's Land, the countryside so much like a painting:

".... Of pleasant mountain country, beautified with woods, vineyards, fruits of all sorts, flowers also, with springs and fountains delectable to behold. Then he asked the name of the country. They said, 'It is Emanuel's land'..."

Leaving his wife and child behind, Christian sets out on his journey "to save his own soul." Along the way, he is accompanied by Mr. Great-heart; Mr. Evangelist; Mr. Honest; Mr. Valiant-for-the truth and Mr. Sagacity." And so, the odyssey begins.

However, Christian also meets Mr. Ready-to-halt and Mister Feeble-minded. These are, as we Christians today may know, caught on the hinge of every wind, and like them, we tremble and wonder whether our faith may have abandoned us in our moments of despair.

We know Bunyan was himself an evangelist, imprisoned in the Bedfordshire jail for refusing to attend one church over another when the uncompromising Puritans occupied the land.

Fortunately for us today, there is an easily obtained on-line review by Charles Scribner and Sons, written by S. M. Crothers, of Cambridge, Massachusetts, dated May 1, 1918. "The Pilgrim's Progress" (1678) was then 310 years old.

How clearly Crothers wrote:

"Bunyan's own words have this kind of magical power. They are alive. We may be reading a bit of moralizing that promises to be dull. Suddenly out of the old book appears a sentence addressed to our personal experience. It talks to us.

"And we not only hear but see. Our imagination is a picture-gallery. There upon the walls we see the House Beautiful, the Hill Difficulty; Doubting Castle; the street scenes in Vanity Fair; the Interpreters' House; the Delectable Mountains; the Land of Beulah; the Dark River; and beyond it the gleaming towers of the Celestial City."

Crothers goes on to say:

"Here is a book that does not cease to charm. It is pleasant to think that "The Pilgrim's Progress" is still among the best sellers. Bunyan's incantation over his readers has not yet lost its power."

Accordingly, I suggest that today's reader may find a certain reassurance of the joy that lies at journey's end by the pleasurable pastime of this book.

My Earliest Impressions of My Faith in God

I began reading this book in mid-1958 as I discovered 'Fox's Book of Martyrs" and this beautiful book's sketches from early woodblock prints upon its pages. My Christian influence at age 8 or 9 was not from the Internet. It was my Godly mother who ascertained that what was good for George Washington was assuredly good for young impressionable Donnie. I found similar happiness as Crothers described seeing the valiant, ever hopeful, yet often bewildered Christian march onward in his personal battle against lethargy, malaise, and defeatism.

My mother took pains to constantly assure her prodigy of heaven, the "bright, fair land where we'll never grow old." It was therefore real to me that the words in the song "Onward Christian Soldiers" did have meaning, were grounded in supernatural reality and was certainly written, much like the book by Bunyan, a pastime to while away the weary hours even as Bunyan sat in his common prison room. It may have begun as a respite from his dull status as a prisoner, but it quickly became an inspired work for many Christians such as Mrs. Bunyan and their children.

Written in 1680, little could John Bunyan, a prisoner for twelve years, have known that his dear wife would only be the first to read this work of encouragement, this setting down of Bunyan's belief. That book that may have first intended to be only a picturesque series of letters to his wife to be shared with his congregation has now become a hallmark in providing a genuine loving story to millions of children such as I when the well-used volume fell into my eager hands.

I was impressionable as a youth, loving the dragon, knights, damsel-in-distress story of "King Arthur and the Knights of the Round Table". To me, Sir Lancelot and Guinevere were handsome and beautiful, and I recall even now, sixty years later, that I wanted to be in that host of characters, ever ready to wage battle against the oppressors and tormentors of God's people as Bunyan described them so well. It was an innocent time.

At night, my brother James and I were warm and safe, lying in our cozy beds, as I read to him "The Pilgrim's Progress". He was two or three and doubtlessly did not understand the meanings from which I read, or perhaps he sleepily loved his brother's voice. I followed that time-honored dictum "You have not learned something, until you teach what you've read to someone else." James was my willing (if not captive) apprentice. I can visualize him with his head propped on his hand, looking at me wide eyed with anticipation as I read to him.

Today after twenty-five years of bi-monthly letters exchanged between my brother James and I, we still write of our exploits though it may be mundane activities. We manage to shrink the 3,000 miles that separate us.

You see, my brother James lives in Syracuse, N.Y., and has subsisted on a hand-to-mouth existence for many years, having never been willing to subject himself to the work-a-day forty-hour drudgery as I did for a three-decade long Department of Corrections career. To think that I would voluntarily allow myself to be locked inside a maximum-security prison for eight-hour days, weeks, months and years—who can say which of us was smarter? Perhaps I know a little more now about what John Bunyan experienced and yet remained a spiritual blessing in his writing.

My brother James walks by faith and when his eye lights on a coin, he retrieves it from the ground and comments to his fellow traveler: "Look, it says 'In God We Trust!"

We share the same heritage of giving freely, thankfully with no expectation of return, both to God in our offerings on Sunday, or to others in random acts of kindnesses—the very thing our mother taught us to do as children.

James uses his pickup truck, to drive his neighbors—many are aged widows or young, single mothers—to cash their checks, buy groceries, and pay their bills. His truck is often in need of repair and frequently James cannot make ends meet at the end of the month. James manages on prayers and the goodwill of his friends. His is not a 'hope so', but a 'hope secure' attitude, having placed his trust for his future in the living Lord Jesus. The motto 'In God We Trust' for James, is true.

James' letters are filled with many examples of his providing transportation with little remunerations to those in his rough and tumble neighborhood. Neighbors constantly seek his services. He should be an Uber or Lyft driver, though I think insurance would prohibit that occupation. He paints churches and does legitimate housing repairs to anyone who requests his services.

What Have we Learned about Trusting God?

In the complexity of our fast-paced modern life, does "The Pilgrim's Progress" offer to teach young people? What is the straight and narrow path leading to our final reward? How shall we pursue the daily demands upon our own salvation when the gloom of the shock and awe daily television news seems designed to thwart our countenance of joyful smiling?

The Life of a Writer Amidst Confusion and Unrest

The awesome power of Nature is seen amidst the extreme firestorms burning out of control from Yuba County up north all the way to the outskirts of Solano County. It began in eight separate fires that consumed trees and vineyards and homes of Napa and Sonoma counties early Monday morning. As Les mentioned in the last chapter, I will address this catastrophe just since the total eclipse of the sun this summer. Our nation and the world have experienced an unparalleled three hurricanes that ripped apart Florida, Texas, and Puerto Rico, and a devastating earthquake in Mexico. Last month, a madman unleashed a ten-minute hail of bullets and death upon concert attendees with a mind boggling 550 injured victims; all from the wrath of a deranged sniper high atop the thirty-second floor of a hotel in Las Vegas, where fifty-nine innocent victims died.

Next came four countywide fires with much death and fear left in its path in California's beautiful wine country. Contrary to what some may think, this was not an act of God. I am convinced that we serve a loving God who does not wish that any should perish, but that all would come to salvation through repentance. This fire continues to the very borders of Solano County where my family resides.

You may recall that I work as a substitute teacher. This day, I am sitting at Mr. Isaac Bartsch's desk where I look past the fifteen students and can see clouds of gray colored smoke filling the usually blue Vacaville sky. I am teaching at Vacaville Christian High School. It is second period.

There is a lull in our classroom, for I have a prep period. I am joyful that I can work in this place of peace in our community. Today, I'm blessed to teach Advance & Graphic Design while Isaac is away. Earlier was a chapel service in which the students honored grandparents for their courage and leadership in raising these pupils in Godly families.

Some students were leaders in chapel witnessing their faith by the singing of praise songs including "What a Wonderful Name it is, the Name of Jesus" as recorded by Hillsong Worship. The Baptist sanctuary is nearly full of students, parents and grandparents. It's wonderful that Vacaville Christian has a church of the beauty and size of this building for their use to accommodate the school's worship schedule.

After singing, five students representing each level of the High School came individually to the front of the assembly. Each boy or girl gave a short heartfelt talk about what their grandparents (here in the audience) meant to them in their early development as children. One tall exchange student warmed the hearts of all of us, as he clearly and deliberately told of his grandparents who remain in China. He shared typical boyhood fun times and recalled his austere, "fearsome-seeming Grandfather who now is fun and makes me laugh. But not always; when I was a boy, I was afraid of him. He was always serious; he was a TEACHER!"

The audience erupted into laughter, getting the emphasis on all the teachers in our audience. Knowing the similarities in our own youthful upbringing, the talks were wonderfully done, and each student's presentation brought smiles, applause and giggling to the grandparents who embraced the students as they returned to their seats.

At nine a.m. I drove from Chapel several blocks and turned into the Marshall Drive lot, adjusted my tie, and walked in to the high school. I felt free and light having enjoyed the fellowship of the singing and student testimonials.

Now room 104 was full of students, four sets of grandparents and me. A large concert piano sat invitingly in the center of the spacious room. Several students entertained us with well-accomplished piano numbers. I even added to the mirth and played "Angel Baby," by Rosie and the Originals, one of my daughters, Alison and my favorite songs to harmonize together. Today was a day of celebration with little classwork expected with a limited curriculum.

I occupied my time by taking attendance and greeting the grandparents. Meanwhile the students filmed their projects and I monitored the hazy sky outside that was turning gray-white with ashes sprinkling all the cars in the lot. I was concerned that we might be in the progression of the wildfires, so I led the class in a prayer for all the first responders of fire and police and especially for the Kaiser Hospital nurses who remained on their duty posts for eleven hours on Monday, the day before. A day earlier, a neighbor nurse had explained to me the nature of shorthanded doctors and nurses during the crisis.

As well on Monday, I had sent a message to Les in Waikoloa requesting prayer on behalf of all victims and those who are relocated from their family homes. Far away in Waikoloa, Les has a heartfelt affinity for the people of Vacaville, as many are his former church members. My message consisted of:

"Ali was here this weekend. Got very ill and now I'm with Liz and Ali at Kaiser. She is suffering from upper respiratory cough and fever. Luckily, she stayed here in Vacaville. I could not have driven on highway 29; I-37 or I-101. All closed. Fires started in eight hot spots after 80 mph winds swept embers into 30,000-acre fires."

"Mostly in the city areas whole trailer parks burned. Many expensive homes—gone! Kaiser Petaluma and Kaiser Santa Rosa evacuated all its patients to Marin. Fire containment is lacking due to current 40-50 mph winds and ultra-low humidity. Older people in S.F. having smoke lung/congestion complaints."

"Doctors and nurses being summoned to Queen of the Valley Hospital Napa. They can't get in due to road closures.

I-101 north clogged with hundreds of EFF & Cal Fire Units trying to get to Napa, Petaluma, Santa Rosa."

"God is so good. Little deaths, if any reported. Later established at 30 deaths and climbing."

"Massive four a.m. evacuations helped save lives. Much prayer and Red Cross donations needed from churches America-wide according to the Governor. FEMA chief said all their resources are already thin due to hurricane responses."

Les began to pray on behalf of this situation and this was his response:

"Wow! I'm speechless after reading your synopsis of the damage done. I am thankful that Ali is in Vacaville and that there have been no reports of fatalities. Please know that we in Waikoloa will be praying for all of you."

This communication encapsulated 24 hours of non-stop news feeds from local and national outlets. It is included here to show in a few lines what sincerity exists between we two writers as we were creating this book. Life is not lived in a vacuum; the world continues despite us.

As co-writer and pastor, Les mentioned, we try to lay out the difficulties we experience in life's many events during our season of writing. As we approach our 70th birthdays, we take inventory to see what works in our lives. I have been blessed immeasurably with four healthy, beautiful kids and the Lord continues to shine His ever-merciful light on me. As Les wrote in the last chapter, so do I agree: God has provided me with a jeweled gift in the person of my wife, Liz. She is, as King Solomon once said, an adornment to me like a crown upon a prince's head. Liz continues to embolden me to teach both in Sunday school on my 18th year at Bethany Lutheran Church, and as a substitute teacher at Vacaville Christian School.

During the pandemonium all around us, it may be hard to see God's plan and His future for us. These events are only trials and tests of our faith. We know who holds our future and we know our story's end is a good one if we are faithful. The Lord has promised His children that He will never leave nor forsake them.

The Lord is Faithful to Those Who Love Him

Today, feeling tense with home evacuation plans made, I was privileged to hear a recorded 1989 sermon on my car radio by Dr. Charles Stanley. I was keen to hear his message and I was not disappointed. Many times, his uplifting messages resound within my soul during periods of distress.

In brief, Dr. Stanley said his mother entered his room on the morning of the Dr. Stanley's first sermon many years before. She told her son she felt that God had laid it on her heart to quote to him from Joshua, Chapter 1, verses 3-5. It must have produced a warm healing feeling as Mrs. Stanley quoted God speaking to Joshua:

"I will give you every place where you set your foot, as I promised Moses. "Your territory will extend from the desert to Lebanon, and from the great river, the Euphrates—all the Hittite country—to the Mediterranean Sea in the west. No one will be able to stand against you all the days of your life. As I was with Moses, so I will be with you; I will never leave you nor forsake you" (Josh. 1:3-5, New International Version).

Mrs. Stanley then commanded her son, Charles:

"Three times God also commanded Joshua to 'be strong and courageous, because you will lead these people to inherit the land, I swore to their forefathers to give the land.

"Have I not commanded you? Be strong and courageous. Do not be afraid; do not be discouraged, for the Lord your God will be with you wherever you go" (Josh. 1:9, New International Version).

As Dr. Stanley told this dynamic story—I could visualize how God's instructions had such a profound effect in the re-telling. This reminds me of a Godly woman, who wrote the book,

"Psalm 91" and then continually passed out her books to GI's departing US bases for overseas assignments. Peggy Joyce Ruth was writing a love letter to her fellow countrymen. She wanted to urge the twenty-somethings (and younger) soldiers, to take heart and do not be afraid for "no arrow will come near you". She wanted them to know what the Bible's King David knew;

"You will not fear the terror of night, nor the arrow that flies by day...if you say, 'The Lord is my refuge' and you make the Most High your dwelling, no harm will overtake you, no disaster will come near your tent. For he will command his angels concerning you to guard you in all your ways" (Ps. 91:5, 9-11, New International Version)

Ruth had testimonials of hundreds of airmen, sailors, soldiers and marines who embraced this little traveler's book, and now, decades later, "Psalm 91" is reverently referred by these servicewomen and men as "The Soldier's Psalm."

As Les Seto says, that behind every good man stands a great woman who blesses him, instructs him and honors him and his work. Superior strength comes to them that love God and so it is true, Psalm 91, verse 14-15 says:

"Because he loves me, says the Lord, I will rescue him;

"I will protect him, for he acknowledges my name. He will call on me, and I will answer him:

"I will be with him in trouble,

"I will deliver him and honor him."

Verse 16 completes this promise:

"With long life will I satisfy him and show him my salvation." (Ps. 91:14-16, New International Version).

Forty years ago, Dr. Stanley heard his mother's encouraging commands. He has prospered in his ministry even today. His many sermons continue to draw sinners to repentance and his listeners find comfort in what he preaches throughout the airwaves.

Forty years ago, Peggy Joyce Ruth's desire was to share the words of Psalm 91 to her friends, then to strangers, and now to the world. She has published many books centered on this wonderful strategy to trust in God. How many soldiers have held her book in army hooches in a far-away foreign land, only their rifle, that book, and their training to rely on? How many men and women who rely on God, fearlessly protect our country from foreign enemies? Do we remember the guardians of our nation's safety? "Psalm 91" was written, including the testimonies from military leaders, so today we can appreciate what Mrs. Ruth's desire was: to comfort a grieving, frightened cancer patient. Mrs. Ruth was writing about trusting God's covenant and grabbing fast to His available promise. She emphasized that our God is always faithful to keep His promises. She likes to say we must run to God like little chicks and hide under the wings of our Protector.

As I pen this, authorities are calling citizens in the neighboring towns of Fairfield and Suisun Valley to prepare for evacuation from their homes. Fires continue throughout the town of Santa Rosa, population 170,000, where 3,000 homes, hotels and stores, have been destroyed in the first day. Outside, the smoke is hovering over our town of Vacaville. The prayers of many have been heard—terrific winds have died down. Thankfully, 8,000 fire fighters with 500 fire-trucks have responded.

Tuesday, my substitute teacher assignment was cancelled due to the emergency closing of all schools in Vacaville, Fairfield, Napa, Suisun City, Santa Rosa, Petaluma, and Calistoga. Over 9,000 citizens, including 5,000 from Calistoga have been evacuated to centers in safe areas. The wine country streets remain covered in ashes and the air is not conducive to being outdoors. Many are wearing protective masks and small animals and horses have been carted off to the stalls at the Solano County Fair Grounds in Vallejo for safekeeping. The animals' owners no longer have homes to shelter the pets.

In this unsettling time, newspapers captured the humanity of those who are volunteering to make sandwiches for the firefighters; others are giving their store's profits to buy water and food for the homeless. Many companies have donated materials and food. In all these calamities, God is touching the hearts of men, women and children to do what each can provide comfort and support. As we have proclaimed, be proud to be an American and a follower of Jesus Christ. Let your light shine for Him and if you are able, witness the light of Jesus in your writing.

Chapter Sixteen

A BLIND PILGRIM PROGRESSES

LEAVING A LEGACY

In the beginning of Chapter Fifteen, Don stressed the value of leaving a written legacy. By doing so God might bless generations after us. Don pointed out how the seventeenth century English author and pastor John Bunyan left an inheritance of eternal wisdom and truth to readers in his era and in epochs thereafter. Little did Bunyan know that his book Pilgrim's Progress, written in prison, would inspire millions of pilgrims. One of those exhilarated by Bunyan's masterpiece was a girl with blindness who lived across the Atlantic from Bunyan two centuries after him. She would in turn invigorate millions of Christians in her time and in the centuries after her.

During our correspondence in 2015 and 2016, Don often referred to other influential writers besides Bunyan. One of those was Frances "Fanny" Jane Crosby, who left a treasure of inspirational hymns and poems to countless people during her lifetime and in the decades after her death in 1915. Not surprisingly, Crosby read Pilgrim's Progress, as did many Christian children in her time.

Bunyan's book must have made an impression upon Crosby because as an adult, she wrote forty poems for publisher Philip Phillips based on Pilgrim's Progress. As a descendant of Elder William Brewster and other voyagers on the Mayflower, she could relate to the ordeals and joys of Bunyan's character Christian, a pilgrim like those on the Mayflower, journeying to the Celestial City.

Fanny Crosby wrote between 8,000 to 9,000 hymns, maybe the most hymns by a single writer in all history. Because many hymnbook publishers were hesitant to overload one writer in their publications, Crosby used about 250 pseudonyms. By doing so more of her hymns would be printed. Amazingly Crosby began writing hymns at age 43, which is rather late in life for someone who wrote as many hymns as she did. Her first published hymn was "There's a Cry from Macedonia" which was released in 1864. She would then publish 8,000 to 9,000 more hymns in the years after that, an incredible accomplishment, achieved only by the grace of God.

More astonishingly, Crosby was blind when she wrote her miraculous number of hymns. She was stricken with blindness when she was six months old. Most scholars attribute Crosby's blindness to a caustic mustard plant compress, which some biographers say a man pretending to be a doctor applied upon her eyes. Other researchers say that Crosby was already suffering from a congenital eye condition, which would eventually have caused blindness anyway. In either case, Crosby suffered a severe setback. Many would have been angry with God their whole life or filled with malice toward the imposter who claimed to be a doctor.

Yet at age eight, Fanny Crosby wrote this poem about her blindness in which she expressed only gratitude for her condition:

O What a happy soul am I!
Although I cannot see,
I am resolved that in this world
Contented I will be.

How many blessings I enjoy?
That other people don't,
To weep and sigh because I'm blind,

I cannot, and I won't.

No doubt her Christian upbringing by her devout mother Mercy and her grandmother Eunice fostered the upbeat attitude that she had toward her blindness. Crosby did not blame God for her condition. Neither was she surly toward life. Nor did she vent outrage toward the quack doctor who fled and was never apprehended. Through reading her Bible, Crosby had learned about Abraham, Joseph, Moses, David, Elijah, Job, Paul, and other heroes, including, of course, the Son of God and Man, Jesus Christ, who suffered colossal pain and injustice and yet still praised His Father God. As a young girl, Fanny Crosby already was living out the Apostle Paul's exhortation, "Rejoice in the Lord always: and again, I say, 'Rejoice" (Phil. 4:4, King James Version). As a senior citizen, I have a lot of catching up to do to rise to the level of spiritual maturity, which the eight-year-old Fanny Crosby had.

In Chapter Fifteen, Don described the unfair confinement imposed upon John Bunyan, his wrongful imprisonment. In a sense, Crosby, too, suffered from an undeserved restraint, her lifetime loss of vision. As Bunyan, however, ultimately assessed his incarceration to be an opportunity to write what would become an epic for the Lord, so did Fanny Crosby see her blindness as an advantage.

As an adult, she commented,

"It seemed intended by the blessed providence of God that I should be blind all my life, and I thank him for the dispensation. If perfect earthly sight were offered me tomorrow, I would not accept it. I might not have sung hymns to the praise of God if I had been distracted by the beautiful and interesting things about me."

The Power of Imprinting

In Chapter Fifteen under the section "My Earliest Impressions of Faith in God" and in letters to me over the years, Don has cited how his mother Sister Vina Bonnie encouraged him to read the Bible and other books which are in harmony with it. Don mentioned that at age eight or nine, he read Foxe's Book of Martyrs for the first time. He was captivated by the courage of those Christians throughout history who suffered horrific torture and death because of their allegiance to Jesus. In numerous letters to me, Don also wrote about the value of memorizing verses in Scripture to give us strength and wisdom from the Lord to endure any adversity.

Because Fanny Crosby's father died when she was an infant, her mother Mercy needed to work outside the home, and so Fanny's grandmother Eunice took on the role of being the primary care provider for Fanny. Both Mercy and Eunice introduced Fanny to the Bible and encouraged her to memorize Scripture just as Don prescribed for everyone to do in many of his letters.

Whether it was due to her blindness, which aided in concentration or to her simply being blessed with keen recall, Fanny had an extraordinary memory. As Mercy and Eunice cheered her on, by age fifteen, Fanny had committed to memory the first five books of the Old Testament, the four Gospels, Proverbs, Song of Solomon and many Psalms. The tons of inspiration from these books of the Bible stored in Fanny's memory bank undoubtedly contributed to her radiant writing and to her sterling, stable commitment to Christ.

For some of us who are now adults, Fanny's dedication in memorizing Scripture might prompt us to commit to memory even a verse a week. As I write this chapter, I have made this a priority. We may not be able to memorize whole books of the Bible as Fanny did, but even if we imprint in our minds a verse of Scripture a week, the Lord will strengthen our hearts and minds for greater service to Him just as He did for Fanny.

Amid Pandemonium

As Don wrote Chapter Fifteen, the most devastating fire in the history of California was raging ten to thirty miles from his home. He could smell the thick smoke, which was congesting the city of Vacaville, California where he lives. Don also alluded to recent hurricanes that had defaced large sections of Texas, Florida, and Puerto Rico, a destructive earthquake in Mexico City, and the deadliest mass murder shooting in U.S. history, which took place in Las Vegas. As I am writing this chapter, national news outlets are covering the story of a mass shooting in a church in Sutherland

Springs, Texas where twenty-six people were killed. Don chose an apt word "pandemonium" to describe the last two months in Central and North America.

Yet despite the trauma around us, Don affirmed,

These events are only trials and tests of our faith. We know who holds our future and we know our story's end is a good one if we are faithful. The Lord has promised His children that He will never leave nor forsake them.

In similar ways did Fanny Crosby calm the agitations of people in her era and in the decades after. An example of the consolation from the Lord that Crosby conveyed is her hymn "All Will Be Well". This hymn's fourth stanza and the refrain especially give reassurance for the calamities which Don described in the previous chapter and in the aftermath of a mass shooting during a Sunday morning church service in Texas:

Only Thy presence when wild is the gale,
Only Thy presence when rent is my sail;
Only Thy presence my vessel to guide
Into the harbor and over the tide.

Refrain: What tho' the billows like mountains may swell;
All will be well; yes, all will be well;
Under Thy shadow in peace I shall dwell;
All, all will be well.

In turbulent storms, the Lord is always present just as Jesus was on a fishing boat with his disciples in a squall. What comfort the Lord whispers through Fanny Crosby's words taken from Scripture to offset the howling winds around us.

Faithful Pilgrims Along the Path

As he remarked in Chapter Fifteen about the important lessons from John Bunyan's Pilgrim's Progress, Don made note of how faithful people gave support to Christian on his journey to the Celestial City and how Christian in turn aided others, too, along the path. In a similar way, it is crucial that we help and receive help from fellow pilgrims of Christ.

Don wrote,

"Along the way, he [Christian] is accompanied by Mr. Great-heart; Mr. Evangelist; Mr. Honest; Mr. Valiant-for-the truth and Mr. Sagacity." How crucial it is that God places Christians into our lives at key junctures. What greater results for God's glory occur when Christians help each other?"

Don's observation is true. When Christians share with resources with each other, the outcome is more abundant than if Christians lived their lives in isolation. Fanny Crosby knew this Biblical principle well.

God endowed her with an astounding ability to write poetry and lyrics. At times, she would incredibly write six hymns a day. An example of the speed, which God supplied her in writing lyrics, took place on April 30, 1868 when Crosby wrote one of her most famous hymns "Safe in the Arms of Jesus." A well-known Christian composer named William Howard Doane made an unexpected visit to Crosby's home. Doane who was a friend of Fanny said that he had forty minutes before his train left for a Sunday school convention in Cincinnati.

Doane knew that what he was about to ask Crosby would be extremely difficult to accomplish, but he asked her anyway. He explained to Crosby that he had just composed a tune to a hymn, which he wanted to introduce at the convention in Cincinnati. But he needed lyrics plus a title for the hymn. He said that he would play the tune on Crosby's piano and then let her write verses and a title for it. Crosby said she was willing to take on this tremendous challenge.

And so Doane played the tune once on the piano and immediately Crosby said that tune was begging for the title "Safe in the Arms of Jesus", a very fitting theme, too, for boys and girls in Sunday School. As Doane continued to play the tune over and over on the piano, Crosby wrote lines that formed stanzas. The refrain that echoed in Crosby's mind and heart was the following:

Safe in the arms of Jesus,
Safe on His gentle breast;

There by His love o'ershaded,
Sweetly my soul shall rest.

After twenty minutes, she astonishingly completed scribbling the words for the hymn and gave the sheet to Doane and hastened him on his way so that he would not miss his train.

Doane got on his train in time, and upon arriving in Cincinnati, he taught the hymn to the delegates at the Sunday school convention. The delegates were delighted with the new hymn. "Safe in the Arms of Jesus" eventually became one of the most popular hymns of Crosby and Doane and is so even today. On August 8, 1885, this hymn, the words of which Crosby wrote in twenty minutes, was sung at the funeral of President Ulysses S. Grant. Such was the aptitude that the Lord gave to Crosby in writing immortal hymns within minutes to match tunes that she had just heard for the first time.

Although Crosby could play the harp, piano, guitar and other instruments and was trained in music theory and music composition, she chose not to devote much time to writing tunes and setting her lyrics into music. She let composers, like William Doane, gifted by God in writing tunes, to create the music for her texts. She would write the text and then composers would set her text to music, or at other times, they would first write the music and then she would provide the text. The Lord blessed both sequences.

Besides Doane, other Christian composers like William B. Bradbury, Phoebe Knapp (who wrote the tune for Crosby's text "Blessed Assurance"), and Ira Sankey collaborated with Crosby in producing many of the most beloved hymns in Christendom. As John Bunyan included in Pilgrim's Progress faithful servants of the Lord to assist and to receive help from Christian, so did Franny Crosby give to and receive support from many composers in producing masterpieces of music for God.

Fanny Crosby's collaboration with Christians was not limited to only composers but also to Christians with other gifts. One of the most blessed collaboration in Fanny Crosby's life was that with Dwight L. Moody who had the magnificent gift of evangelism. Dwight L. Moody who partnered with singer and composer Ira Sankey embraced Crosby's lyrics set to music. Moody shared her words from God to millions especially in the United States and the United Kingdom. Through her association with Moody and Sankey, Fanny Crosby's hymns brought the joy and comfort of Christ to countless persons.

As Ira Sankey helped Fanny Crosby by setting many of her words to tunes and welcoming her to be part of Dwight Moody's evangelistic team, so did Crosby help Sankey. In his later years, Sankey was stricken with glaucoma and lost his sight. If there were anyone in the world who could relate to and give encouragement to Sankey in his last years on earth, that would have been Fanny Crosby. In the same manner that Sankey had shared the compassion of Christ with Crosby, so did Crosby do for him.

Such is the fruitful outcome when pilgrims traveling to the Celestial City give to and receive from fellow pilgrims the resources, which God gives. As the Apostle Paul declared, "Now there are diversities of gifts, but the same Spirit" (1 Cor. 12:4, King James Version).

Hell's Kitchen, The Tenderloin, The Bowery

Just as the Bible, Pilgrim's Progress and other books gave shape to Don's character, so did these books also mold the life of his younger brother James. Don wrote how his brother James especially took to heart the lessons in the Bible and Pilgrim's Progress about helping those in distress. Don expressed;

"James uses his pick-up truck, to drive his neighbors—many are aged widows or young, single mothers—to cash their checks, buy groceries, and pay their bills. His truck is often in need of repair and frequently he cannot make ends meet until the end of the month. James manages well on prayers and the goodwill of his friends. His is not a 'hope so', but a 'hope secure' attitude, having placed his trust for his future in the living Lord Jesus. The words 'In God We Trust' are true. . .. James' letters are filled with many examples of his providing transportation with little remunerations to those in his rough and tumble neighborhood. Neighbors constantly seek his services."

James loves the Lord, and James especially loves to help the Lord's people who are struggling to just make it through the day. In the latter years of her life, Fanny Crosby also had such a love for those who lived in rough neighborhoods in New York City. As a youth and young adult, Fanny was understandably focused on helping those who were blind as she was. When Crosby was in her forties, however, while actively writing hymns, and speaking on behalf of blind persons, she also felt compelled to help the hurting people in the most destitute sections of New York City. She began to devote more time in helping those in Hell's Kitchen, the Tenderloin, the Bowery and the harbor. She also visited prisons and jails, rugged environments with which Don is very familiar.

The residents of the impoverished neighborhoods where she lived and served called her "Aunty Fanny." When she was eighty-eight years old, she said in an interview that she wanted to be known foremost as rescue mission worker over and above her fame as a hymn writer, poet and advocate for the blind.

In 1868, Crosby spoke at a worship service in a New York City prison. She was grieved when some inmates expressed fears that the Lord would pass them by. Crosby reassured them that Jesus would never walk pass a person pleading to be saved. After that incident, Crosby wrote a hymn and named it "Pass Me Not, O Gentle Savior." William H. Doane set her words to music, and Dwight L. Moody and Ira Sankey often included that hymn in their evangelistic gatherings. "Pass Me Not, O Gentle Savior" eventually became Crosby's first hymn that was sung around the globe. In the first stanza of "Pass Me Not, O Gentle Savior", we can grasp the deep compassion that Crosby had for the lost and forgotten:

Pass me not, O gentle Savior,
Hear my humble cry;
While on others Thou art calling,
Do not pass me by.

Besides her empathy for the blind, the disabled, and the impoverished, Fanny Crosby also had a heart for the plight of slaves in America. She unabashedly supported the abolition of slavery. Early in her life, she belonged to the Democratic Party that supported slavery, but she later joined the Whig Party and then the Republican Party, both of which opposed slavery. She was an avid supporter of President Abraham Lincoln and the Union Army. She wrote many powerful, patriotic poems and songs that boosted the morale of the Union troops. Crosby once almost got into a physical altercation with another woman. The woman was sympathetic to the Confederacy, and she told Crosby to remove a Union Flag emblem pinned to her dress. Crosby refused, and a fight almost broke out, but was quelled.

As Don's brother James has made it his mission in life to help people in a bind often in rough neighborhoods and as Don served most of his adult life in prisons, going out of his way to encourage inmates to reform and to share the Gospel with them without breaking institutional policies, so did Fanny Crosby dedicate her whole life to help and to proclaim Jesus to the blind, the impoverished, the imprisoned and the enslaved. Along with Don, James, and a host of pilgrims in all ages, Crosby heeded Jesus' words, "Verily I say unto you, inasmuch as ye have done it unto one of the least of these my brethren, ye have done it unto me" (Matt. 25:40, King James Version).

Freely Received and Given

Closely related to helping the needy, Don noted how his mother Vina Bonnie instilled in him and in his brother James the joy of giving freely what they freely received from the Lord. Don wrote in Chapter Fifteen, "We [Don and James] share the same heritage of giving freely, thankfully with no expectation of return, both to God in our offerings on Sunday, or to others in random acts of kindness—the very thing our mother taught us to do as children."

Don and James' generosity generated by the Holy Spirit is akin to that of Fanny Crosby. As mentioned, she lived a frugal life, often residing in some of the most underprivileged neighborhoods in New York City. She disclosed, "From the time I received my first check for my poems, I made up my mind to open my hand wide to those who needed assistance." She did not have a set price for speaking at functions. She often declined honoraria, and when she did accept a donation, she often gave what she received to one of the many city rescue missions in New York City. Her husband, Alexander van Alstyne, Jr., an accomplished organist, also had a charitable spirit. He and Fanny would organize concerts and donate half of the proceeds to urban mission work. Fanny's formula for finances was to keep only what money was needed for bare survival and the rest be given to the poor.

As a child memorizing whole books of the Bible, Fanny internalized what Jesus said about giving to the needy: "It is more blessed to give than to receive" (Acts 20:35, King James Version). As Don, his brother James, Fanny Crosby and her husband Alex van Alstyne, Jr. did, may we do likewise?

God's Joy Overcomes Grief

During 2015 to 2016, Don and I encouraged one another in letters in response to events leading up to and following the deaths of three dear Christians in our lives: Don's father in law, Dr. Robert Mitchell; World War Two Veteran Navy aviator Bill Sheehan, and my mother Carolyn Seto. In our letters, we reassured each other that each of them trusted in Jesus as their Savior and so are with Him in the Celestial City that John Bunyan described in Pilgrim's Progress. We comforted each other by writing that we would see Dr. Mitchell, Bill and Carolyn again one day in Heaven. As we trusted in the eternal care of Jesus, the Holy Spirit consoled us.

Dr. Mitchell, Bill, and Carolyn were senior citizens who had lived long, blessed lives. Yet their loved ones including Don and I mourned over their deaths. Much more traumatic, however, is the death of a young parent leaving behind a spouse and children or the death of a child. In these occurrences, surviving family or friends often become angry with God or with life.

Fanny Crosby's father John died when she was six months old, and so she never knew her father. She could have lived her whole life feeling cheated, but she by the power of the living Lord Jesus held no grudge against God.

Later in life, Fanny Crosby and her husband Alexander van Alstyne, Jr. were shaken to the core when their infant daughter Frances died while sleeping in her crib. Alexander had a more difficult time than Fanny in coping with this tragedy. He became increasingly reclusive in the years after Frances' death. Fanny did not go into isolation as her husband did. She instead chose not to speak about her daughter's death even though she had the peace in knowing that her little Frances was in Heaven. Years after her daughter's passing, she surprised a writer who was interviewing her when she confided;

"Now I am going to tell you of something that only my closest friends know. I became a mother and knew a mother's love. God gave us a tender babe, but the angels came down and took our infant up to God and to His throne."

What a glorious testament did Fanny Crosby declare about the everlasting life and love that God gives us through His Son Jesus. Even while grieving in her heart, Crosby affirmed that her daughter Frances was sitting near the dazzling throne of our living God. Fanny Crosby could visualize the many descriptions of Heaven in the Bible, including the vision of the glorious throne of God where all the living in Christ surround and praise Him:

"And I beheld, and I heard the voice of many angels round about the throne and the beasts and the elders: and the number of them was ten thousand times ten thousand, and thousands of thousands; Saying with a loud voice, Worthy is the Lamb that was slain to receive power, and riches, and wisdom, and strength, and honour, and glory, and blessing" (Rev. 5:11-12, King James Version).

The death of her father when Crosby was six months old did not embitter her soul as a youth or adult. Her poetry in her younger years and her hymns in her older years projected hope, life, joy, and gratitude to the Lord. There is no trace of feeling cheated in her writing.

The same could be said about Crosby's hymns written in the years after her daughter Frances' passing. Though she chose not to talk at all in public about Frances' death, Crosby still had a strong faith in the goodness of God. She continued to write hymns that were as vibrant and uplifting as she had before Frances' death. Consider one of Crosby's many signature hymns "To God be the

Glory" copyrighted in 1875, sixteen years after Frances passed away. The first stanza and the refrain resonate only pure gratitude and celebration, no gloom or scorn toward God or life:

To God be the glory, great things he has done;
So, loved he the world that he gave us his Son,
Who yielded his life atonement for sin?
And opened the life-gate that all may go in.

Refrain:
Praise the Lord, praise the Lord; let the earth hear his voice!
Praise the Lord, praise the Lord; let the people rejoice!
O come to the Father through Jesus the Son,
And give him the glory; great things he has done.

The Lord of Life Jesus has triumphed over death. No matter how painful the passing of a family member or friend may be, no matter how young or old they were, Jesus will sustain us. Crosby reflected the confidence in the Lord that the Apostle Paul proclaimed,

"Nay, in all these things we are more than conquerors through him that loved us. For I am persuaded, that neither death, nor life, nor angels, nor principalities, nor powers, nor things present, nor things to come, nor height, nor depth, nor any other creature, shall be able to separate us from the love of God, which is in Christ Jesus our Lord (Rom. 8:37-39, King James Version).

The Pilgrim's Path

If Fanny Crosby had not written a single hymn in her lifetime and not spent one minute or one penny in supporting inner city rescue missions, many would say that she lived an incredible life. She personally met and spoke with twenty-one presidents to discuss the needs of the blind. How many of us have met and spoke with even one president? Not I. Crosby was also the first woman to address Congress when she was invited to speak on behalf of the blind. She wrote about one thousand secular poems and about a hundred romantic, patriotic, and entertaining songs. She was an ardent defender of human rights, denouncing slavery.

However, all these wholesome and enormous accomplishments were preparing her for the crown of her legacy bestowed upon her by the Lord. This crown was brought to light when at age forty-three, she wrote her first hymn and when around that same time she began to devote herself more fully to the support of inner-city rescue missions.

Crosby's pilgrim path was relatively straight in contrast to many others and mine. She did not have a prodigal son type of departure from the path that others and I have taken. From childhood when her mother Mercy and grandmother Eunice were encouraging her to memorize whole books of the Bible and through her teen and adult years, Fanny remained faithful to Christ. There were no long deviations from the straight and narrow pilgrim's path that God had laid out for her. Yet she did not look condescendingly upon those who veered off the trail blazed by Christ. She understood what the Bible teaches that we are either all wayward wanderers or would be such if it were not for the grace of God in Jesus Christ our Lord. Both the pilgrim and the wanderer depend fully on the mercy of the Lord for salvation.

For those of us who have strayed off the sure trail, may Fanny Crosby's consistency be ours, too, by the work of the Holy Spirit. This might be an appropriate time to reflect upon the second stanza of Crosby's hymn "All the Way My Savior Leads Me" which urges us pilgrims to follow Christ's lead upon His path:

All the way my Savior leads me,
Cheers each winding path I tread;
Gives me grace for every trial,
Feeds me with the living Bread.
Though my weary steps may falter,
And my soul athirst may be,
Gushing from the Rock before me,
Lo! A spring of joy I see;
Gushing from the Rock before me,
Lo! A spring of joy I see.

Some biographers state that Fanny Crosby wrote her last verse shortly before she died on February 12, 1915 at age ninety-four. She jotted, "You will reach the river brink, some sweet day, by and by." The word brink can mean a bank such as a bank on the river.

How apt that Fanny Crosby's last written verse evokes imagery expressed by John Bunyan at the end of Part One of his Pilgrim's Progress. Christian and Hopeful are on the last leg of their journey to the Celestial City. They enter the land of Beulah where the glorious city is located. They need to cross a river to enter the city gate where residents are joyfully waiting to welcome them. Bunyan explains that the river is a symbol for death where only two persons in the Bible, Enoch and Elijah, have bypassed. All others must cross it to finally reach the Celestial City.

It is fitting that Crosby's last written verse paints a serene picture of a pilgrim crossing the river to reach the brink, the bank on the "by and by" of the Celestial City. Crosby was thankful that she was of Pilgrim heritage. She was a member of the Daughters of the Mayflower that was strict in admitting only women who were bona fide descendants of someone who sailed on the Mayflower. Through marriage in previous generations, Crosby was a descendant of Mayflower Pilgrims William Brewster, Edward Winslow and Thomas Prence.

Don began Chapter Sixteen by illuminating how John Bunyan left a legacy of inspiration to millions in the centuries after him. Fanny Crosby is one of those millions upon whom John Bunyan energized. Fanny Crosby of Puritan and Pilgrim lineage then in turn by the providence of God left an impression upon millions of new pilgrims. Her words will continue to live on because they declare the eternal Word of God in poetry set to music.

Might you, O Reader, write a short autobiography, even ten pages, typed on your computer and then printed on paper, or in a hard bound, pebbled composition book, of how the Holy Spirit has given you faith in Christ Jesus and how that faith in Him has carried you through your pilgrimage in this life as you walk to the land of Beulah where the Celestial City awaits. Someday a great-great-great grandchild might read your testimony and be saved. She or he will become a pilgrim walking on the path that leads to the Celestial City. This is possible only because of Jesus.

May this be our pilgrim's prayer: "Make me to go in the path of thy commandments; for therein do I delight" (Ps. 119:35, King James Version).

Chapter Seventeen

IGNITING A FIRE UNDER A WRITER

In the awesome summer days of nineteen eighty-five, I returned to college for an expository writing class. I was 36 years old and freshly engaged to be married. Three years earlier, I had moved from Marin to Solano County, and now was dwelling in a modest apartment in Fairfield, California.

I began a rudimentary pursuit of educating myself through reading. I loved anything by Robert Frost; Ezra Pound; Goethe and John Gardner. Even the suicidal remnants of Sylvia Plath's poems spun and danced in my thoughts. Plath's "Lady Lazarus" injected into my quiet morning and soon began to cause me to brood. I felt I needed and shouldn't resist fellowshipping with other predisposed journalists of short verse. It was thus that I enrolled in school.

The first awkward morning in class, I knew I was a decade older than my fellow students. I also knew at 10:30 each day I'd arrive early and do my best to receive a good grade. I was studying to earn a teaching credential. I'd leave class after two hours, drive to my apartment, and I'd suit up for my afternoon shift at the prison. As a State worker, I'd be "Lieutenant Fortin" and spend hours draining several ink pens on redundant bureaucratic reports for which I would be paid handsomely. But I felt little personal achievement in doing this work.

I was soon to marry, and my heart overflowed with joy.

Day One

That first summer morning, I eased into a chair, took out a loose-leaf pad, and noticed our teacher seemed friendly and at ease; her short, red hair and quick, yet pensive smile was welcoming. Teacher and I were the oldest of the class and therefore able to bond quickly.

The teacher asked us to write plainly and write only personal feelings in her class. She introduced herself: "My name is Mrs. Johnson, but my friends call me Deni." I felt as if I was back in my high school English class and Miss Smith, the teacher was tapping my slender shoulder telling me 'I love your use of adjectives'. In that moment, I felt free to think outside the margins of my dulled prison-awareness view of the world. Suddenly I felt lightness again. I could do what I wanted in this class—I could express myself! What a powerful feeling.

And so, I did.

Deni, as we called our teacher, said "Write a paragraph today and call it "Who Am I." Tomorrow we'll explore your personal language. If you want to write hip-hop or if you have a published writer you enjoy, feel free to sync your story with her or his style—that's okay providing you list the author's work."

I raised my hand: "Can it be personal, even a little emotion-filled," I asked? Deni smiled at my unexpected question.

"Of course, you can put it in poetry or prose form" Deni said, "and we'll all share together in class."

'I'm going to learn how to write; all this and POETRY too!' It seemed too good to be true, given the loneliness in my apartment reading the famous poets. This was liberating not to have to follow rules or a paint-by-number writing assignment. A cool, young hipster began his oral hip-hop and we all laughed. It was good to express one's self.

I hadn't written anything for sharing in twenty years and I guess that I was primed to explore. My first hand-printed story was quite tentative; "The Tree Cannot Heal Itself," and was a few pages reporting my mother's bizarre decline, told from a 13-year-old son witnessing the unfolding of his mother's mental breakdown. It seemed forever since I was able to unlock my thoughts of this one memory.

We fellow students were pleased to receive Deni's praise. Daily, she took seven classes of students' homework with her. The next day Deni told us it took her four hours to review and notate on all our writing. I appreciated this and thought this should be what all teachers do. Less energetic teachers would have us exchange our 'work,' eliminating the middleman—the teacher; I could see Deni honored us and placed a premium on her budding authors' efforts. We were to be rewarded many times in the coming weeks.

I kept my papers, amazed that Deni allowed we students to do an in-house bound booklet that contained our short stories. How nice it was to see our work printed for the first time with our names on the booklet's flagstaff. I know that my writing style matured through Deni's critiques. Once she wrote: "Don, you act humble and say you're unsure of the value of your work; but your attached note to me from your desk pad says: "I'm So Good;" is there a contradiction? Learn to write exactly as you feel. Don't compromise."

"However, your phrasing has a quality I like because you both command and encourage." She said that beyond my "purple prose and too many descriptive words, where one good adjective would suffice," she continued, "you write with a deft encouraging gracefulness." Deni went on: "Someday, I'll see your work in print." I certainly took her comments to heart.

Deni reviewed my stories that soon were multiplying from my zeal. Encouragement from Deni's editing (mostly deleting) astounded me—both being necessary. Rarely had anyone remarked that I had the making of an author; or that what I was writing showed truth, value and could be called 'work.' I was thrilled with what I recognized was genuine training. Ideas soon began to take wing in my head.

Without delay, I used my fiancé, Liz's Olivetti typewriter and began turning out poems, short stories and a novella (a mini novel). Almost magically over six weeks, I participated with fellow students in weekly reading groups. It was from those groups that I finished a score of poems and brought them to a print shop owner who produced one hundred booklets. The box of the newly minted chapbooks was an accomplishment that gave credence that I was becoming a writer. More importantly, I was releasing pent up ideas.

One of my booklets, I sent to Washington, D.C. to receive a copyright. Over a few years, I gave ninety booklets to anyone who wanted one. It pleased me to think that poetry was to be given away like little kisses on the cheek of dear friends.

Permitting My Hidden Feelings to Become a Book

I overcame indecision and worrisome thoughts, such as why am I a prison lieutenant, writing poetry? The usual naysayer feeling reared its head. What would my subordinate officers think of their supervisor!

My mother was a poet and Gospel songwriter, and I suppose poetry came naturally to me in the form of a blessing. My mother was tolerant of my playfulness as a boy. I'd sown wild oats and been a carefree, occasionally, irresponsible young man. I'd done pretty much as I pleased and my calibration to become a responsible man was often questionable. At times, I was a light-hearted Peter Pan, and I fancied myself a young Paul McCartney or a rakish "Tom Jones," a kind of irrepressible youth. As with the movie character Jones, there was a bit of unrealistic thinking going on in me. Perhaps I was a poet even then.

I found my new poems had a reoccurring fluid movement as if the poems were able to ascend into heaven's zone like Spanish galleons drifting on clouds. I was experimenting with words looking for rhythm and how to write short Haiku verse. I tried disguising some of my lustful Machiavellian desire within my poetry's revealing titles; "The Dream of the Whorehouse", "Gently, I spread Wide Her Arms" and "Love Comes Softly."

In other poems I explored my mother's hospitalization and my longing for closure to a quest of the unknown status of my birthfather. This I did in a longer poem resembling a short stage play. A longing for the romanticized life of a battle tested leader, resulted in my poem, "The Commander at the Bridge." There was an undercurrent of Holy Scripture, especially from Ecclesiastes meandering through my verbiage.

As I wrote, I realized there remained a fresh wound of having been a divorcee, which was reflected in a Beatlesque poem I wrote as an overture to my ex-wife Joanne. I wrote that poem as if to say, "Will you tell our little children, I was not a bad man—only one who was stuck in the 1960's (Summer of Love)."

That fall, when I completed the poetry chapbook entitled "Unveiling Liberty, A Face Lift", I sent a copy to Deni Johnson. I did not receive her response as she had moved on to new students. I tucked my papers in my portfolio of writing and shut it in a metal cabinet. Many years would pass until I read my work again.

The next year, 1986 was the occasion for Liz and me to marry, settle down, focus on becoming counselors and for the next three decades, raise our family. Liz gave us wonderful children, Alison and William. We used every available hour enjoying our kids along with our lovely daughter, Rachael and son, Christopher, from my former marriage.

We lived our 30's, 40's and 50's in relative ease. My writing was restricted solely to letters. The advent of my retirement from thirty-three years of prison work came about in 2003. The death of my mother, Vina Bonnie coincided in that year. Those events seemed to demand that I revisit fifty years of special memories together—a boy, then a man, who now felt briefly severed from the connection a mother brings to her eldest son. I need to qualify this last statement.

Mama Vina raised her four children and did it exceeding well, chiefly by her own, and as I have said, under often excruciating circumstances. That she was a fine Christian who loved Jesus and witnessed her salvation can scarcely be doubted; it was underscored by her evangelistic sharing the Gospel News.

Mama's interrupting mental issues resulted in hospitalizations, accompanied with doses of psychotropic drugs as well as electro-convulsive shock therapy and all that goes with clinical depression episodes. These things robbed her of any golden years of a genteel life. It is the examination of such things that propel a writer to reveal his or her inner thoughts. My mother's plight had much to do with my need to express my soul.

Thoughts and Actions Process

In 2006, penning a tribute to my mother, I attempted my first hundred-page memoir titled "Faith Beyond Doubt, An Allegory." I published this revealing documentation. Reading it, for me, is like riding a teeter-totter at a playground...up, down, up and down went those years—never dull, sometimes even amusing to me, as well as the hurt I may have caused to love ones left in the wake of my thoughtlessness. The "Faith" book's pages permitted me to analyze my thought process, to set down a record of my simply human hit and miss goals, and to understand what it was that contributed to my failed actions.

We see things clearly once the secrets are dribbled out on paper. Causes and results are illuminated in the morning's light. Fearful things like a failed marriage; failed faith in God; the acts of a prodigal youth sowing his wild oats—all these things I had kept concealed in my head, were percolating just below the surface—now these thoughts were finally released. Caged feelings no longer hidden, allowed that I could breathe freely again. It was like graduating from a fat farm to lose weight. With the release of emotional baggage since my boyhood, I felt lighter and freed. Guilty self-blame and feeling like a victim were released. The healing process often requires simple, clear writing.

It's appropriate that I thank my mother for her reading of my poetry and comically referring to me as 'the Bard of Vacaville'. I also shout out a Thank You to Mrs. Deni Johnson, for trusting her own ability to encourage her students to achieve what their desire may lead them to explore. By her kind methods, the spark that Deni gave to her students ignited a flame of personal self-empowerment. That spark is germane to any student's growth through writing.

Elsewhere in this book, we have repeated that a teacher has the power to shape the future. I know this is true. For many years I've read to second grade students and for several years I've worked as a part time teacher in high school. This has been a training ground permitting me to practice the art of leading students toward the light of dignity and wisdom. It's not easy or always successful, but in the effort to mold young minds, I count their kind loving reception to me as a blessing.

Who Said It Best?

King Solomon declared this in Proverbs, Chapter 1, and verse 1-9:

"The proverbs of Solomon, the son of David, King of Israel; to know wisdom and instruction; to perceive the words of understanding; to receive the instruction of wisdom, justice, and judgment, and equity; to give subtlety to the simple, to the young man knowledge and discretion.

"A wise man will hear, and will increase learning; and a man of understanding shall attain unto wise counsels; to understand a proverb, and the interpretation; the words of the wise, and their dark sayings. The fear of the Lord is the beginning of knowledge; but fools despise wisdom and instruction. My son, hear the instruction of thy father, and forsake not the law of thy mother: For they shall be an ornament of grace unto thy head, and chains about thy neck" (Prov. 1:1-9, King James Version).

My prayer, Dear Reader, is if someone you love and who loves you, should make the effort to place this slender book into your hands, rejoice...not at the sentences of our stories from the pens of we the writers, but of Solomon's keen insightful suggestions.

Indeed, Solomon is known as the wisest man who ever lived. But Solomon asked God, "Give me now wisdom and knowledge so that I may go out and come in before this people: for who can judge this thy people that is so great?" (2 Chron. 1:10 King James Version).

May all the glory, praise, and honor gleaned from this chapter be to God; only the mistakes are mine—and mine alone.

Chapter Eighteen

AN AMAZING WRITER OF 20,000 LETTERS

I Was Wrong . . . Again

During our correspondence in 2015 and 2016, Don Fortin often praised the wisdom, courage, discipline and patriotism of Thomas Jefferson. Don pointed out how I and everyone else could learn valuable lessons from the words and actions of this champion for life, liberty and the pursuit of happiness. When Don was a boy growing up in Thomas Jefferson's home state, the Commonwealth of Virginia, Old Dominion, he learned early to appreciate the gigantic role that Jefferson had in shaping both the foundation and the future of our nation.

In contrast to Don's enthusiasm for President Jefferson, I was privately uncomfortable about magnifying him. Although I had the highest regard for Thomas Jefferson as a patriot and founder of our nation, I remained silent and refrained from lavishing him with praise. I secretly sided with devout Christians who are nervous about a person who used a scissors or another cutting instrument to remove verses from the Bible, even if he did so for noble reasons as Jefferson's defenders convincingly propound. I also agreed with others who find it difficult to laud a man who proclaimed liberty for all but still owned six hundred slaves over his lifetime and only released a few of them. I found it easier to embrace and speak glowingly about less complicated founding fathers like George Washington who freed his slaves and subscribed to the whole Bible.

While having reservations about Thomas Jefferson, I had sense enough never to speak or write despairingly of him. Out of reverence for the greatness of Thomas Jefferson, I made it a point to never criticize him to anyone. "Who am I?" I thought, "a lowly nobody like me, to say anything negative about one of the most intelligent and remarkable persons in all history?" Only when others prodded me to honor him as Don periodically did, would I express mild hesitancy to do so while never mentioning my personal issues with Jefferson's shearing of Bible verses and his ownership of slaves. Opinions like that were best to be left unspoken.

Don must have noticed my cool reticence in response to the many accolades he would write about Thomas Jefferson. And so possibly he sent to me a copy of Jon Meacham's 759-page biography, Thomas Jefferson: The Art of Power published by Random House, 2012. With an open mind, I read the book. Being a slow reader, it took me about thirty-five hours to complete it. The time, however, was well spent in reading this epic chronicle of Thomas Jefferson's life. The information that Jon Meacham skillfully and artistically presented was fascinating. I saw Thomas Jefferson in a completely different light. Here again was an example of how letter writing helps people to look upon perceptions and sometimes discover that they are misperceptions. Don is gifted by God to have that skill of helping people to assess or reassess their opinions and attitudes and look upon them from a different angle and with new information.

Thankful for Imperfect People Like Me

I was wrong in my prior concealed, harsh judgment about Jefferson's Bible clipping and his slaves. As to Jefferson's eliminating of verses in the Bible, Meacham pointed out that Jefferson understood rightly that government should not promulgate any religion upon its citizens, but that government had every right to promote moral conduct conducive to the safety of all individuals and the preservation of their property. Hence, Jefferson cut out all verses in the New Testament that referred to the divinity of Jesus, including His miracles. What was left then in Jefferson's Bibles (his 1804 and 1820 editions) were the moral teachings of Jesus. He then had an easy reference to the verses in the New Testament that could be legally quoted by him as he carried out his public duties.

Some devoted Christians may still maintain, "OK. We'll give Jefferson a pass on snipping verses out of the Bible, but what about his statements that he did not believe that Jesus was divine? In other words, he did not believe that Jesus was the Son of God who had and still has miraculous power and is to be worshiped. We who are authentic Christians must never let Jefferson get away with his statements denying the divinity of Christ." Jon Meacham verifies that Jefferson did make it known that he did not believe that Jesus was divine.

In response to the concerns of some sincere Christians about this matter, might I comment that dedicated Christians can still marvel with thanksgiving for leaders in government who stand up for laws that are in harmony with Christ's teaching even if these leaders do not espouse the same doctrines which Christians hold as sacred. The Apostle Paul had many valid reasons to condemn the debauchery and the despotism of many Roman and local Mediterranean rulers in his day, but might we recall what Paul wrote in 1 Timothy 2:1-2? He urged his readers, "I exhort therefore, that, first of all, supplications, prayers, intercessions, and giving of thanks, be made for all men. For kings, and for all that are in authority; that we may lead a quiet and peaceable life in all godliness and honesty" (1 Tim. 2:1-2,King James Version). Instead of imploring Christians to condemn the outrageous behavior of the kings and those in authority, Paul pleads with Christians to do just the opposite. He instructs his readers to give thanks "for all men" including the scoundrels who ruled over them. I'm not in any way implying that Thomas Jefferson was a scoundrel. No, please. I am not saying that at all. I am just trying to make the point that if Paul directs us to pray for even debased tyrants, wouldn't he also encourage us to pray for at least decent and well-meaning leaders like Thomas Jefferson?

It would be wonderful if all U.S. presidents believed in the Trinity and in Jesus Christ, who was both human and divine, as their Savior, but the Apostle Paul instructs us to thank the Lord for "all men", all humans, even those who are not believers in the divine Jesus, including those in authority. We thank God for all who govern because they have a God given role to maintain order in society. By them as leaders insuring us a safe environment, "we may lead a quiet and peaceable life in all godliness and honesty."

No, Thomas Jefferson did not believe that Jesus was divine. As faithful Christians we can still applaud him, however, because God created him to have a pivotal role in the development of the United States of America where Christians have the freedom to share the Good News of Jesus without interference from the government or anyone. For this we are very grateful indeed.

Do I Qualify to Cast the First Stone?

As far as Jefferson owning about six hundred slaves during his lifetime while still pledging that "all men are created equal," Jon Meacham in his book mentions some points that I had not considered. Meacham documents how Jefferson in his young adult years as an attorney and as a legislator in the Commonwealth of Virginia had attempted in the courts and in the House of Burgesses to end the practice of slavery. However, all his attempts fell upon either deaf or defiant ears, and his measures were turned down.

When Jefferson was assigned the task of writing the draft for the Declaration of Independence, as he did as an attorney and as a legislator in the state of Virginia, he again wrote a statement calling for the elimination of slavery. As in previous attempts, however, a majority or a vocal minority of delegates overruled his efforts. In commenting upon sections of his draft to the Declaration of Independence which were deleted, Jefferson wrote, "The clause, too, reprobating the enslaving [of] the inhabitants of Africa, was struck out". No one can fault Jefferson for earnestly trying to abolish slavery.

After reading Meacham's biography of Thomas Jefferson, I concluded that I was wrong to misjudge him as having a double standard about the rights of human beings, one criteria for those with European heritage and another standard for those with African heritage. Jefferson truly was due diligent in trying to include all people to have equal rights.

Just as Don Fortin's mother Vina Bonnie Fortin, also of Virginia, was ahead of her time in trying to treat all races equally in the 1950s, so was fellow Virginian Thomas Jefferson a century ahead of his time on matters related to race. Just as Don's mother Vina Bonnie received rejection and even retaliation for her efforts in race relations, so did Thomas Jefferson receive the same. Just as I have admired Vina Bonnie's efforts though they fell short for what she had hoped, so do I now value greatly the efforts that Jefferson made to treat all men, women and children as equal.

Some critics, however, are not about to excuse Thomas Jefferson on the matter of race, even though he did try to eliminate slavery but was outnumbered or outpowered by his colleagues. Jefferson's detractors point out that Thomas Jefferson could have still done what George Washington did by releasing all his slaves. Jefferson's detractors complain, "Just because Jefferson was outnumbered by his colleagues on the ending of slavery, Jefferson could have still done the right thing in emancipating his own slaves. Okay, he couldn't control what people around him did, but he could have done at least something. Letting his own slaves go free would have been that something." Meacham addresses this fault-finding about Jefferson by explaining that some states, including the state of Virginia, had a high fee for the release of any slave. The reason for the high fee was so that the state could be assured that the slave would be provided with food, clothing, shelter and employment so that the slave would not resort to crime in acquiring these basic needs out of desperation to survive. Is it possible that George Washington had the wealth to pay for these fees, but Thomas Jefferson did not?

Meacham pointed out throughout his book that even though Jefferson resided on an estate in Monticello and had what we today would call a wealthy lifestyle, Jefferson was almost always in debt often because of inherited debt or because of defaulted loans that out of kindness he co-signed for relatives. Keeping his slaves to run his nailery and to care for his farm operations was then an economic necessity for him. Critics, of course, have no sympathy for Jefferson if his reason for keeping his slaves was for his very economic survival. This same excuse could be used by every slave-owner in the South. Lest I or anyone be quick to condemn Jefferson for not releasing his slaves even though it meant financial ruin for him and his family, may we ask ourselves how many times have we avoided doing the right thing because by doing so we would jeopardize the financial security of our spouse or our children?

It should be noted that Thomas Jefferson did give freedom to his slave Sally Hemings and her children before he died. But those who look sternly upon Jefferson sneer that allowing only the Heming slaves to go free was just a pittance in relation to what he could have done for all his slaves. Jefferson's naysayers also make note that Jefferson and Sally Hemings were intimately involved, and so Jefferson's overture to her was not based on expressing the equality of all people but his decision was rather based on a personal attachment to Hemings and her (many say their) children. Again, may I, and no one else, be quick to judge Thomas Jefferson. Most of us have issues in our lives that are not consistent with doing what pleases God. Very few, if any of us, are qualified to castigate Thomas Jefferson.

After reading Meacham's biography, the Lord has pointed out the many flaws and contradictions in my life. I say I am against abortion, but am I writing my legislators every week, every month or even once a year asking them to repeal abortion except when the life of the mother is jeopardized? If I say I am against all the filth on television, do I cut off the cable service in my home even though my spouse wants to keep cable? If I say that I am against same gender marriage, am I writing up petitions against same gender marriage and going to the Wal Mart parking lots asking people to sign them? The answer to these questions is no, and so I am the least of all persons to pin point Thomas Jefferson for not doing enough publicly and privately to abolish slavery.

Jesus said it concisely, "Judge not, that ye be not judged ... Thou hypocrite, first cast out the beam out of thine own eye; and then shalt thou see clearly to cast out the mote out of thy brother's eye" (Matt. 7:1,5, King James Version).

After coming to terms with the unjustified obstacles that I had raised which preventing me from giving Jefferson the praise which he has more than earned, I could then enjoy the many valuable lessons which I learned from reading about him. Here are just a few insights that I found very applicable to my life and maybe to yours, too.

Virginia's Culture of Grace

What first jumped out at me in reading about Thomas Jefferson was his gentle manner in in the presence of argumentative persons. He would either politely excuse himself or gently guide the conversation into a more pleasant topic. In his writing, however, he could be gruffer than he was in person especially in his references toward his longtime friend John Adams and his longtime foe Alexander Hamilton.

My uneducated impression of the founding fathers (Washington, Adams, Jefferson, Hamilton, Madison, Monroe, and others) was that they were a chummy fraternity of brothers. I must have been dozing off in my American History classes in elementary, middle and high school because Jon Meacham cites sharp division among the heroes after the Revolutionary War. They were often not civil towards each other due to their entrenched political views.

True, the founding fathers were a band of brothers in the years leading up to the Declaration of Independence and during the Revolutionary War. Don Fortin aptly wrote in one of his text messages to me on November 26, 2017,

"I am amazed at what these early Americans did with ingenuity, strong faith and much courage. Jefferson, Franklin and all 55 signers of the Declaration were single minded and of one accord. You can see it in their surviving correspondence. Each day they knew that King George III could have them hanged as traitors to the crown. Yet they wrote hourly and encouraged one another until success would not be denied"

In the time prior to the Revolutionary War, the founding fathers were of one mind and one heart. However, Jon Meacham documents that after the Revolutionary War, when detailed and technical matters about operating the country needed to be decided, the founders had very different ideas as to what would be best for our nation.

I did not realize the intense opposition that the Federalist Party of George Washington, John Adams, and Alexander Hamilton had towards the Democratic-Republican Party of Thomas Jefferson, James Madison and James Monroe.

Jefferson was greatly upset with the Alien and Sedition Acts that President Adams used to arrest members of Jefferson's Democratic-Republican Party for writing what Federalist Party members considered to be treasonous publications. Jefferson did not support President Washington's endorsement of President Adams who pushed for a stronger, bigger federal government, even talking about establishing a monarchy where the successor to the throne would be determined by birthright. So wide were the political differences between Jefferson and Washington that Jefferson thought it wise to not attend any of the ceremonies which honored President Washington following his death in December 1799.

Acrimonious words among the founders often were spewed after the Revolutionary War. After twenty years of friendship, John Adams and Thomas Jefferson gradually grew apart in their political views. When Jefferson took a hiatus from public service in 1794, Adams wrote to his wife Abigail, "Jefferson went off yesterday, and a good riddance of bad ware". During the presidential election of 1800, Alexander Hamilton publicly called Jefferson "an atheist and a fanatic" and therefore unfit to be the leader of the nation. In a letter to English scientist Joseph Priestley, Jefferson referred to the Federalists that included Washington, Adams and Hamilton in the following unflattering way, "Their leaders are a hospital of incurables, and as such entitled to be protected and taken care of as other insane persons are".

Yet in face-to-face situations including dinners, meetings, or social galas, Thomas Jefferson consistently conducted himself as a gentleman. Jon Meacham explains, "Part of the reason for his largely genial mien lay in the Virginia culture of grace and hospitality" (Meacham pp. 308). In the twenty years that I have known Don Fortin, a Virginian in his formative childhood years, I, too, can attest to the truth of Meacham's that there is much to be said about the Commonwealth of Virginia's "culture of grace and hospitality."

I have never seen Don lose his temper or speak disrespectfully to anyone. In the twelve or so times that I accompanied Don into the California State Prison in which he worked, I observed that he greeted every inmate whom he passed with a "Good morning, Sir" or a "Good afternoon, Sir." He conversed with fellow staff and with inmates with the same courtesy that he spoke to persons in church. Five thick three ring binders that contain his letters from the past decade written by Don do not have one sentence of ugly, unkind remarks. Such is the character that I imagine Thomas Jefferson to have had also, reflecting "the culture of grace and hospitality" of Old Dominion.

In a letter to grandson Thomas Jefferson Randolph, Mr. Jefferson explained his rules of engagement in human interactions. One of his maxims was of "never entering into dispute or argument with another. I never yet saw an instance of one of two disputants convincing the other by argument. I have seen many, on their getting warm, becoming rude, and shooting one another".

In that same letter to his grandson, Jefferson commented on his venerable mentor Ben Franklin who also learned the wisdom in not being dragged into verbal confrontation with anyone: "It was one of the rules which above all others made Dr. [sic] Franklin the most amiable of men in society, 'never to contradict anybody".

How refreshing it would be if homes, communities, churches, nations, and the world would be if there were more people like Thomas Jefferson and Benjamin Franklins among us. In this heated political climate of 2017 with name calling and reputation bashing taking place daily, it would behoove all of us to consider the cordial conduct of Jefferson and Franklin, two of the most competent public servants of all time who both relied on tact and calmness to achieve their objectives of improving the lives of the American people, the world, and civilization.

But Not an Air Headed Idealist

Thomas Jefferson may have always used a strong dose of diplomacy as his default mode in approaching any situation, but he was wise enough to understand that sometimes diplomacy was not always the answer. Jon Meacham maintains that in addition to his role as a masterful peacemaker, Jefferson was also a realist who was not averse to use force after all courteous efforts failed. As Governor of Virginia in 1780, Jefferson unsuccessfully tried to reason with armed citizens in the southwestern region of the state who were loyal to England. Jefferson gave the following directive to his military commander George Rogers Clark: "Nothing can produce so dangerous a diversion of our force, as a circumstance of that kind if not crushed on its infancy". Governor Jefferson had given Commander Clark permission to use force if necessary, to quell the armed uprising.

As U.S. President, Jefferson also understood that military action was necessary in dealing with treacherous pirates from the Barbary States of Morocco, Algiers, Tunis, and Tripoli. These raiders were attacking vessels from America and other nations. Jefferson approved the U.S. ship Enterprise to engage in battle against the Barbary State ship Tripoli. On August 1, 1801, the Enterprise prevailed over the Tripoli. In praising the efforts of the U.S. commander of the Enterprise, Andrew Sterett, President Jefferson stated, "Too long ... have those barbarians been suffered to trample on the sacred faith of treaties, on the rights and laws of human nature. You have shown to your countrymen that that enemy cannot meet bravery and skill united". Such was the sober thinking of President Jefferson. Force must never be used as an impulse, but if needed, it can be used as a deterrent.

The formula President Jefferson followed reflects the teachings of the Holy Bible that he read often. Is it possible that verses such as the following helped to shape Jefferson's approach to dealing with people, political parties, and nations? Be profusely gentle first, and then only if necessary, be stern.

"Come now, and let us reason together, saith the Lord: though your sins be as scarlet, they shall be as white as snow; though they be red like crimson, they shall be as wool" (Isa. 1:18, King James Version)

Moreover, if thy brother shall trespass against thee, go and tell him his fault between thee and him alone: if he shall hear thee, thou hast gained thy brother. But if he will not hear thee, then take with thee one or two more, that in the mouth of two or three witnesses every word may be established. And if he shall neglect to hear them, tell it unto the church: but if he neglects to hear the church, let him be unto thee as a heathen man and a publican (Matt. 18:15-17, King James Version).

As a correctional officer and counselor in the California State Prison System, Don Fortin dealt with inmates and staff in the same manner as Thomas Jefferson, and more importantly, Jesus Christ. "Come let us reason together." And if the inmates or staff members reject that overture, then tougher measures need to be taken.

Hope for the Future

Meacham's Prologue to Thomas Jefferson: The Art of Power began with a drowsy fifty-eight-year-old Thomas Jefferson getting out of bed and immediately soaking his feet in a bucket of invigorating, cold water, a ritual that he did every morning, believing it to be conducive for good health. Heavy on his mind and heart was the undecided outcome of the 1800 Presidential Election. The election was in the hands of the electoral voters with the field of candidates narrowed down to three: Pro-Small Government Thomas Jefferson, Pro-Big Government John Adams and Volatile and Unpredictable Aaron Burr. Jefferson had won the popular votes but was tied with Burr in the electoral voting. Tensions between the two major political parties were feverish, the Federalists (strong centralized government, even monarchial) and the Democratic-Republicans (small centralized government, anti-monarchial).

The election had been heated because of many dynamic factors. Supporters of Former President George Washington saw the election as a referendum for or against the legacy of the first President. A vote for the incumbent John Adams, a zealous supporter of President Washington, was a vote of affirmation for Washington. On the other hand, a vote for Jefferson and Burr was a slap in the face to the revered Washington. Supporters of Thomas Jefferson and Aaron Burr viewed a vote for John Adams as a vote for the establishment of a monarchy with successors chosen by birthright. Jefferson saw the election in terms of a vote for the preservation of the rights articulated in the Declaration of Independence or a vote to reject those rights. To Jefferson, a vote for him insured that the values of the Declaration of Independence would be defended for at least the next four years.

Jefferson expressed his frustration in a letter to his eldest daughter, "[I am] worn down here with pursuits in which I take no delight, surrounded by enemies and spies catching and perverting every word which falls from my lips or flows from my pen, and inventing where facts fail them.

These lamentations of Jefferson could be describing the U.S. political atmosphere at the time in which I am writing this chapter. It is 2017, and many as Jefferson did, "take no delight" by the rancor which buzzes in the air. Many are upset that we have a victorious president of the 2016 election who did not win the majority popular votes but instead legitimately and fairly garnered the majority of the electoral votes unless the FBI can prove that any collusion with Russia took place. Many citizens feel "worn down" by cable news stations like CNN and Fox News devoting almost 24 hours of news daily, featuring stories of partisan "enemies" tearing away at their counterparts non-stop. We hear or read about political "spies" plants and news leakers, people obsessed with "catching and perverting every word which falls from" the lips of opposition party members "inventing stories where facts fail them" (fake news).

Many are calling the political vitriol the new normal. However, after one reads about the life of Thomas Jefferson, she or he might conclude that the intense competition in politics experienced in 2017 is really the old normal, refusing to take a breather since the years following the Revolutionary War. Great honorable leaders such as Washington, Adams, Jefferson, Madison, Monroe, and J.Q. Adams, the first six presidents of our nation, often fiercely disagreed.

By the grace of God, however, our nation inched forward despite powerful, differing opinions among some of the most intelligent persons in history. As Meacham highlights throughout his book, Thomas Jefferson was wise to temper some of his entrenched values for the survival of our nation. One example of Jefferson's core beliefs was that the central government of the U.S. should be as small as possible in size and power, a position antithetical to George Washington, John Adams and the Federalist Party. However, when faced with the need to purchase the vast western territory of Louisiana from France before Great Britain or other unfriendly countries acquired it, President Jefferson used his executive powers in a vigorous way to broker the purchase. He orchestrated the deal with France in an assertive manner similar to what a Federalist president might have done.

For us in 2017 and in other times when the heat of verbal political polemics seem unbearable, may we find encouragement by reflecting upon the life and times of Thomas Jefferson. In critical times, God somehow forges unity among U.S. citizens with divergent almost uncompromising opinions. The beauty of a republic and democracy is that its citizens can have clashing points of view but can also come together for a common cause that will benefit all citizens.

About three years after Thomas Jefferson retired from public service, he and John Adams restored their friendship that had been tattered by partisan strife beginning in the 1790's. In 1812, they began to correspond. Between 1812 and 1826 when they both passed away, a period of 14 years, they exchanged 158 letters. In their lifetimes, they wrote a total of 326 letters between them.

Their letters, especially between 1812 and 1826, reflect the most honorable traits of the American ethos. All their letters abound with dignity, respect, open mindedness, congeniality and thoughtfulness. Jefferson and Adams continued to disagree on many topics, but each articulated their positions without venom toward the other. Adams sought reconciliation with Jefferson when he wrote "You (Jefferson) and I ought not to die before we have explained ourselves to each other".

Jefferson often composed gracious words about Adams in his letters. In his first letter, dated January 21, 1812, in reply to Adam's first letter to him, Jefferson wrote,

"A letter from you calls up recollections very dear to my mind. It carries me back to the times when, beset with difficulties and dangers, we were fellow laborers in the same cause, struggling for what is most valuable to man, his right of self-government. Laboring always at the same oar, with some wave ever ahead threatening to overwhelm us and yet passing harmless under our bark we knew not how, we rode through the storm with heart and hand, and made a happy port".

The restoration of friendship between Jefferson and Adams in 1812 gives us much hope in 2017 or in any year of verbal wildfire over how our government should be run. The history of our nation gives us vibrant reassurance. When our nation needs to come together as one, the Lord will break down barriers and join us as one. Just as Jefferson and Adams rejuvenated their friendship despite their differing strong political convictions, so can the Lord draw us near to Him and to one another.

As the Lord was with our nation during the times in which Thomas Jefferson lived, so will the Lord be present with us when we trust in Him. Trusting in Him leads us to the next section of this chapter dealing with Thomas Jefferson's wall between church and state being misunderstood.

A Wall of Separation

A topic that hits a sensitive nerve in many Americans is a metaphor Thomas Jefferson once used, "a wall of separation between Church and State." Some Americans interpret the wall to mean taking "In God We Trust" off all coins, striking out "one nation under God" in the Pledge of Allegiance, stopping all invocations in Congress, or ceasing to use government funds to pay the salaries of Armed Forces chaplains. In other words, many interpret Thomas Jefferson's metaphor of the wall to mean remove God from government and put Him on the other side of the wall.

In one of Don Fortin's letters, he expounded on why Jefferson's wall metaphor never meant the removal of God and prayers from government. He referred to a letter which President Jefferson wrote on New Year's Day 1802 to the Danbury Baptist Association in Colebook, Connecticut. He wrote to the churches there because two months prior in October 1801, they had praised President

Jefferson for his protection of religious liberty. In appreciation for their recognition of him, Jefferson wrote,

Believing with you that religion is a matter which lies solely between Man and his God, that he owes account to none other for his faith or his worship, that the legitimate powers of government reach actions only, and not opinions. I contemplate with sovereign reverence that act of the whole American people which declared that their legislature should 'make no law respecting an establishment of religion, or prohibiting the free exercise thereof,' thus building a wall of separation between Church and State.

Based upon President Jefferson's own words then, "the wall of separation between Church and State" meant that no town, city, county, state or federal agency would pass any law or ordinance which would identify or promote through words or practice any religion as preferable to another or which would prohibit any religion from worshiping or promulgating their faith. Jefferson was specifically referring to legislators and legislatures in our nation. Nowhere was he suggesting that prayers and references to God on coins or in pledges and anthems be prohibited.

To this day, therefore, "In God We Trust" is still included on many coins, pastors and church leaders still lead in invocations in Congress, Armed Forces chaplains' salaries are still funded by the U.S. and citizens still declare "one Nation under God" in the Pledge of Allegiance. Thank God, people have not yet thrown these practices over the wall to be kept entirely separate from government.

The increasing challenge for Christians will be, however, to work out the details as to what religious liberty entails. For example, at a public high school graduation in Little Rock, Arkansas, will the high school administration allow a Muslim to say a prayer to Allah making reference to Mohammed as the most blessed prophet of all? Will Congress allow a Buddhist monk to chant an incantation to begin a session? Will the City Council in Duluth, Minnesota permit a practitioner from the Church of Satan (recognized by the IRS as a bona fide church) invoke a prayer to the Devil? These are among the hundreds of intricacies related to the practice of religious liberty today in the realm of civic sponsored activities.

No matter how complex the practice of religious liberty in government functions may be, the fact is that President Thomas

Jefferson's wall of separation did not mean to kick God out of government. The wall meant that government separates itself from passing legislation which will either promote or prohibit any religion. For that, we can be most thankful. As the Danbury Baptist Association in Colebrook, Connecticut did in October 1801, we also thank the Lord that President Thomas Jefferson stood up for religious liberty so that Christians have the right to worship and share their faith without interference or preferential treatment from the government.

All Created Equal

As the Danbury Baptist Association hailed President Thomas Jefferson for guarding and fostering the growth of religious liberty for all, we end this chapter by thanking the Lord for the many facets of liberty for which President Thomas Jefferson defended and cultivated. This includes the liberty extended to all people.

No, Jefferson was not successful in his many conscientious attempts in the Commonwealth of Virginia and in the Continental Congress to grant liberty to the thousands of slaves in America. No, he did not release his own slaves that he could have done as a private citizen but with financially devastating consequences for his family. (All of us always do the right thing, don't we? And all of us would do the right thing even if it meant financial ruin to our spouses and children, wouldn't we? I'll be the first to admit that I would be severely tempted to not do the right thing if my spouse and children were to greatly suffer by me doing so. I pray that I would indeed do the right thing even if it meant misery for my family, but I wouldn't sanctimoniously judge others who didn't.)

Despite his unsuccessful attempts to gain liberty for all humans and despite his personal shortcomings (which are infinitely less than mine), Thomas Jefferson will long be remembered as the titan of liberty in all its dimensions. When many think of the name Thomas Jefferson, they immediately associate it with liberty for all humans.

In ways that are beyond our human comprehension, God often chooses to work slowly, according to our definition of slow, in eliminating injustices. He took four centuries to release the children of Israel from slavery in Egypt. God could have released them in a second if He elected to do that. God waited thousands of years after Adam and Eve sinned to send the Savior Jesus Christ to free us from the slavery of sin. God could have instantly sent the Savior from sin the second after Adam and Eve disobeyed Him, but God decided that letting thousands of years pass would be a better plan. God has his beneficial reasons for working slowly according to our perception of slow. We on earth cannot comprehend why He prefers to take action in this manner. We simply trust and affirm that what He does is always in the best interest of those who love Him.

In a similar way, God chose to end slavery in the United States steadily, too steadily in the eyes of those who dare to criticize Him. According to most historians, the first African slaves in America arrived in Jamestown, Virginia (interestingly, the home state of Jefferson) in 1619. Slavery was officially abolished in the U.S. in 1865 with the enactment of the 13th Amendment to the Constitution. That's a period of 246 years, roughly 200 years less than the slavery which the people of Israel endured in Egypt, but still fraught with unspeakable suffering and indignity.

Within those 246 years, however, there was a pulsating progression leading up to the 13th Amendment in 1865. Just a few of the many momentous events contributing to the 1865 abolition of slavery include the Great (Religious) Awakening in the 1740s when clergy spoke against slavery and their sermons became the roots of the formidable Abolitionist Movement from the 1780s to the 1860s; the Territory of Vermont, the first entity associated with America prohibiting slavery in 1777; the State of Pennsylvania, the first state in America abolishing slavery in 1780; of course, the Declaration of Independence in 1776 which at least put into writing that "all men are created equal"; a number of northern states ending slavery during the 1780's, the start of the Civil War in 1861, and President Lincoln's Emancipation Proclamation in 1863.

Each event added another shovel of coal to the burner that heated the boiler that produced the steam to churn the engine powering the freedom train toward its destination, the elimination of slavery in the U.S.

Jefferson's words "all men are created equal" was a wagon full of coal that boosted the train toward its next stop. Many, maybe most, of the signers of the Declaration of Independence did not realize that someday those revolutionary words would apply to not only males of European descent but to men, women and children of all backgrounds, all over the world.

In the next chapter of this book, Don Fortin has allowed me to be privy of an American of African descent. He, like all of us, is a recipient of the liberty that Thomas Jefferson cherished. The writer whom Don will introduce to us is a poet with an elegant style and a robust message. His poetry will remind us that America has made commendable advancements in putting into practice Jefferson's call for liberty but still has more miles to travel. The sublime poetry of this African American writer will be just another confirmation that Thomas Jefferson's words are self-evidently true that "all men, women and children are created equal" indeed.

I won't spoil the delightful surprise in store for you as you read Chapter Nineteen of this book. May this chapter close with this Scripture, a quote from our Lord Jesus Christ, which I have no doubt the gentleman from Don Fortin's home state read:

"And ye shall know the truth, and the truth shall make you free" (John 8:32, King James Version).

Chapter Nineteen

BRAVE AMERICAN WRITER IN HIS DAY

As Les and I have defined, letters can be written in many fashions, be they correspondence to a loved one; an editorial opinion to a newspaper; a heart-broken love song, or a majestic hymn of lush worship. A letter can be a novel of entertaining fiction or a life biography.

One of America's most expressive letter writers did so in collections of short verse. I would have loved to include his poetry in this little book; but having checked, the permission was too costly to include quotations of his works. I must then keep his name anonymous. This man came of age during the Great Depression and his writings celebrated the modern-day urban dweller; the blues singer; the penniless gambler; the rough and mismatched street hustler, and all the while reminding his nation of the sins of unjust southern treatment of Dixieland's black sons and daughters with the use of Jim Crow laws that pervaded those times.

Today, the pendulum of politics seems once more to hover between the calm and progressive status quo versus a return to the times of those Jim Crow laws, when lynching of black men for the dubious act of recklessly eye-balling southern women of a different ethnicity was a real action. We pray that our better angels will finally prevail in these times in which divisive forces are trying to undermine the last sixty years of progress. It is good to remember that Jesus told us to love one another, even as He loved us.

As writers, Les and I deliberated on how our subject matter should be included in this book. Neither of us are African-Americans: I am Caucasian, and Les is a Pacific Islander. We desired to avoid the trap of being one dimensional, that is, to overlook one of the strongest, courageous voices of the twentieth century. So, I chose to joyfully reflect on this man's poems. Not to include a small section of his voluminous work would be a tragic omission however there are copyright considerations based on the intellectual property rights. You may purchase any number of titles under his name, of which 35 he himself wrote.

In the years 1921 to 1968, he published poems of heartbreak; of solitary existence; about men who recalled the herding of men.

He was an acclaimed scholar having graduated with a Bachelor of Arts degree from Lincoln University in Pennsylvania in 1929, just a few years after his first poem was published in a nationally known magazine. A poem which first launched his career appeared in Crisis in 1921. The first of his books was published in 1926. He was awarded a Guggenheim Fellowship in 1935; he received a Rosenwald Fellowship in 1940. Writing unceasingly, he published plays, essays, song lyrics; short stories and that included his own life story among a compendium of books.

This writer of magnificent letters was documenting the teamwork concept of together building this great nation of ours. By doing so, he was calling out the contributions of his brothers in their quest for unity among all Americans. He was showing how together, we could be stronger.

Of these publications beginning in 1930 until his death in 1967, his voice was a clarion call for awareness of injustice. He spoke the truth when it was unpopular and dangerous to do so. His voice was needed at a tumultuous time in America. Perhaps you can guess his name by now.

Influenced in My Early Years

As I reached manhood, many things had changed for the better. In our country, there was just beginning to develop a sense of purpose for inclusion, rather than exclusion, for none-white men and women. Maybe it was the Vietnam War with the national military draft as Les Seto ably described that period in which we both grew up.

What I was doing was as natural as riding a bicycle or rolling along on a skateboard. I was living in California and had graduated from high school. Radio was perpetually blasting Motown music from Detroit and everybody knew who the big music groups were. Kids in the 1960's were listening to the music of The Temptations and The Supremes. We were reminded of getting onboard the Peace Train that the writer of poems advocated from the East Coast to the other coast out West.

During a year and a half, from 1970-'72, I was working alongside 'hard hats,' African-American and white men loading weaponry aboard cargo ships. This was a dangerous job as an ammunition stevedore during the Southeast Asian conflict known as the Vietnam War. From there, I segued into a year of state hospital duty on the psychiatric wards at Napa State Hospital. Having turned 22 years of age, I began what would be the next 33 years of laboring alongside correctional women and men in four California prisons until my retirement in 2003. Close contact with prisoners of all backgrounds exposed me to their rough dialogue and mannerism of all ages of men under restraint; among them, were Latinos, Whites and African Americans. I viewed convicted felons first as gentlemen who had children, with wives, and desires just like myself.

Second, because of the nature of prison work I understood the need for the safety of the public and security of the prison workers. This is such a complicated manner of work for anyone who enters that employment to help others. I think my job on the docks and in the psychiatric hospital helped me immeasurably. I provided significant training to staff to be ethical and professional. There are always a small number of employees who did not embrace this concept, choosing to see the inmates as only criminals unworthy of respect and common courtesy. Most, however, were colorblind to the inmates, and still guardedly believed rehabilitation possible.

The poet's poems of tough urban lives of black men and women resonated with me. In those poems, I could hear the joyless, doomed future many blacks feel based upon prejudice endured in their lives. It was inevitable that I would see prejudice's effects close-up inside the barbed wire fences and walls of state prisons. I was interested to learn that when prejudice rears its head, the white man saw it as individual racism; the black man saw it as institutional racism. The poet saw all racism as destructive and futile.

Writing my earlier book, Sister Vina's Boy, I tried to capture the singular 'face' of many life sentence inmates whose stories I learned as those men crossed my path. Some were vicious, themselves with lives of pain, suffering and little chance for personal achievement; of these, many were black men, physically and chronologically aged by long stretches in county jails as their crimes were repeated until at last, they hit the 'big jolt' and earned a sentence in the Department of Corrections. I often reflected that if there had been a steady father role model in the young man's life, how different their position now might be. We can hear a little about the situation, but the poet put a human face on the story of any American caught in the web of hopelessness.

At San Quentin, I heard their conversations; I watched their movements and I witnessed their ever-vigilant circling to avoid their enemies, running like a tribe with their fellow conspirators. I overheard their conversations and I listened with an understanding ear, just as the Black poet listened to the forsaken ones whom society had no place for and whom 'good citizens" held in fear and reprehension I remember saying to a group of prayer friends at Bethany Church, "I'd love to see two pews in our church filled with parolees and ex-prisoners finally turning their hearts to Jesus Christ." In part, my desire was to be answered.

My favorite poet's poems reminded me about that revealing moment when a man admits to himself that he has been dealt the 'raw deal.' On occasion, inmates told me of a brawling drunken father beating them, remembering it as a child falling asleep afraid and sobbing; the lack of love in their youth almost too agonizing to bear; wearing the same tattered clothes to school with ill-fitting shoes and no clean underwear; sent off with no lunch money; no pencil; no paper; and feeling 'poorness' creeping into their being. When the boy returned home from school, gnawing poverty awaited him. A once-held dream to escape poverty slowly slipped away. I could understand that sentiment.

Part of my own childhood, I knew about living in crowded, dumpy government housing. I knew about walking into a kitchen to see roaches scurrying across the floor. At the end of the month, I knew what it was like to make a sandwich with baloney and a crust of bread. I certainly knew what it was like to wear the same clothes to school day after day. And like those inmates, I turned briefly to the streets to find excitement to blur the pain of reality.

I understood and related to the stories I heard from the inmates. I knew they were not always making an excuse for their bad behavior. As a grown man, I was no bleeding-heart, but I learned that I had to stand up and be counted for something or I would fall for anything.

I learned from my mother's example that anything worth doing was worth doing well. Practice started with my letter writing. Inch by inch with some lucky breaks and my mother's constant prayer, I was able to pull myself out of the mindset of poverty. This applied to my three siblings as well. When I began to realize that I didn't want to exist in substandard conditions, I made up my mind to organize my life instead of permitting life to disarrange me. That takes grit, elbow grease, perspiration and tough lessons learned from the school of hard knocks. But it can be done, as many others will tell us.

I used myself as an example in the prisoner orientation classes. Some found my story believable and they would ask, in private, about my recipe for success. I'd respond that it was having a God-centered plan, as I'd point to my Bible on my desk. Sometimes that interaction was the first opportunity given to that inmate to understand he, himself could take control of his own life. Perhaps it was the first time he felt anybody had truly given him permission to change! I recall my words; "If you're looking for permission to change, Mr. Fortin gives you permission today." It is such an easy thing to say, with the potential for amazing results.

I knew also, it was a one in one-thousandth of a chance for me or for that inmate to succeed; fortunately, I, Don Fortin, took the opportunity to beat the odds. Some inmates made the decision to set aside their repetitious acting out behavior that always brought about the same dismal results. Through education, work training, spiritual growth, sound nutrition and dental care, as well as drug avoidance, those men (inmate gentlemen) discovered that success and change could be attained.

A Brave Man

It's interesting to me to see how fearless so many writers of letters have shown themselves to be. It takes courage to stand up and say the right thing. It takes courage to speak out against evil. Even in prison (so much more), it takes courage for one inmate to tell another "Put the shank down." It takes courage to be a black life prisoner walking across the big yard at California State Prison, to carry his bible under his arm and walk past inmates who earlier had spit in 'Preacher' Brown's face. Preacher was then serving his 20th year of a life term. That day he was on his way to the Good Shepherd's Chapel to conduct a morning service. He wiped his face, continued walking on that straight and narrow path to service. After all Jesus Christ, was Preacher's Savior, too. How difficult it would have been for me to turn the other cheek as Preacher did that day.

One of my favorite Black poets, would have marveled at Preacher's courage and as Ernest Hemingway coined it, Grace under pressure. I knew Preacher and his Christian friends, some of whom made up the prison gospel a capella group. Sometimes these inmates practiced spiritual songs in the counseling office in the state prison. The men met on Friday afternoons after their work assignment and five African-American singers encouraged me with their song. I was their keeper, but in our walk of faith, we were refreshed hearing the harmonies of spiritual praise at the end of the day. One of their choice songs talked about God and how He has smiled on them, setting them free. What a way to end my week by their serenade as I sat composing Warden's responses to inmate appeal letters.

God certainly did smile on me. When at last I retired, I walked out of the prison on Aug 1, 2003, after thirty-three years of employment. I still fondly recall my sense of sadness and elation. We leave our footprint wherever we are assigned. I pray my actions then and now brought glory, praise and honor to God.

I felt it would be good to include the passage remembering what it was like to be friendly to black inmates (Hispanic and white inmates too) inside state prisons and to have one ex-convict come visit my Sunday school class upon his parole from prison. We know God's power is always at work if our spiritual eyes are opened to God's marvelous miracles all around us. Many times, I was in danger with violence around me, yet not one hair on my head was harmed, though I was assaulted once. God used me to be watch commander of the afternoon shift as a lieutenant and for five years to serve as commander of the prison honor guard. How good is our God! From little beginnings, God raised me in his purposes.

In one of this favorite poet's poems, he told us the universal plight of the enslaved black man. He spoke of the great hope of someday being free. He felt within his own brown skin what it must have been to shine the boots of George Washington and to serve the supper to Thomas Jefferson, whose faces are on Mount Rushmore. Those presidents were great orators who were men born before their time, whose minds were keen enough to envision what democracy could be to all people.

The poet wrote of freedom's dream; gave us his interpretation of how our manifest destiny of the American Way would leave the black man behind, those who carried the heavy bricks to build the American physical dream like the pyramids, now left out of the prize. He told how the black sons of America would die at Anzio, defending what Washington and Jefferson had held forth, that blazing torch of freedom.

The poet showed us our American colonial history.

He told us that many hands were preserving in their hearts the seed of liberty and he wanted us to know that the most cherished word, a fondness for liberty was always there.

The poet examined the productivity; the creations; the building; the great enterprise of American white hands and American black hands laboring to achieve today's America. Clearly it was the perspiration and the toil that together, men of different skin colors worked mightily to build all that is our Nation.

This poet's words make me remember that personal thing I knew from my own mother's style of Virginia and New England living—she would tell me: "Treat everyone the same as you want to be treated." Mother would sing to me the songs of Bible verses and as a very young boy I learned: "Jesus loves the little children; all the children of the world: red and yellow, black and white; they are precious in His sight. Jesus loves the little children of the world." (Clarence Herbert Woolston & George Fredrick Root)

I entered manhood in 1968 and I worked my muscles loading heavy ammunition pallets, as the winch man lowered the crates of weaponry into the holds deep within the Victory ships from the piers and out of railroad boxcars. We received the weapons from Bangor to be sent to troops serving in Vietnam to support Les Seto's cousin US Army Specialist 4 Terrance Ogata and the thousands of other American military men.

We loaded those pallets sweating eschewing the rain that came soaking us on the docks. We were working black men and white men, simply stevedores doing our duty. We were 19-year-olds and 40-year-olds, making America and the world safe for Democracy.

Here in the U.S., we felt the draining fatigue, but we went home safe and sound each day. 58,000 other men, equally young, died on those Vietnam battlefields giving their last ounce of devotion to that symbol of freedom, the Stars and Stripes. Stateside, on the first and fifteenth of each month, we lined up to receive our pay packet. I think we knew that we were part of the great adventure of our times. And we were comrades and compadres in our work, the living embodiment of the poet's words.

Chapter Twenty

A HUMBLE COMMUNICATOR

Throughout our exchange of letters, Don Fortin and I seemed to unintentionally flow into a pattern about once every eight months. Don would recommend that I read a biography usually about a famous person. I would balk and put off reading the book. I would eventually, however, give in and read the book. I would then be delightfully surprised in reading it. I would thank him for insisting that I read the book. Don would be pleased and then recommend another book to me soon thereafter.

Such was this recurring sequence in which Don sent me the biographies of Thomas Jefferson, Ronald Reagan, Oral Roberts, World War Two aviator and POW Louis Zamperini, and Billy Graham. Don pleaded with me to read these books, which I did. This chapter will highlight one of the books Don begged me to read, the autobiography of Rev. Dr. Billy Graham, Just as I Am (1st and 2nd Editions). Sadly, Reverend Graham passed away as I was writing this chapter on February 21, 2018 at the age of ninety nine.

More than ten years ago Don gave me the first edition of the autobiography of Reverend Graham, an evangelist who has traveled more miles and spoken in person to more people in a span of a lifetime than any other evangelist in the history of human kind including, may I even dare say, the Apostle Paul. I struggled, however, in picking up the book and reading it. The reason? I knew that if I read Reverend Graham's autobiography, I would have to grapple with painful issues in my own life like those, of which Reverend Graham struggled.

One of those discomforting issues is the stinging criticism Reverend Graham received especially in the 1980's and 1990's for not speaking out enough against abortion. Devout pro-life Christians have also levied that same condemnation upon me. In the 1980's, I was heavily involved in the chartering of a Pregnancy Center in Granite City, Illinois, a town across the Mississippi River from St. Louis, Missouri. The purpose of that Pregnancy Center was to support expectant mothers, traumatized at the thought of having a baby. The Pregnancy Center staff and volunteers supported these mothers physically and spiritually so that they would give birth to their babies rather than to have abortions.

Some of the dedicated, pro-life Christian leaders in that Granite City, Illinois project would often comment to each other, "Isn't it sad that Billy Graham seldom, if ever, speaks out against abortion in his many crusades. We know he's against abortion. But he constantly has more than 100,000 people in his audience, and millions more on television, and he doesn't even mention abortion. He speaks out all the time against murder and sexual immorality in our country. Those topics are related to abortion, but Reverend Graham just shies away from taking abortion head on."

Those same pro-life Christians would often direct their anger and frustration against me. They would say to me, "Pastor, we know you are pro-life. That is not the issue we have. We also know that you support our local Pregnancy Center. You have even held up signs on the sidewalk when we protest abortion. But why is it that you only preach against abortion, maybe two or three times a year. We just can't understand why the murdering of almost a million babies a year in our nation doesn't move you to denounce abortion in your sermons at least twice a month. Also, why don't you include the elimination of abortion every Sunday in your prayers during church? You always pray for our nation and our leaders in government and our soldiers. But you seldom pray that abortion be made illegal."

These criticisms have shaken my conscience to the core. Comments like these must also have hurt the sensitive soul of Reverend Graham who has made it clear on his website and in his publications, that he has always been pro-life. For many years, I had saved a clipping from a magazine article in which Reverend Graham addressed the scorn lashed out against him for not preaching more about the sin of abortion. However, in my many moves in residences, I have since lost that article. I have gone on line to search for the article or one like it, but I have been unsuccessful.

Here's what I recall Reverend Graham saying. He affirmed that God has called him to be an evangelist for the primary purpose that people be saved. To be saved they need to accept Jesus as their Lord and Savior. Reverend Graham went on to acknowledge that other very important issues such as the sin of abortion and homosexuality need to be discussed also. But such topics can be discussed later, not when an unbeliever is wrestling with the first and most important question, "Who is Jesus and why do I need Him?"

Reverend Graham noted that an unbeliever who is struggling with accepting Jesus as his Savior has enough on his or her plate to partake. If an unbeliever is wrestling with the question "Who is Jesus?" the unbeliever would be greatly distracted if asked to come to terms with other weighty issues such as abortion, homosexuality, evolution, the Trinity, smoking, drinking, predestination, the rapture, the Book of Revelation, infant baptism, and the legitimacy of the Pope. Crucial subjects such as these need to be addressed but only after the unbeliever comes to faith in Jesus.

In Reverend Graham's perspective, the assignment of the evangelist is to share the Gospel in one location so that people will be saved and then move on to a next city or town to share the Good News of salvation in Christ there. After the evangelist leaves a community, then pastors and teachers will take over and follow up in instructing the newly saved about the crucial topics mentioned. These concerns need to be discussed in depth but not when the evangelist is trying to preach whom Jesus is.

I feel for the heart of the evangelist Reverend Graham and for pastors such as I who have a clear understanding that priority number one is the salvation of a soul. Meanwhile, I also feel for the hearts of faithful pro-life Christians who are horrified by the mass murder of unborn infants and demand that Reverend Graham and other pastors like me speak out more on this issue.

Many pro-life Christians have been harsh on Reverend Graham, but he has never responded with malice. He has truly obeyed Christ's command in dealing with those who lash out against us: "Ye have heard that it hath been said, An eye for an eye, and a tooth for a tooth: But I say unto you, That ye resist not evil: but whosoever shall smite thee on thy right cheek, turn to him the other also" (Matt. 5:38-39, King James Version).

His Greatness is His Humility

Reverend Graham's gentle response to dear pro-life Christians who have castigated him is indicative of how he handles all attacks against him. After reading both editions of Reverend Graham's autobiography Just as I Am, I am in awe not only of his incredible courage, intelligence, faithfulness and knowledge of the Bible, but I am even more astounded by the kind manner in which he dealt with malicious reporters, arrogant aristocrats, egotistical intellectuals, judgmental Christians, cunning politicians, and hostile tyrants.

In almost every chapter of Just as I Am, people were doubting, insulting, ignoring or threatening Reverend Graham. Yet in response to each negative remark made toward him, he responded with the compassion of Christ.

Reverend Graham points out that he wasn't always this gracious in handling people and situations. However, when he was a teenager, after he committed his life to Jesus Christ at a revival led by Dr. Mordecai Fowler Ham, Reverend Graham noticed that a change had come over him. He reflected,

Before my conversion, I tended to be touchy, oversensitive, envious of others, and irritable. Now I deliberately tried to be courteous and kind to everybody around. I was experiencing what the Apostle Paul had described, "Therefore if anyone is in Christ, he is a new creature: The old has gone, the new is here!" (2 Cor. 5:17, New International Version). (Graham pp.32).

And "courteous and kind" did Reverend Graham try to be for the rest of his life. An example was how he coped with snarky church leaders and members at the first church he served as pastor. What church wouldn't want Reverend Graham as their pastor? Apparently the first church, which Reverend Graham served, didn't. Many of the deacons and church members didn't take kindly to townspeople with unsavory reputations coming to church to hear the young Reverend Graham preach. Reverend Graham and his wife Ruth found these new but rough on the edges Christians to be "refreshing" because of their enthusiasm in having been saved by Jesus. However, many long-time church members expressed to Reverend Graham their disfavor in having people with sordid pasts worshiping with them.

Instead of reacting in the same ugly way that church leaders and members were relating to him, Reverend Graham continued to treat them with graciousness as he always had. Finally, when the Lord laid it upon Reverend Graham's heart to leave that church to become an evangelist for the Youth for Christ organization, Rev. Graham resigned peacefully expressing only sincere gratitude to the congregation. Graham noted that a considerable number of members and leaders were all too happy to receive his resignation. However, he chose not to harbor or convey any ill will at all. (Graham pp.625).

How Reverend Graham handled opposition towards him and toward his outreach to the spiritually and even physically unwashed at the first congregation he served became a template for the courtesy he would extend to anyone who was antagonist toward him or his work in the future. Throughout the decades following his first pastorate, Reverend Graham daily demonstrated the remarkable calmness of Jesus toward any cruel person.

The More Hostile, The Better

Because Reverend Graham had learned early in his calling the time-tested formula of Christ in responding to any antagonistic person, Reverend Graham had the courage to go anywhere in the world to share the Gospel. He already knew in advance that when he would encounter hateful rejection, he would automatically respond with benevolence. He impeccably followed the instructions of the evangelist Apostle Paul who wrote, "Recompense to no man evil for evil. . . If it be possible, as much as lieth in you, live peaceably with all men" (Rom. 12:17-18, King James Version).

It seemed as if the unfriendlier a region was to the Gospel and to Christians, the more Reverend Graham wanted to go there. His reason, of course, was that those most spiteful toward Christ were the ones most needy of His salvation. Again, like his role model, the Apostle Paul, Reverend Graham's mission statement was, "Yea, so have I strived to preach the gospel, not where Christ was named" (Rom. 15:20, King James Version).

I am dumbfounded at the many dangerous places that Reverend Graham and his evangelistic team traveled: North Korea, which boasted to be the most atheistic nation in the world. The Soviet Union in its glory years of communism. China with its wretched treatment of Christians. Africa, still raw with its outrage against colonialism, which was associated with Christianity. Central and South America teeming with murderous dictators and revolt.

The more brutal a region was, the harder Reverend Graham and his team prayed that the Lord would open doors for them. The Holy Spirit had imparted upon Reverend Graham a heart for those who hated Christ the most and who would therefore hate him the most, too.

Again, following the example of St. Paul, Reverend Graham always began his sermons to hostile persons by pointing out any truthful God pleasing qualities that even people who abhor or ignore Christ have. In addressing the Epicurean and Stoic philosophers at Mars Hill in Athens who had ridiculed him, Paul began his sermon with these complimentary words: "People of Athens! I see that in every way you are very religious. For as I walked around and looked carefully at your objects of worship, I even found an altar with this inscription: TO AN UNKNOWN GOD" (Acts 17:22-23, New International Version).

As the Apostle Paul did, Reverend Graham often defused a raucous crowd by first speaking winsome words about how precious they were in God's eyes, how much they have contributed to humankind by the grace of God, and how much God loved them, so much so, that He sent His only Son to die for them.

In China, Reverend Graham praised the Chinese university students for emulating scholars instead of movie stars. In Russia, Reverend Graham commended the people for their endurance demonstrated by how the Russians wore down the Nazi invaders during World War Two. In North Korea, he acknowledged what loyal citizens they were to their government and how Christ could make them even better citizens. In a rock concert in Miami, he pointed out to the many unruly teenagers that Jesus was a non-conformist, too.

What a valuable lesson do the Apostle Paul and Reverend Graham teach me and maybe you, too, on how to deal with people who dislike us and the Gospel of Jesus which we share: Look for ways to truthfully and sincerely complement our adversary. Then somehow link what admirable quality our opponent may have to the death and resurrection of Jesus. Commend them for not being lukewarm. We could then share how Jesus was the only person who could keep his powerful emotions in check and how He died for the sins we commit when we use our strong emotions wrongly. Then share how Jesus rose from the dead to give a new life to Christians who formerly hurt people with their words but who now bring healing with the words of Jesus.

Just as Jesus Was Criticized . . .

One of the biggest "gripes" that the religious leaders in Jesus' day had against Him was that he was friendly toward sinners: "But the Pharisees and the teachers of the law muttered, 'This man welcomes sinners and eats with them'" (Luke 15:2, New International Version).

Until I read Just as I Am, I wrongly thought that Reverend Graham was a fire and brimstone fundamentalist preacher who condemned not only sin but sinners, too. As I read chapter after chapter of his autobiography, however, I realized how wrong I was.

In 1949, William Randolph Hearst wanted his papers to portray Reverend Graham as a young, fiery, self-assured, Bible thumping preacher from the South who was barnstorming through Los Angeles and major cities in the U.S. warning people to repent or perish. Such a caricature of Reverend Graham, however, was grossly inaccurate.

What is ironic is that the critics who were arguably the harshest on Reverend Graham were not only liberal agnostics, atheistic communists or militant Muslims. Rather the ones whose snide remarks hurt Reverend Graham the most were the many every-Sunday-in-church Christians and their pastors who condemned Reverend Graham for being soft on sin, weak in theology, unfaithful to Biblical truths, and too friendly with sinners especially despicable Hollywood stars and corrupt politicians. These unfounded charges were the same reproaches that the Pharisees spewed upon Jesus.

As with Jesus, Reverend Graham did not condone sin, was faithful to the Scriptures, and was friendly toward sinners but without approving of their thoughts or actions. Like his Savior, Reverend Graham loved lost sinners. He embraced them with kindness and counseled them to receive Jesus as their Redeemer and Lord. He conveyed to them the danger of their sin and trusted in the Holy Spirit to make changes in their lives.

If Reverend Graham were a fire and brimstone preacher, as I had erroneously perceived, he would have hammered President Richard Nixon and President Bill Clinton. But much to the dismay of many Christians, Reverend Graham censured neither. If he were a hardliner against sinners as I had conceived, he would have condemned former North Korea dictator Kim Il Sung and many movie stars who were involved with infidelity and multiple divorces. But instead Reverend Graham showered kindness upon them as Jesus did.

A preacher obsessed with pouncing on every sinner is the farthest portrayal one could make of Reverend Graham. He truly strove to fit the description of an authentic Christian as the Apostle Paul outlined, "Put on therefore, as the elect of God, holy and beloved, bowels of mercies, kindness, humbleness of mind, meekness, longsuffering; Forbearing one another, and forgiving one another, if any man have a quarrel against any: even as Christ forgave you, so also do ye." (Col. 3:12, King James Version).

Why Did So Many Flock to Hear Him?

As I read Just as I Am, it was as if I were reading a continuation of the Book of Acts. People filled stadiums around the world to hear Reverend Graham proclaim the Gospel. There were 150,000 in Sydney, Australia, 110,000 in Barbados, 100,000 in Chicago, 250,000 in Rio de Janeiro, and 500,000 in South Korea are just a few of the gigantic crowds that sought to hear Reverend Graham preach. Thousands at every crusade prayed a sinner's prayer asking God to forgive them and then receiving Jesus as their Savior and Lord.

If there is a formula to Reverend Graham's sermons, it was a Biblical one, which the evangelists in the New Testament followed. First, Reverend Graham connects in a favorable way to his audience. As mentioned earlier, he expresses his love and good will toward them, as an ambassador of Christ, by mentioning at least one truthful God pleasing trait, which they have.

Second, Reverend Graham points out that despite our positive traits, sin lurks in each of us. He always conveys either explicitly or by his humble tone of voice that sin is swirling in him, too. Sin is disobedience to God and separates us from God.

Third, Reverend Graham explains how sin creates restlessness in our soul, which includes a feeling of emptiness. In his sermon in North Korea, Reverend Graham said, "Down inside we sense that something is missing in our lives. There is an empty space and a loneliness in our hearts that we try to fill in all kinds of ways, but God can fill it"(Graham pp. 625).

Then, fourthly, Reverend Graham identifies the cure to our restlessness, emptiness, and frustration. The cure is Jesus Christ. He forgives our sins, the cause of our restlessness. But we need to confess our sins, receive Jesus as our Savior and Lord, and then turn our lives over to Him.

Many theologians and intellectuals consider Reverend Graham's preaching to be too simplistic. Many life-long, dedicated Christians consider what Reverend Graham asks of people in the audience to be too easy. Many Christians also want Reverend Graham to stress more of the other doctrines of the Bible such as infant or adult baptism, the Trinity, the rapture, the millennium, predestination, and the sins of abortion and homosexuality.

Some of the key reasons, however, why Reverend Graham reaches so many listeners is that his message has the following elements: the commandments of God, the sins we commit when we break the commandments, the love of God who sends His Son to die for our sins, and the need for us to receive the forgiveness and the eternal life which Christ gives.

It is the love of God for us through His Son Jesus and the Holy Spirit that rings out loudest in the crusades of Reverend Graham. He emphasizes the mercy and kindness in Jesus even more than sin and punishment. He is anything but the angry hell and damnation preacher that I long associated him to be. I was totally wrong, and Don Fortin unintentionally helped me to recognize my error by prevailing upon me to read Reverend Graham's autobiography.

How Not to Be Flustered by Hostility

At the time I am writing this chapter, people in our nation and our world are experiencing what seems to be increasing hostility. In race relations, many of us thought that peace among ethnic groups in the U.S. was increasing. However, as the quarter mark of the Twenty-First century approaches, black and white relations continue to be tense. What to do about illegal aliens and children of illegal aliens are also topics that raise blood pressures between those who want to allow them to stay and those who don't. Building a great wall along the southern boundary of the U.S. is causing a great stir among voters.

In America, many families have a no discussing politics rule when they gather for Thanksgiving, Christmas, New Year's, Fourth of July, and other holidays. A reason for the no discussing politics rule is to prevent wildfire arguments from flaring up at family gatherings.

Road rage is a big problem in my home state of Hawaii. Fights between drivers are common. Injuries and even deaths often occur, not caused by vehicular collisions but caused by scuffles between motorists after an accident or near miss accident.

A false missile attack alert occurred in Hawaii a couple of weeks prior to the writing of this chapter. It traumatized many residents. A retiree I know was so nauseated after hearing the alert that she almost fainted. Children were trembling and crying. Thankfully, the alert was false, but it reminded the people in our state that hostility between nations is a reality, which needs to be reckoned.

The message of the Bible that Reverend Graham preached is helpful today. If verbal or physical confrontations pop up with people, please don't be shaken. When dealing with bitter or angry people, Reverend Graham always responded with calmness and gentleness. He followed Proverbs 15:1 on countless occasions, "A soft answer turneth away wrath: but grievous words stir up anger" (Prov. 15:1, King James Version). We would do well to do what this verse says. Reverend Graham has.

If a hostile nation launches a nuclear missile to where we reside, there is little we can do other than seeking shelter. However, we can have peace in our souls by remembering the many reassuring messages of Scripture to which Reverend Graham often referred in his sermons. One of those verses was "Yea, though I walk through the valley of the shadow of death, I will fear no evil; for thou art with me; thy rod and thy staff they comfort me" (Ps. 23:4, King James Version).

Reverend Graham always reassured his listeners that no threat or danger will rattle persons who have confessed their sins, received Jesus as their Savior, and turned their lives over to Him. Hence, at Reverend Graham's crusade, millions have responded to God's call to seek the comfort that only the Holy Spirit can give. What courage in their souls did those millions of people receive as they placed their trust in the One who controls the universe and in His Son Jesus who has saved us from eternal destruction. We can't lose with God watching over us.

I am thankful to God and to Don Fortin by whom God used to direct me to read Billy Graham's autobiography. I would have not done so otherwise. The life of Rev. Dr. Billy Graham has inspired me to extend the kindness of Christ to all who have a mean or a dismissive spirit towards God or me. That's what Reverend Graham did whether he had just one person or 300,000 with whom to communicate the Gospel. He always treated each person or each crowd with the grace of our Lord and Savior Jesus.

As the Apostle Paul wrote and as Reverend Graham put into practice,

"To speak evil of no man, to be no brawlers, but gentle, shewing all meekness unto all men. For we ourselves also were sometimes foolish, disobedient, deceived, serving divers lusts and pleasures, living in malice and envy, hateful and hating one another. But after that the kindness and love of God our Savior toward man appeared, Not by works of righteousness which we have done, but according to his mercy he saved us . . . (Titus 3:3-5, King James Version).

Chapter Twenty-One

BEN, THE AMERICAN PRINTER

"But sanctify the Lord God in your hearts: and be ready always to give an answer to every man that asketh you a reason of the hope that is in you with meekness and fear: Having a good conscience; that, whereas they speak evil of you, as of evildoers, they may be ashamed that falsely accuse your good conversation in Christ" (1 Pet. 3:15-16, King James Version).

In this book, Pastor and writer Les Seto has given an honest account of which he can say is a firm foundation of his belief that Jesus Christ is Lord of all. He has told us of his struggle to be accepted, and then to enter the seminary with his young wife. Les said he was certainly more than fortunate to be accepted.

He revealed how he and his beautiful partner, Bernadette sought to choose Godly living as they began their journey together raising up children, Kili and Mewlan. He was candid.

We learn from reading this that there are many faithful who have had such a journey as Les and Bernadette, some to a more well-known degree, as those men and women we have studied in this book.

Thomas Jefferson with his substantial number of letters to correspondents, including churches and others, dealt with the freedom and liberty of worship and pursuit of truth. Thus far, you have read here of the lives of not only Jefferson, of Amy Carmichael, Fanny J. Crosby, an unnamed poet; and now we come to another writer, publisher and well-known American thinker- Benjamin Franklin.

You may know the basics of his life, that he was a framer of the Declaration of Independence; an ambassador to England, and Franklin served in the Continental Congress. We know of his scientific exploits having learned of his experiments and inventions. We see his visage on the $100 (one hundred dollar) bill and we know he did much to help modernize living in the early United States. Much of this he did before America won its independence from Great Britain.

He is assuredly the founding father all others in his day looked to for wisdom trusting his authority, and knowledge to lead the hearts and minds of Americans.

Franklin's creative mind invented the Franklin stove and he was an early harnesser of electricity. In fact, until Thomas Edison was able to refine the incandescent filament light bulb, we were in a candle-lit world; yet it was other men including Franklin who developed the working theory of electricity.

We know about Poor Richard's Almanac, sold for twenty years, one of the most widely relied upon booklets after the Holy Bible in Franklin's day. Of course, Benjamin was the writer under the alias of Richard Saunders. Certainly, we know about the lending public libraries that he set up in Philadelphia. Andrew Carnegie and Franklin Roosevelt's WPA program later made the library a widespread institution in many American cities. But it was the success of Franklin's first free library that made this educational facility an acceptable blueprint for community use for all people.

As elementary school students we have learned of Franklin's political genius and his common-sense quotes that our grandparents often relied on in their daily regimen of living. Dear Reader, perhaps your parents reminded us of this little jewel of a homily? "Early to bed; early to rise; makes a man healthy, wealthy and wise."

If so, you may thank Mr. Franklin for that little sage advice and many more like it.

Those proverbs of Franklin are a basis by which we find continuity, grace and assuredness in the daily going about our lives as men, women, girls and boys. We are indebted in many ways to this giant figure of early Americana. Though he read Pilgrim's Progress, the Holy Bible and everything he could turn his eager curious mind upon, Franklin, like Lincoln, had a tremendous curiosity and a capacity for learning. Like Lincoln, he knew he had truly learned any newly discovered information after he wrote out the contents of his well examined thoughts and put them down on paper for others to consider. Unlike the lawyer Lincoln, Franklin being a printer and a publisher by trade, took his newfound knowledge and promptly distributed his writings largely in South Carolina, Pennsylvania, Washington and New York. In doing this extensive writing and printing, he assured his place in literary history.

The books he wrote and letters to the editor Franklin began writing at age 16, continued unabated for the next 65 years in his long, illustrious full life. One book, the Autobiography of Benjamin Franklin was and continues to be a massive best seller. Experiments in science and his development of useful machinery have become a boon to society. Imagine the world today without volunteer firemen working to suppress the damage to life and property from fires. Imagine a world without access to free books to learn from and to enjoy. Imagine homes without efficient and affordable heat even before electricity. A litany of other ideas we take for granted today, would not be possible in America if not developed logically by the engaging galvanizing of ideals of liberty and freedom from tyranny that Franklin helped to generate in his useful witty writing.

I quote Michael Zuckerman in his section of the reprint of the Autobiography of Benjamin Franklin. As one of the co-authors of the 2005 Penn Reading Project Edition, University of Pennsylvania Press, he said the following:

"In the conventional understanding Franklin personified the opportunity America afforded people who were not well-born to seek their own aggrandizement. He was the poor boy who made good. And in doing so he embodied the best aspects of America: the chance that the country offered all to get ahead, the individualism at the core of the culture." (Franklin pp.154).

Zuckerman gives a review of Franklin's Autobiography placing emphasis on the developing mind of Franklin's "chicanery and sharp practice where wary attentiveness to one's own needs was necessary." Zuckerman was describing young Franklin, an impoverished run-away from his father's plan to place 12-year-old Benjamin in a ten-year indentured servitude apprentice, in a printing shop, under the supervision of Ben's elder brother James. Will be seen, that Franklin flees, destitute, without any means of support, to Philadelphia where he begins a mature march becoming an intelligent, able young man. Perhaps it was this scary action, as much as any, that drove Franklin to seek freedom and embrace a liberty of his spirit. Much of his adult writing would reflect this.

A Yearning To Be Magnaminous

Using the print shop as a jumping off spot to write criticism and anonymous letters to the editor, Franklin began a lifelong search for a religious understanding of God, and he desired to know the cause of his faith. Because of his adventurous spirit and a challenging view of the world around him, he was poised to become a messenger and a role model of meritorious living. His acquaintance and lifelong friendship with the noted minister of the Gospel, George Whitefield, had much to do with Franklin's departure from the Calvinist background of his parents and his sister, to a more enlightened belief system. He began a conflicting argument within himself that ''men are naturally benevolent as well as selfish."

Zuckerman continues: "His Autobiography is in many ways an account of the many ways by which he cultivated his own benevolence, weaning himself from the gratification of aggression and the delights of defeating others."

Today, we can see that Benjamin Franklin desired to live a life dedicated to doing good to help others prosper and become self-sufficient. At an early age he adopted the pseudonym of "Silence Do-Good" reflecting his youthful maturing thinking.

As Franklin developed his journeyman skill as a printer, he published many documents and letters including The Way to Wealth (1758). Author Thomas S. Kidd's "Benjamin Franklin The Religious Life of a Founding Father", documents:

"[Which…] distilled his best thoughts on frugality and industry, [and] illustrated the spirit of capitalism in near classical purity and simultaneously offered the advantage of being detached from all direct connection to religious belief."

Here, Kidd was quoting from Max Weber's classic study The Protestant Ethic and the Spirit of Capitalism (1905).

Franklin, having been raised as a boy by his strict Calvinist father, knew about sincerity in one's vocation and calling, and that this would provide moneymaking and success as products of "competence and proficiency." No doubt, young Benjamin's dexterity, single-minded pursuit of the work ethic and wide-ranging curiosity provided the perfect canvas upon which he would paint his portrait of ideas and later implement these thoughts into action. Franklin demonstrated diligence to duty.

If one reads Poor Richard's Almanac, one can note the origins of his words inspired from The Book of Proverbs in the Holy Bible. He took these time-honored verses and distilled them to single sonnets or jingoisms. The charm of his work made whole theories of intelligent teachings highly memorable and quotable.

Franklin's keen memorization of much of the Holy Bible was as Thomas Jefferson had also done; both absorbed the verses to show themselves well qualified to quote from scripture. In their long lives, first as colonists and ultimately as America's founding fathers, the Age of Enlightenment had a profound effect on both Franklin and Jefferson who studied these theories. This included the act of elimination of all things of institutional religion even to the rejection of the idea of a Supreme Being in the rational logic of philosophers of their day. Having once been trained in the truth of God and the mystery of the Holy Spirit, Franklin's faith in God went through an extended period of self-examination, rebuttal and refuting what he once accepted as truth. Yet we can surmise that the moral and imaginative desires of Franklin were always pushing his thoughts to the forefront in his conduct. Indeed, frugality and avoidance of wastefulness were primary in his day-to-day living. In his Autobiography, written between 1759 and 1790, the year of his death, Franklin wrote:

"It was about this time I [conceived] the bold and arduous project of arriving at moral perfection. I'd wished to live without committing any fault at any time; I would conquer all that either natural inclination, custom or company might lead me into. As I knew, or thought I knew, what was right or wrong, I did not see why I might not always do the one and avoid the other." (Franklin pp. 154).

Franklin went on to explain his ideology:

"Thirteen Names of Virtues, [is] annexed to each a short precept, which fully expressed the extent I gave to its meaning. These names of virtues, with their precepts were:"

1. Temperance
   Eat not to dullness; drink not to elevation.

2. Silence
   Speak not but what may benefit others or yourself; avoid trifling conversation.

3. Order
   Let all your things have their places; let each part of your business have its time.

4. Resolution
   Resolve to perform what you ought; perform without fail what you resolve.

5. Frugality
   Make no expense but to do good to yourself or others; i.e., waste nothing.

6. Industry
   Lose no time; be always employed in something useful; cut off all unnecessary actions.

7. Sincerity

Use no hurtful deceit; think innocently and justly, and, if you speak, speak accordingly.

8. Justice
   Wrong none by doing injuries or omitting the benefits that are your duty.

9. Moderation
   Avoid extremes; forbear resenting injuries so much as you think they deserve.

10. Cleanliness
    Tolerate no uncleanliness in body, clothes, or habitation.

11. Tranquility
    Be not disturbed at trifles, or accidents common or unavoidable.

12. Chastity
    Rarely use venery [the indulgence of sexual desire] but for health or offspring, never to dullness, weakness, or the injury of your own or another's peace or reputation.

13. Humility
    Imitate Jesus and Socrates (Franklin pp. 66-67).

I've included these points of confession so that we can see how and where Franklin derived these pure virtues of rectitude. Understand Dear Reader, that the primary reason given for Autobiography was so Franklin could provide a recipe for success, a roadmap of the life he had traveled and then bequeathed the sum of his experience to William Templeton Franklin, his surviving son who had been born out of wedlock.

Recall that Old Testament's King David penned his wonderful instructions to his son Solomon in the Book of Proverbs. Franklin industriously wrote his Autobiography in hopes of edifying God and as a way of teaching his offspring. Such a permanent record is a loving gift that lasts well beyond the demise of the giver.

Often, we see this expansive habit from writers to their children in the form of memoir. It is like the simple act of nature that an elephant returns to his birthplace when he knows its date of expiration is at hand. So, it was that Franklin labored to eliminate vices and to propagate virtuous acts. What we now can learn from Benjamin Franklin is that we as individuals are accountable to govern ourselves in our personal and public lives. These things he wanted his son to know.

Order Begat Journaling

Faithful to his written scheme of Order, another practice Franklin daily kept became my goal. I set upon writing my lengthy journal entries after reading Franklin's book. Daily, without exception, I went about my task for five years. These entries, I saw, were like Franklin's Order, in which by morning, I wrote of the preceding day's progress in my way of Christian thankfulness. I also required of myself to read and to seek understanding of the multitude of wisdom found in Scripture.

I can point out successful habits of others, but I can only judge myself as whether I am in line with God's commandments. This becomes a concern as I reach the latter part of my life. I know my children watch and consider my decisions. It is of paramount importance that I remember I am a role model; it is a 24/7 responsibility whether it be teaching Sunday school, a high school Bible class or participating in family activities in our home or in public places. Les has enumerated for us, this device of memorializing each of our allotted days.

In these journals, I used a daily salutation of "Dear Heavenly Father" thereby hoping to record a truthful version of my day. As with other authors, I found I could eliminate vices such as intrusive, untoward thoughts, by dedicating myself first as a husband to my wife and a good father to my children. Scripture tells us, "But if any provide not for his own, and specially for those of his own house, he hath denied the faith, and is worse than an infidel" (1Tim. 5:8, King James Version). And I believe this to be true.

I see a correlation between writing down my daily activities and soon after, reviewing what it was that brought me joy; this causes me to imitate that good behavior in future days. Like Franklin's scrutiny, anything that lent itself to irritation and demoralization, I arduously refrain from repeating it. Through the Holy Spirit's discernment, I began to eliminate worthless activities. In this way I was able to accomplish meaningful things avoiding procrastination.

Learning and "unlearning" is easy with rote repetition. I tell any interested students, "if you practice your penmanship, your handwriting will soon garner compliments for you. If you dash off thoughtless scribbling, that too will point to a careless attitude to the act of writing". As well, it takes practice to eliminate profanity from one's vocabulary and it takes self-restraint to avoid bingeing on liquor and illicit drugs as common among today's college students. Thoughtful, quiet prayer will lend itself to produce the courage required to make honorable decisions.

Kudos to a man or woman who says, "No thank you; I'm not interested in joining in that behavior." This is because it takes courage to swim against the stream. It may appear to be lonely on the pathway of righteousness. It may seem difficult to avoid turning and keeping your eyes firmly on the path of excellent living. But it is not impossible. Remember, Christ has given us His promise never to leave us nor forsake us. We must remind ourselves that Jesus is always just a prayer from us. I have found that often the closeness between a problem and its solution is the distance between our knees and the floor (in prayer).

Making Your Voice Heard

As has been said, Franklin wrote many letters-to-the editors, often giving a point/counter point discussion. In this way, one could readily examine opposing points of view, as if he were looking carefully at two sides of a coin. Franklin would show how a situation had both positive and negative attributes. He was judicious, careful not to offend his reader's sensibilities. When he did take umbrage with a minister's sermon (or other religious actions) in Philadelphia, he chose wisely to write using a pen name.

As was his habit, he did not use hurtful deceit or speak unjustly of anyone. In this way he could guard against violating those virtues Franklin held dear.

In a new book released in May 2017, Benjamin Franklin The Religious Life of a Founding Father, author Thomas S. Kidd, gives dramatic insights into how Franklin progressed from a youthful arrogant resistance to the organized church, finally changing when he met and heard the Evangelist George Whitefield preach in a manner that supported the teachings of Christ. Franklin strongly believed the Bible's Book of James, where it says: "For as the body without the spirit is dead, so faith without works is dead also" (James 2:26, King James Version).

Franklin considered Whitefield's sermons and he began to embrace what hitherto he had resisted. Once, Franklin had denounced formalized religion having little good to say in his writings about the grace of God being sufficient for his salvation. After much soul searching and the lessons taught in his middle age, Franklin voted to have sessions of Congress opened with an establishment of a chaplain's prayer. Earlier, he was instrumental in submitting a proposal, to Anglican minister Richard Peters for an academy in Philadelphia to be created as a university of higher learning (Page 164); he published "Proposals Relating to the Education of Youth in Pennsylvania" (1749) and laid out plans:

"for the academy, with educational goals of virtue and practical service. Theology and ancient languages (Greek, Hebrew, and Latin) were deemphasized. English grammar was a primary emphasis, because it was more useful than "foreign and dead languages…".

Quoting John Milton's Of Education (1644), Franklin noted that students would find the historical basis of law "delivered first and with best warrant by Moses in the Pentateuch". Reading about moral exemplars in the past would remind students of the "advantages of temperance, order, frugality, industry, perseverance and other virtues". It would also reveal the "necessity of a public religion", he argued. [Although terse] Franklin noted that pupils would learn of the "excellency of the Christian Religion above all others ancient or modern." (Kidd pp. 165).

As his plan unfolded, we know that Franklin's dream for a college became a reality. In 1755, under the direction of Anglican minister William Smith it became the "College Academy and Charitable Schools of Philadelphia, precursor to the University of Pennsylvania" (Kidd pp. 169).

Caring for the Afflicted

With equal exuberance, Franklin committed his considerable skills, both in writing a pamphlet entitled Appeal for the Hospital and his plea in fund-raising toward his concept of a public health facility, a hospital for indigent Philadelphians to receive free care. He reasoned correctly that proper care and treatment of the ill was not only a preeminent Christian obligation but would...

"help contain the effects of disease and enable those treated to remain productive...". Franklin believed that taking care of suffering people was "essential to the true spirit of Christianity", Franklin contended, "and should be extended to all in general, whether deserving or undeserving".

The need to create a lending library, hospital, fire stations, and a university, amazingly were all from one man, Benjamin Franklin, and all from a deeply held promise he made to himself. Poor Richard reflected his belief in charity as a condition of being welcomed into "God's sheepfold". His alter ego, Poor Richard, commented in 1757, "godliness surpassed all earthly goods, for our good or bad works shall remain forever recorded in the archives of eternity."

Little did Franklin realize that his philanthropy would grow to not only benefit Philadelphia but also to many future American cities. This seems to prove the Letter is indeed more powerful than the sword.

In summation, Les and I have projected just how important it is to maintain a vigorous desire to do good and to advance those peculiarly American values of community endearment and peaceful co-existence between men; for indeed we are God's children, brothers and sisters all.

It is hoped we have resurrected examples of leaders both in thought and in action that caressed and helped to foster a kinder, gentle world.

With that in mind, remember we cannot change 180 degrees overnight; but with prayerful practice and attention to duty we may succeed in changing a little to gain much.

Bibliography

Brande, Dorothea. Becoming a Writer. J.P. Tarcher, 1981. pp. 43-44,142.

Brande, Dorothea. Wake up and Live! Jeremy P. Tarcher/Penguin, a Member of Penguin Group (USA), 2013. pp. 124-126.

Franklin, Benjamin, and Peter J. Conn. The Autobiography of Benjamin Franklin. PENN/University of Pennsylvania Press, 2005. pp. 66-67, 154

Graham, Billy. Just As I Am: The Autobiography of Billy Graham. Harper Collins, 1997. pp.32, 625.

Kevin Larimer, "Vote of Confidence: The Life-Changing Support of an NEA Fellowship," Poets & Writers Magazine, May/June 2017. Reprinted by permission of the publisher, Poets & Writers, Inc., 90 Broad Street, Suite 2100, New York, NY 10004. www.pw.org.

Kidd, Thomas S. Benjamin Franklin: The Religious Life of a Founding Father. Yale University Press, 2017.

Meacham, Jon. Thomas Jefferson the Art of Power. Random House Trade Paperbacks, 2013. pp. 308.

Steinbeck, John, and Robert J. DeMott. Working Days, the Journals of "The Grapes of Wrath", 1938-1941. Penguin Books, 1990. pp. 56.

The Holy Bible, New International Version®, NIV® Copyright © 1973, 1978, 1984, 2011 by Biblica, Inc.® Used by permission. All rights reserved worldwide.

The Holy Bible: King James Version, https://www.biblegateway.com/King James Version.